THE LIGHT
WE GIVE

THE LIGHT
WE GIVE

*How Sikh Wisdom Can
Transform Your Life*

SIMRAN JEET SINGH

Riverhead Books
New York
2022

RIVERHEAD BOOKS
An imprint of Penguin Random House LLC
penguinrandomhouse.com

Copyright © 2022 by Simran Jeet Singh

Library of Congress Cataloging-in-Publication Data
Names: Singh, Simran Jeet, author.
Title: The light we give : how Sikh wisdom can
transform your life / Simran Jeet Singh.
Description: First edition. | New York : Riverhead Books, 2022.
Identifiers: LCCN 2021060426 (print) | LCCN 2021060427 (ebook) |
ISBN 9780593087978 (hardcover) | ISBN 9780593087992 (ebook)
Subjects: LCSH: Religious life–Sikhism. | Sikhism–Doctrines. | Sikhism.
Classification: LCC BL2018.37 .S4785 2022 (print) | LCC BL2018.37 (ebook) |
DDC 294.6/44–dc23/eng20220408
LC record available at https://lccn.loc.gov/2021060426
LC ebook record available at https://lccn.loc.gov/2021060427)

Printed in the United States of America
1   3   5   7   9   10   8   6   4   2

Book design by Alexis Farabaugh

To my parents, who taught us
To live with love and give with love.

CONTENTS

Part I

SEEING WITH FRESH EYES

Part II

RADICAL CONNECTION

Part III

FROM CONNECTION TO LOVE

Part IV

CULTIVATING OUR VALUES

Part V

SEVA AS A SPIRITUAL PRACTICE

PROLOGUE

I was a teenager when I learned how much people spent on haircuts—
and I was *floored*. I thought that maybe the Sikh gurus were on to something with the whole no-cutting-hair thing. Think of the money my
family saved.

I mentioned it, half-jokingly, to my soccer teammate Anton, who replied, "Yeah, but think about how much you spend on shampoo and
conditioner."

We all see the world from our own eyes.

Ever since I was a boy, I've tried to understand how my life experiences might differ from those of my friends and neighbors. As I grew
older, I sought to make meaning of another kind of difference. I viewed
myself a certain way, but people perceived me differently. How would I
reconcile these two understandings? We all go through this process on
our own journeys. Perhaps this is what it means to mature.

By virtue of who I am, a Sikh man in modern America who was born
and raised in Texas, I experienced the aftermath of 9/11 as a pivotal moment in my life. Your experience may be similar to mine; you might have
been more directly affected by it than I was; you might have seen it from
a distance, or from the corners of your eyes, or even from memories
passed down to you.

We have shared experiences, yet we experience them differently.

I have grown immensely by opening myself up to the world. Rather than being judgmental about different perspectives and ways of living, I am now intrigued and curious. *Why do you think so? What experiences inform that outlook?* Taking this approach reveals that there's more to us than the attributes we are born with or our experiences at the surface. We all have it in us to journey together to our shared interior, to the inner struggles that make us human and that we hold in common. Traveling together can help us make meaning—of ourselves and our world—and can help us find answers to questions we never even thought to ask.

Besides, I prefer to travel with support and company. Life is so much more enjoyable when we feel connected and move with purpose.

If we can learn to see the humanity in ourselves and in one another, we can mitigate so much of the self-inflicted pain we feel daily. It's a simple upgrade, really, and it's intuitive, too. Even my two young daughters understand: *Being kind to others makes them happy and makes you happier, too.*

(This is what I tell them every morning as I try to convince them to let me sleep in.)

This way of life is not a cure-all or a ready-made solution for all our problems. There will always be things beyond our control. But calming our inner tumult *is* within our control. To paraphrase Guru Nanak, "If we can conquer our minds, we can conquer the world."

All this might make sense in theory, but finding inner peace is hard work. It takes time and commitment and effort, and don't we all have enough to do already? I'd also love to be more generous and caring and compassionate, but the truth is that dealing with people can be annoying, even the ones we love.

And as we look around at our world on fire, there are plenty of reasons for us to be frustrated, outraged, and angry. The negativity that surrounds us can be overpowering, turning simple acts like turning on the news or checking our social media into fraught, anxiety-provoking experiences. In the words of civil rights leader Fannie Lou Hamer, we're sick and tired of being sick and tired.

So how do we go on? Here's some real-life inspiration.

Jaswant Singh Khalra wasn't always a human rights hero.

In the 1980s, Khalra was a director in a cooperative farmers bank in Amritsar, Punjab, when two of his colleagues suddenly went missing. Khalra began looking for them, and his search led to a horrifying discovery: evidence that the Punjab police had illegally killed and cremated thousands of Sikhs. Worse still, Khalra would soon realize that the files he'd first unearthed represented just a fraction of the large-scale persecution targeting the Sikh community. Despite threats to his life from government and police authorities, Khalra continued to investigate for years, and he ultimately estimated approximately 25,000 extrajudicial killings and illegal cremations of Sikhs in the state of Punjab.

In 1995, Khalra disappeared like the thousands before him, never to be seen again. Witnesses implicated the police in his murder, and it took ten years for them to be held accountable. On November 18, 2005, six Punjab police officials were convicted for Khalra's abduction and murder.

Just before his disappearance, Khalra visited Canada. He planned to tell the world about the severity of human rights atrocities in India. Some of his supporters, worried about the increasing threats to his life, urged Khalra to stay in Canada as a political asylee. With characteristic grace and gentleness, Khalra responded that a truly wise person knows that truth and justice are greater than fear. From the stage of a gurdwara in Ontario, in his last speech before his own abduction, Khalra shared a Punjabi folktale about a lantern that insisted on challenging the darkness, no matter the consequences:

> There is an old tale about when the sun was first setting. As her distance narrowed to the horizon, the light on earth slowly diminished. This made way for darkness to creep over the land. The people were afraid that when the sun would finally set,

darkness would be permanent. "What will happen to us?" they
said.

Far, far across the land, in a small hut, a little lantern lifted
its wick. It said, "I challenge the darkness. In my small corner,
I will not let the darkness settle itself around me." With this
example many other little lanterns in other small huts lifted
their wicks to the darkness. And the people watched in amazement as so many little lanterns illuminated the earth, prevent-
ing the mask of darkness from taking over.

The lantern in Khalra's parable did not seek to end darkness entirely. It
was humble enough to recognize that this was not a reasonable objective,
and instead it focused on its own small corner. By doing its part, the lantern's flicker of light inspired those around it to do the same. It modeled
a way forward that could be emulated, collectivized, and scaled. As other
lanterns followed, it became apparent that the little lantern's humble action effected meaningful change.

Although the lantern achieved an ideal outcome in this case, let's also
note that it would have been just as happy if other lanterns did not join its
cause. Why is that? Happiness is a function of our individual expectations. The lantern did not set out to save the world. Its satisfaction came
in understanding the needs of those it could reach and in seeking to meet
those needs. This is what it means to serve selflessly.

This insight resonates at a time when it feels like the world is falling
apart all around us. We see suffering and injustice everywhere we look:
climate change, lack of health-care access, gender inequities, racial injustice, widespread corruption, mass incarceration, voter suppression. The
list is endless. Our soulful compassion (hamdard) makes us want to act,
but being inundated with endless concerns leaves us feeling paralyzed.
Add to this that our culture of performing outrage demands an impossible standard, making us feel like imposters if we don't try to fix every
problem, or at least pretend to.

Khalra's life and his parable offer us a different way of engaging, what we call "seva" in the Sikh tradition. Seva demands humility, disabusing us of our desire to bear the weight of the entire world on our shoulders. Yes, there is endless suffering and injustice in our world, and yes, there are infinite issues to address. But aiming to fix all the problems around us or expecting ourselves and others to always do the right thing is not realistic. If that's the goal we set for ourselves, then we are setting ourselves up for perpetual disappointment and frustration.

Sikh philosophy presents a different way of understanding and engaging with our world. Rather than seeing the individual self as the starting point (as in Descartes's "I think therefore I am"), the Sikh outlook is that the entire world is fundamentally interconnected. Seva, therefore, is a way of caring for others, and it's also a way of caring for ourselves. With each selfless act, we become slightly less selfish; with each loving action, we become slightly more loving. On their own, single acts of seva might seem random, but taken together, they bring light into our world and into each of us.

This book is about you, about Sikh teachings, and about a way of life that enables a happier, more fulfilling engagement with the world, one that has shaped a vibrant community and tradition that remains unknown to so many. It speaks to the ways in which Sikh spirituality helped me survive the many challenges of life in America—especially racism—while preserving a sense of happiness, compassion, and justice for all. In showcasing the spiritual tenets of Sikhi that I have been studying, practicing, and teaching for much of my life, I also hope to share how anyone can adopt and cultivate these perspectives to enhance their lives.

At its core, this book is about that outlook we try to instill in our own kids: *Being kind to others makes them happy and makes you happier, too.* We have seen the best among us embody this wisdom, including Khalra, Mandela, and Malala. Yet we don't even have to rise to their level to be effective in changing the world and enhancing our own lives. We can do our part by living like that lantern, insisting on doing what we can to challenge the darkness. And who knows? Perhaps others will see our flames flickering in the darkness, and maybe they'll feel inspired to light their flames, too.

Khalra's life might be an extraordinary case, but his parable offers us light for our everyday lives. Over the past few years, I've developed a practice for when I feel ready to throw up my arms in exasperation and give up on people. I shut off my devices, step onto the sidewalks of New York City, and notice the small acts of kindness. *A man in a suit notices a baby lose a shoe and chases the woman pushing the stroller to return it. The handle breaks from a teenager's shopping bag, and the fruit vendor offers his own bags to help her. A construction worker realizes she is a dollar short at the bagel and coffee cart, and the seller replies: "Don't worry about it. Get me back another time."*

Like many people, I used to describe these as random acts of kindness. But once you start noticing, you'll see that there's nothing random about them. They're happening all around us, all the time. While our world is filled with pain and suffering, and while our culture focuses on the negative, there's beauty all around us, too. Noticing it can restore our faith in one another and in life itself.

When I watch people help one another, a number of questions come to mind. I wonder what they get out of giving to others. I wonder what moves them to give up something of their own for someone else's benefit. I wonder who they are and who they care for at home.

More than anything, I wonder how much better our world would be—more generous, more compassionate, and more just—if we could infuse these small acts of kindness into our way of living. In each of these moments, we get a glimpse of the light we have within us, the light we share with one another.

Introduction

WHERE I'M COMING FROM

"If I love you, I have to make you conscious of
the things you don't see."

—JAMES BALDWIN

I was eleven the first time someone called me a terrorist.

I was in middle school, and our club soccer team had a game near Dallas, Texas. During our pregame equipment checks, the referee came straight to me and demanded that I let him pat down my turban.

"Hey, little terrorist! You're not hiding bombs or knives in there, are you?" he said. "I know how you people like to blow shit up."

My fists clenched tightly and my body tensed. I wanted to punch him. But in that moment, I decided to lean my head forward instead. I hadn't ever let someone touch my turban before. But I wanted to play. And I was a kid.

You might praise me for not reacting with violence, but my response came from pragmatism, not principle. As an eleven-year-old boy, I wasn't about to fight a grown man.

I hated being put in that position, and I hated even more how I responded. For the rest of that game, the six-hour car ride home, and in the days and nights that followed, I seethed with anger. I resented the referee for how he treated me—like a criminal—and I resented myself for not having the courage to take a stand.

After a few weeks of reflection and talking through it with my family, I became less angry with myself for giving in to an ignorant man's racism. I started to see this interaction as a learning moment. I couldn't change what had happened, but I could promise to do better in the future.

———

Less than a year later, I found myself in a similar situation. We were in the locker room after basketball practice at my middle school in San Antonio, and like typical adolescent boys, we skipped our showers and instead doused our clothes and underarms with way too much of our dads' cologne. We would often play fight while getting changed, and this afternoon I was shadowboxing with Monroe, a teammate I'd become close to over our years of playing basketball together. We pretended to swipe at one another, and then he said, "Y'all can't fight. No wonder y'all use bombs on us instead." All the guys laughed, or at least that's what it felt like. I knew that he was joking and even remember thinking that, although his comment was racist, at least it was pretty clever. Suddenly, he reached forward and yanked the turban off my head. As before, my fists clenched and my body tensed. I flashed back to that moment with the soccer referee, recalled the overwhelming regret, recalled the promise to stand up for myself. And then my fists started flying, landing punch after punch on my friend's face. It all happened so fast.

Our teammates broke us up, but not before I gave him a bloody nose and opened up a cut on his cheek. He went to the sink to assess the damage and wash off. I silently packed my bag to go home. No one spoke in the locker room then, and none of us discussed it later. I think Monroe and my teammates knew he had crossed a line. I felt as if I'd crossed a line, too.

Was I right to fight a friend over a racist joke? Was this what standing up for myself looked like? And most perplexingly, if this was an overreaction and if my response to the soccer referee was an underreaction, then what might an appropriate reaction look like?

I was confused. And I was still only twelve years old.

Here's the reflection that began to take shape in my mind. Our species is wired to deal with anger and frustration in one of two ways: fight or flight. Yet neither of these addresses our problems sufficiently, and neither of them brings us satisfaction. Whichever of the two paths we choose, we find ourselves—as I did after both incidents—wrestling with regret, wondering what we could have done differently, and confused about how to respond the next time we're in a tough situation. Worse still, we walk away feeling more upset, not less.

This is how we get mired in cycles of anger and frustration.

=====

About twenty years after my fight with Monroe, a conversation with my student Kyla reminded me just how painful these cycles can be. I was teaching Islamic studies in the religion department at Trinity University in 2017, which must have been confusing for people in Texas meeting a Sikh for the first time. There I was, looking exactly like America's stereotype of a Muslim, teaching courses on Islam, yet claiming I was not a Muslim, but a Sikh. I welcomed their curiosity, however, because each question created an opportunity for education.

Kyla had been in my course on the Qur'an the previous spring and signed up for another course with me the following semester. One day, she visited my office hours and shared that she was feeling emotionally wrought after a falling-out with her parents. The trouble had started over the summer, when Kyla heard her father make racist comments while watching TV. When Kyla asked him why he had said what he did, her father dismissed them as harmless jokes. Kyla didn't want to cause more tension, so she decided to ignore them. But as the summer went by and the racist comments kept coming, Kyla felt her anger grow. The rage built up inside her until one day the dam burst. Kyla and her family were having dinner at a restaurant, and as a Sikh family walked by, her father announced: "Holy shit! It's ISIS!" That's when the floodgates opened. Kyla called her father a racist and told him that one of her professors (me) was a Sikh whose family had been hurt by negative stereotypes. What she once hoped would be an open and honest conversation turned into a series of heated arguments and, ultimately, a breakdown in her relationship with her father.

When Kyla shared the story with me, it had been six weeks since she and her father had last talked to each other. I could tell she was hurting. Her father was surely hurting, too. Kyla said she'd wanted to tell me sooner, but that she worried about my feelings. I thanked her for her concern and compassion and told her not to worry about me. I've dealt with far worse and have developed a thick skin. I also told Kyla how proud I was of her for doing the right thing and speaking out against anti-Muslim bias, especially given how difficult it must have been to stand up to her own father.

We talked for nearly an hour that afternoon, and as I sat there listening to her, I realized that we all have our own version of Kyla's story.

Life gives each of us our own challenges. We don't choose them and we can't predict them. All we can do is prepare ourselves to deal with them. When challenges confront us and we consider how to respond, we tend to take one of two imperfect paths: ignore or agitate. Ignoring our problems can give us momentary escape, while agitating against them can be an emotional release with consequences. As Kyla found with her father, limiting ourselves to these two options can leave us angry, embittered, and dissatisfied.

We know that these two approaches are unproductive and self-destructive. But often we don't know how to react any differently. As I spoke to Kyla that day, I recognized in her the same confusion I had felt myself at her age. When the most obvious answers fail to meet our needs, we need a fresh vision. One that helps us meet the challenges of our lives in ways that make us feel proud of our past, confident about our present, and hopeful for our future.

━━━

No faith or school has exclusive claim to wisdom. *Homo sapiens* literally means "wise person." The Sikh faith—the world's fifth largest religion, which I was born into and try my best to follow—is intensely focused on what it takes to journey through life with the beautiful inheritance of our bodies and to manifest wisdom in each moment. And yet, especially since the attacks on September 11, 2001, people the world over associate our flowing hair and wrapped heads with terror, fear, and intolerance. This reaction explains the urgency behind our efforts to distill Sikh traditions for ourselves and for others. To know ourselves, and to make ourselves known, are matters of life and death.

As I watch my fellow Americans watch me, I see faces flash with uncertainty—willing to be corrected yet unwilling to be convinced. What guides us in moments like these, when we feel doubt and confusion? How do we embody wisdom in ourselves and in our actions? These are daily questions for those of us who live on the margins of modern America, whether because of our race, religion, gender, sexual orientation, or otherwise. These are also the questions we all must answer regardless of our backgrounds, because answering these questions is part of our journey together.

This is where Sikh wisdom has come to serve me. It doesn't purport to give answers for these probing questions, nor does it offer an oversimplified view of the world. Rather, Sikh teachings prepare us to meet the challenges in our lives with core principles, frameworks, and practices. At a time when failing to convince someone can be fatal and where an easy answer is sometimes a cultural betrayal, Sikh wisdom offers a necessary balm in an age of daily provocation.

I'm aware that most of what distinguishes me physically is a personal choice. (Aside from my ridiculous handsomeness, of course.) I could stop wearing my turban and start shaving my beard if I wanted. Yet, every morning, I make the decision to brush my beard, comb my long hair, and tie my turban.

I choose to maintain my Sikh appearance because I believe the benefits far outweigh the hardships. I have experienced firsthand how Sikh teachings can equip and empower people to live with authentic happiness in the face of enormous difficulty. I have also seen how Sikh wisdom can help balance one's spiritual, ethical, and social being through consistent practice, and how doing so can help us maximize our potential in a meaningful and holistic way.

That is what this book is about: sharing wisdom that is personally transformative and spiritually uplifting, with the potential to change how we view ourselves, one another, and the world around us.

The beauty is that these teachings are meant for everyone and apply to people from all walks of life. The Sikh gurus lived their truth and shared their truth, yet they don't make an exclusive claim to truth. They believed there are many paths to the destination we all seek, and that you don't have to be a Sikh to be a good person or to live a joyous, loving, and fulfilling life.

The Sikh gurus taught that we are more likely to reach our goals when we get guidance from those who have already achieved them. They also advised that if you take these teachings just as knowledge—known as vidya (from Sanskrit)—they will remain nothing more than intellectual curiosities. In order for them to become part of your own wisdom—gyaan—you have to put them into practice. This is the Sikh way, and it's why we'll focus on the wisdom *and* its daily application. The teachings are part of a framework that apply to us all, but there is no clear-cut formula and there are no shortcuts. Each of us must journey into ourselves to discover joy and truth.

The Sikh ethos also proclaims that we're all interconnected, and therefore we're all in this together. Our individual liberation is bound up with one another's; we seek our own freedom while seeking freedom for all. It is this spirit that drives me to share the relatively untapped font of Sikh philosophy with the world. This worldview is not mine alone, nor is it exclusive to our community. Secret-keeping and gatekeeping have never been the Sikh way. From its outset five hundred years ago, the Sikh tradition has sought to smash power inequities and to democratize access to personal happiness for all. If we truly see ourselves as interconnected, we must endeavor for others as we endeavor for ourselves.

As I search for ways to navigate our tumultuous world, I realize that I would be lost without this guidance. Through studying and trying to live into this philosophy, I have found answers to some of life's most urgent questions. What does it look like to truly love our neighbors, including those who don't love us back? How do we prepare ourselves to fight hate with love, even when the hate threatens to harm us and our loved ones? What might we do to nurture humility, authenticity, and ethical fortitude in our own lives? In weaving this wisdom together with personal stories and contemporary accounts that bring these ideas to life (and occasionally with what I hope are good jokes), this book aims to offer a unique perspective to help cultivate empathy and a fresh vision for finding contentment in our lives, all while making visible a community and tradition that has remained unseen for far too long.

Part I

SEEING WITH
FRESH EYES

I t used to bother me a lot when people shared their racist views to my face. My anger would keep me from responding clearly—even responding at all. Even now, as a grown man, I still don't always know the right answer, in part because I believe there's no winning when it comes to racism, and in part because each situation requires its own measured response.

Yet I have developed different ways to meet each racist encounter, confident of who I am and unapologetic about how I look.

I have learned that deflecting ignorance and hate doesn't help anyone, and that we won't ever truly care for one another until we connect with one another. I have also learned that we can't lecture our way into people's hearts, and that opening ourselves up to strangers takes courageous vulnerability. The greatest payoff of sharing ourselves with one another is going beyond our individual experiences and seeing life from other viewpoints. Every day we can give the gift of empathy, to one another and to ourselves.

Sharing our stories is hard and uncomfortable, but as with my choice to wear my turban, I believe the rewards far outweigh the costs. It is in this spirit that I invite you into my own life. My sincere hope is that you might see and feel what it's like to walk in my shoes, as a brown-skinned, turban-wearing, beard-loving, sports-playing dude, trying to create a life of happiness for himself and his family in modern America.

One

HOME?

A few years ago, I was just outside my apartment building in New York City when I saw an elderly white woman trip and fall as she was crossing the street. I rushed over to help her and extended my hand. She reached up gratefully, but when she saw the turban on my head she jerked her arm back. Her face scrunched up, then opened back up to release a voice from deep within: "Go back to where you came from!"

I didn't expect my offer to help would trigger such a reaction. When I was younger and heard similar comments, my body would tense up, unsure whether to lash out in anger or shrink back in fear. Though both responses are natural and justifiable in their own way, neither struck me as right in these situations.

Coming face-to-face with hate regularly over the years helped prepare me for this moment. I had come to understand that there are other ways to respond that go beyond fear and anger, a middle path to dealing with the painful moments we encounter that can help us receive hate without internalizing it. While she saw me as a foreigner who threatened her safety, I saw her as I've learned to see all people: a fellow human being trying to bring security, coherence, and joy into her life. Isn't this concern for and interest in one another what makes us human?

Within seconds of the woman's exclamation, I knew what I wanted to do. I called over onlookers to help get her off the street and out of danger, standing by her until she was safe before going on my way.

I chose to care for this stranger, even though she clearly didn't care for me. In a moment when it would have been easier to feel hurt and to walk away, I decided instead to double down on her humanity—and my own.

⸻

I'm still amused when people tell me to go back to where I came from. It's not that I don't know what they mean, and it's not that I don't know what racism is. I grew up in Texas with a turban, beard, and brown skin, so I've been dealing with racism my whole life. I was born and raised in San Antonio and am an American. My family and I watched American movies growing up. Many of the athletes in the posters that hung on my bedroom walls were American, including David Robinson, Mia Hamm, and Muhammad Ali. I was even terrible at world geography as a kid— and what's more American than that?

Yet when people tell me to go back to where I came from, I know what they mean: *You look foreign and dangerous, and we'd feel better if you left.*

When it's safe and appropriate, I respond with a tactic that I've come to love over the years: humor.

Sometimes I have a little fun at their expense by putting on a thick Southern drawl: "Well, bless your heart!" I exclaim, drawing out each word as if it had at least two syllables. "My mama would love you. She keeps telling me to move home to Texas, too!"

I watch them squirm with confusion, and before they can figure out what's going on, I reach up to my turban and give it an imaginary tug, as if tipping a ten-gallon cowboy hat.

Other times I might reply earnestly, as if unaware of their malice: "Thank you *so* much for your thoughtful advice. I *really* appreciate it."

When people are being especially hateful, I prefer to ignore their nasty comments and continue on with my day, as if I didn't have a care in the world and they didn't exist. Nothing bothers them more than realizing their hate doesn't bother me.

Some friends who don't deal with racism have asked how I can find humor in these moments. I'm never quite sure how to answer that question. From my viewpoint, it's hard to imagine enduring daily provocation *without* humor.

What I do know, and what many people from marginalized groups also know, is that it's possible to remain calm in the face of hate. One can learn how by maintaining perspective—and with *lots* of practice.

It has also helped to recognize that people telling me to "go home" says more about them than it does about me. I've come to understand that their words reveal cultural ignorance, that underneath their statement is a pair of twin assumptions: that the United States is not a place for people who look like me, and that there is a place in this world where I truly belong.

———

My parents and ancestors hail from Punjab, a region in South Asia that spans northwestern India and modern-day Pakistan. We speak Punjabi, one of the ten most widely spoken languages in the world. And we eat Punjabi food—roti, daal, sabji, cholay—or at least many of us do. I personally prefer pizza to roti, to the embarrassment of pretty much everyone I know.

My family maintains a distinct appearance as part of our Sikh faith, which is known in the West as Sikhism and in Punjabi as Sikhi. "Sikhi" is the original Punjabi term for the tradition, pronounced with a long *e* at the end as in "queen." Sikhism is the later English form popularized through colonialism.

In 1469 CE, a boy named Nanak was born to Hindu parents in the village of Talvandi (now Nankana Sahib, in his honor). From childhood, young Nanak noticed the unhappiness, divisions, and inequities all around him. As he matured, Nanak began to offer a new vision for finding joy and purpose that centered around the daily practices of spiritual growth (nam japna), ethical living (kirat karni), and selfless giving (vand chakna). Nanak saw all existence as interconnected, and he decided to establish a new community that would live by a set of core principles, including equality, humility, integrity, service, and love. For many Sikhs, including myself, wearing the turban is a public commitment to living by these values.

I started wearing a turban when I was three years old. Not because there's something holy or special about that age. That's just when my hair grew long enough to wrap into a bun on top of my head. Until then, my mom would braid my hair into pigtails every morning. Pigtails are a common look for Punjabi Sikh toddlers—we're nothing if not trendsetters. Moreover, I think my mom secretly loved the pigtails because she *really* wanted at least one daughter.

Each morning, before school, my mom would line the four of us up at the kitchen counter. We would chatter over peanut butter toast and milk while she stood behind us, combing, braiding, and twisting our long, uncut hair until it was taut but not too tight. She'd then tie a small turban called a patka on each of us, adjusting it until it felt just right. If it came off in elementary school (which happened often enough during recess), my brothers and I would dash to one another's classrooms to get help retying it. As we became teenagers, we learned to do this ourselves, and we also started wearing larger turbans (dastaars and pagris) that are more typically worn by adults. There's a formal ceremony that Sikhs undergo when they begin wearing a larger turban (dastaar bandi), usually as adolescents or teens. My brothers and I never had one of these, and I don't quite know why not. My recollection is that it wasn't really on our radar and that our parents preferred that we ease into the new turbans without feeling the pressure of a formal ceremony.

I still wore the smaller patka when I played soccer in high school. It's a bit tighter on the forehead and felt more practical for heading the ball.

Having a turban helped me with my form, too. If I didn't hit the ball squarely with my forehead, my turban would loosen and I'd have to fix it. I can only remember one time that my turban came off while playing soccer. It was the second half of a tense playoff game against Madison High School. I rocketed a header into the goal so hard my hair exploded out of my turban and flew down to my knees. I remember it vividly because the goal, as well as my hairy celebration, were all over the local news that night. But the news reports focused less on me and more on my brothers in the stands, who had painted their faces blue and gold, wore matching blue and gold turbans, and were leading the fans in raucous celebrations. Not that I'm still bitter or anything, but *they* got all the attention after *my* glorious goal.

People often ask about the colors and styles of turbans. While it's true that it all comes down to personal preference, it's also true that I enjoy pulling people's legs. Sometimes I answer by saying that God will punish us if we don't wear certain colors on certain days. Sometimes I tell people that the larger your turban, the more God likes you. Once I told a friend who accidentally touched a turban sitting in a laundry basket that she had defiled holy cloth and that I would have to take it back to Punjab to get it resanctified. I was kidding, of course, and I still feel a little bad about the joke. But the look of horror on her face was priceless.

In reality, Sikhs can choose whatever color or style turban they want. I tend to wear a circular style that's a bit different from my father's, partly because it's more traditional, partly because it's more comfortable, and partly because it's a style that's cool among younger Sikhs (and among people like me who wish they were cool and young).

I also believe it's important to know one's own limitations, and here's one of mine: I'm definitely not stylish enough to pull off neon or floral, printed turbans. I tend to stick more with the muted colors—my go-to turbans are black, gray, and white, which, uncoincidentally, are the same colors as my beloved basketball team, the San Antonio Spurs.

Sometimes people ask me if wearing a turban is heavy or hot, especially while playing sports. I joke and say I wouldn't know because I've never taken mine off (though of course I do, when I shower, sleep, or even just relax at home). The truth, though, is that I don't *really* have a point of comparison. Yes, it can get sweltering, especially when I run marathons and half-marathons, but even then, I've been wearing a turban my whole life and it feels like an extension of my own body.

My turban has become an integral part of who I am, to the point that it's hard to imagine going through life without one. My identity as a Sikh, like my turban, has been wrapped into my own sense of self.

———

Guru Nanak's unique message attracted a community of followers, who would be known as Sikhs, pronounced with a short *i* and an aspirated *k* as in the word "sick." (While it's also common to pronounce "Sikh" with a long *e* sound, as in the word "seek," I prefer the former because that's how it's pronounced in the original Punjabi; the latter pronunciation was popularized through colonization.)

The word Sikh literally means "student," and to be a Sikh is to strive to practice these teachings daily. Sikhs referred to their teacher as guru, a word derived from Sanskrit that means moving from darkness to light—an enlightener.

Guru Nanak's following grew rapidly during his own life, and he appointed a successor, Guru Angad, who could continue growing the community and its institutions before appointing a successor of his own. There would be ten successive gurus in the line of Nanak, each of whom contributed to Sikhi's expansion until 1708. Before his death, the tenth leader, Guru Gobind Singh, passed authority to two entities—the community of committed and initiated Sikhs, known as the Guru Khalsa Panth, and the scriptural text, Guru Granth Sahib, which contains the wisdom of the Sikh gurus and some of their spiritual peers.

The Sikh community continued to grow under this new leadership over the next three centuries. Today, there are nearly 30 million Sikhs globally, making Sikhi the world's fifth largest religion.

Sikhs remain unknown to many people in the West, despite their sizable presence and despite having been in the United States for more than a century. A recent study conducted by the Stanford Innovation Lab found that 70 percent of Americans couldn't identify a photo of a Sikh while looking at one. In 2016, I appeared on a segment of *The Daily Show* to talk with correspondent Hasan Minhaj about the racism Sikhs face (and to dazzle Hasan with my brilliant wit). The first disappointment was that the interview didn't launch my stand-up career. The second disappointment came when Hasan asked several Americans to look at a card with four images—birds, binoculars, children playing peekaboo, and a turbaned Sikh man. He asked each of them to identify a Sikh. None of them could.

This is what it's like to be a Sikh in modern America. People notice me wherever I go: walking down the street, playing frisbee in a park, and most definitely at the airport.

EVERYONE notices me at the airport.

And yet, people don't actually *see* me. Hardly anyone who sees my turban, beard, and brown skin has an accurate sense of who I am or what I'm about.

Some who tell me to go back to where I came from assume that, somewhere on our planet, an entire society of people is walking around with turbans on their heads, free to express themselves as they please. But no such place exists. Even in India, where Sikhs are most populous, they still comprise only 2 percent of the country's population. What's more, Sikhs in India have long been targets of government abuse and human rights violations. My own parents left India to escape the cycle of discrimination against Sikhs and to find a home where their children could live freely and with equal opportunity.

More than anything, my father—Gurvinder Pal Singh—left at his own father's advice, who urged him to pursue his education in the United

States. My father first arrived in the U.S. in 1974 for graduate school in Philadelphia, and my mother—Parvinder Kaur—joined him after they got married in 1980. It turns out that they escaped India just in time, only four years before the Indian government launched a full-scale attack on its Sikh citizens, including a military assault on the most significant of Sikh sites—Darbar Sahib of Amritsar (known popularly as the Golden Temple and Harimandir Sahib). For comparison, imagine the Italian military attacking St. Peter's Basilica at the Vatican, or the Saudi Arabian government attacking Ka'ba in Mecca. A few months later, in November 1984, the Indian government, operating from ideologies of cultural supremacy, helped orchestrate a campaign of anti-Sikh pogroms in the Indian capital city of New Delhi. I was born in San Antonio, Texas, the same year that tens of thousands of my people were massacred by their own government.

———

It's no coincidence that my newly immigrated parents named me for the political activist Simranjit Singh Mann. They hoped I would grow up to serve the world with generosity, ferocity, and fearlessness.

While we were enjoying our comfortable lives in San Antonio, police forces in Punjab rounded up tens of thousands of Sikhs as part of their campaign to wipe out the entire community. Sikhs suffered human rights violations. Torture. Extrajudicial killings. Mass cremations.

My parents didn't experience the genocidal violence or witness any of it firsthand. But people they cared about were impacted, which moved my parents to become active in efforts for awareness and justice. This included educating Americans about the attacks on Sikhs in India, as well as teaching my brothers and me about the violence when we became old enough to understand it. Over the years, I have met survivors and listened to their stories of trauma and loss. I came to understand that their stories could have been ours; and just as importantly, I realized that, however connected we might be, my story was different.

My own experiences pale in comparison to these accounts, yet I have dealt with enough harassment from Indian law enforcement to know the seriousness of their threats. In 2011, while in the midst of my PhD training in religion and history at Columbia University, I received a prestigious fellowship from the American Institute of Indian Studies to conduct archival research in northern India. When Punjab police began harassing and threatening members of my family, several senior advisers urged me to take their threats seriously and do what I needed to do to ensure our safety. On their advice, I surrendered the fellowship and did not return to India. My advisers and lawyers counseled me to keep the police harassment confidential, and I have done so for several years. But more than a decade has now passed, and I have still been unable to visit. I share now with the hope that my story might help you see life from my perspective.

That some people see me and think I belong in India is confounding and laughable. I'm not better off there, nor is it a safe place for my community. For as long as I can remember, I have declined to identify as Indian, choosing instead to identify with that part of my heritage as Sikh, Punjabi, or South Asian.

Yet I have a hard time identifying as American, too. While I have always considered the United States my home, many people see me as an outsider. I know this because they have told me so, including with that tiresome demand I've heard more times than I can count: "Go back to where you came from!"

If only they knew where my family comes from, how we got here, and what we're about.

Two

BETWEEN WORLDS

L iving between worlds and never fully belonging to either is part of my family's inherited experience.

Both sets of my grandparents lived in western Punjab (what is now Pakistan) when the region was abruptly truncated in 1947 to carve out countries for larger religious groups: India would be for Hindus and Pakistan would be for Muslims. Caught between the politics and between new borders, a large portion of Sikhs moved east to the Indian side of Punjab. To this day, the partition of India and Pakistan remains the largest and most lethal mass migration in human history; an estimated 15 million were displaced and 1 million were killed in the ensuing violence.

My grandparents were among the millions who left behind everything they owned and arrived in a new country as refugees. My mother's parents, Kanwal Deesh Kaur and Inder Singh, began again with nothing and rebuilt their lives, eventually starting their own business selling spare parts for tractors. They settled in Rohtak, a small town in Punjab that would later become part of the state of Haryana. That's where my mother grew up, the oldest of four siblings. In typical Punjabi style, they each had their traditional Sikh names and their endearing "house names." My mother, Parvinder, went by Winkey, her sister, Kulvinder, was Ashu, the youngest brother, Amar Deep, was Giky, and their other brother, Harmohan, had the most Punjabi nickname of all time—Bunty.

My father's parents, Partap Singh and Kartar Kaur, also left their comfortable lives in western Punjab and came to India as refugees. They were physically separated in the chaos of the migration, and after losing his family, my grandfather went from camp to camp for days, desperately searching for his wife and kids, not knowing if they were still alive. With good fortune and lots of effort, he found them at a refugee camp in Amritsar. Having survived the horrors of losing one another, their entire extended family decided to live together, which meant seven adults and seventeen children would live under one roof. The family eventually settled in Bareilly, which is in the state of Uttar Pradesh. My grandfather began working for Indian Railways as a ticket inspector on its trains and gradually worked his way up to become a district traffic superintendent. My father, Gurvinder Pal Singh, was the second youngest of his eight siblings. The way he tells it, the extended family was so tightly knit that they didn't know until their teenage years who was a sibling and who was a cousin.

My father's oldest brother, Pritam, was the first to visit the U.S. He came in 1964 for a post-doc position at the University of Kentucky; he later became a renowned entomologist. I think of him often when I feel alone: I can't imagine how alone he must have felt.

The year he arrived in the U.S., a colleague learned that Pritam was from India and asked: "I once met a man named Ahmed Mostafa who was visiting from Egypt. Aren't your countries close together? Did you know him growing up?"

Pritam Uncle, as we called him affectionately, didn't have the heart to call out his colleague's ignorance. So he kindly responded: "I don't know him, but I'll keep an eye out next time I visit home."

My father had two more older brothers who moved to the U.S. before him. Harbhajan Singh came as a chemist and laid roots in New Jersey, and Jasbir Singh trained as an architect and eventually settled in Atlanta. In 1974, my father was admitted to a PhD program in engineering at Drexel University in Philadelphia. At the age of twenty-one, my father left India for the first time and arrived in the U.S. All he brought with him was $11 in his pocket, the clothes in his suitcase, the dream in his heart, and the turban on his head.

Well, actually, he *left* India with $11 in his pocket, but by the time he landed in New Jersey he was already down to $8. He had felt hungry during his layover in Paris and went to order breakfast. Not knowing French, he pointed to a delicious-looking omelet. He was devastated when the cashier took his crisp $5 note and returned two crumpled singles. This was how my father spent nearly a quarter of his savings before even stepping foot in America. On a damned omelet.

My father was fortunate to have family support when he arrived. His brother Harbhajan and sister-in-law Surjeet helped him get settled and showed him how to navigate life in the United States. His graduate adviser mentored him with care and attention, investing wholeheartedly in my father's academic training. And even though he had a better support system than many when they first immigrate, he still felt socially isolated. For the first time, my father was in a place where people didn't know about his Sikh faith. Experiencing discrimination regularly and being constantly asked questions about his background prompted my father to ask himself questions he had never considered before: Why do I choose to wear a turban when getting rid of it might make my life easier? In what ways does my faith contribute to my overall happiness? And if Sikhi is something I want to prioritize for myself and my future family, then how do I preserve my traditions in a foreign land?

After two years of serious reflection, these questions deepened my father's convictions and spurred him to enlist his parents' support in finding a life partner who had the skills, worldview, and fortitude to help raise an American family rooted in the Sikh faith.

While his vision was commendable, the way it played out in the matchmaking process sounds less like reality and more like reality TV. Unbeknownst to my dad, Gurvinder, his parents already had a partner in mind for him. Their longtime family friends had a daughter, Parvinder

Kaur, who had just completed her master's degree in English. Parvinder's parents and Gurvinder's parents conspired, informing one another what their children were looking for in a partner. Learning of Gurvinder's desire for a partner who could preserve Sikh singing traditions and teach them to future generations, my mother's parents immediately enrolled her in classes to learn traditional Sikh music (kirtan). Meanwhile, aware of Parvinder's aptitude and language skills, my father's parents began to suggest how important and special it would be to find a partner who was well educated and proficient in English. Their parents orchestrated it all so well that by the time Gurvinder and Parvinder finally met one another in India, there was hardly a chance that they wouldn't get married.

After my parents finished their degrees—my mother's master's in English literature from Maharshi Dayanand University in north India and my father's PhD in mechanical engineering from Drexel University in Philadelphia—they had their Anand Karaj (wedding ceremony) in Chandigarh in 1980. The year before, my father had accepted an offer to work at Southwest Research Institute in San Antonio, Texas, so after their wedding, my mother moved to Texas to join him. It was a transition for both of them, but they both felt good about San Antonio because the city reminded them of home. The people were kind, open-minded, and family oriented. The weather was warm all year round and blistering hot in the summer. And the food was the spiciest they could find.

To this day, my parents say what they once gleaned from a bumper sticker: They weren't born in Texas, but they got there as soon as they could.

Three

TURBANS IN TEXAS

y parents settled into their first home as a couple in 1980, and life as a newly married immigrant couple was hard. They had bills to pay and jobs to work, all while learning a new culture. The first week in her new home, my mother found a three-liter bottle of Coca-Cola that my father had stowed in the cabinet. Growing up in India, soda had been a luxury that they only enjoyed in sips when guests visited. But now she found herself face-to-face with an entire three-liter bottle of her own. She took a swig. Then another. And before she knew it, she had drunk the entire bottle. Then her stomach hurt for two days straight. Life in Texas would take some adjusting.

My older brother Harpreet was born three years after my parents settled in San Antonio, and I followed him thirteen months later. Darsh came two years after me, and then Raj two and a half years after Darsh. In a span of five and a half years, my poor mother gave birth to four rambunctious, troublemaking boys. Growing up, it wasn't uncommon for strangers to see the four of us in tow and say things to her like, "God bless you" or "You're such a saint." I thought maybe my mother had done something to help them, or that maybe they were trying to convert us (which happened more often than you might think). But now that I have two kids of my own, I see why people felt moved to offer their admiration and sympathy.

My brothers and I were typical American boys. All our free time went to playing sports, reading books, and hanging out with our friends. On the rare occasions that we were bored, we'd pick fights with one another, doing whatever we could to get under one another's skin. I was especially fond of messing with my younger brother Darsh, at least until the summer when he sprouted four inches and suddenly towered over me.

As with many immigrant families, there were more people in our homes than bedrooms. We lived in a small house in an affordable neighborhood the first few years of my life. When my parents learned the importance of being zoned for good public schools, they began saving up for another move. In 1988, we moved into a new home in Braun Station that was just big enough for our growing family. Our youngest brother, Raj, was born the next year, so he slept in a crib in his own room. My parents had their own room. And the other bedroom was for Harpreet, Darsh, and me.

Although my father was working full-time, he and my mom had also started a new software technology business out of their garage. They would work on the business in the evenings and early mornings while we were sleeping. As their business began picking up steam, my father began traveling more often. The more he traveled around the country, the more racism he faced. My brothers and I could hear our parents discussing it at night through our bedroom wall. The business was still in its early stages and needed nurturing, so they wanted my father to go out and attract new clientele. But the biggest priority was our family's physical safety. Perhaps it was best to put that money toward a home in a more secure neighborhood.

We moved again just before I began second grade, this time to a two-story home in a gated community. Each of us would have our own room, and we'd have a backyard big enough for a soccer field and a makeshift basketball court. The house was like heaven, and the neighborhood was even better. We were outdoors all the time, riding our bikes through the streets as if we owned the subdivision. For basketball, we preferred

playing next door with the Mieras boys—Ryan, Shawn, and Michael—
because their hoop went low enough for us to dunk. For football and
soccer, all our neighbors would come to our backyard because it was flat
and open. On rainy days, we'd all get together at the Washingtons' house
across the street; Anthony had a Sega Genesis, and we'd play *NBA Jam*
tournaments for hours.

Our families had so much trust in one another that we would all be
out for hours unsupervised, until our parents wanted us home for dinner.
We were supposed to keep them informed of where we would be, but
we'd often forget to do that. On those occasions, they would have to call
around—and sometimes drive—to collect us and bring us home. Even
then, we'd often convince our parents to let at least one or two of our
friends stay for dinner.

Looking back now, I realize the absurd beauty and privilege of our
childhood. We had trust and freedom and mutual respect. We had safety
and security. We had a diverse group of neighbors—the Mieras family
was white, the Washington family was Black, and the Lewis family was
mixed race, East Asian and white. We even lived on a cul-de-sac, the
quintessence of American suburbia. So much of our life experience mirrored the American dream.

And yet, while we saw ourselves as typical American boys, we also
knew that people didn't see us that same way. On the basketball court, in
our schools, at the grocery store, in our neighborhoods—we never fooled
ourselves into thinking we could blend into a crowd.

For the most part, people saw our turbans and long, uncut hair as
matters of curiosity. We became accustomed to answering people's questions about who we were and why we wore "that thing" on our heads. I
still remember my standard script, which I recited hundreds of times
while growing up: "Thank you for asking. It's called a turban, and it cov-
ers our long hair, which we don't cut as part of our Sikh faith." Our
parents taught us to respond clearly and politely, reminding us that every
interaction was an opportunity to educate people about our culture. I

realize now that this education was not just for the good of others; it was a way for my parents to create empathy, understanding, and safety for their children.

Not all the attention we received was well intended. Some saw our turbans and long hair as objects of ridicule. I could share dozens of stories from childhood. The time in preschool I wanted to cut my hair after a pair of boys insisted that my long hair meant I had to be the princess at playtime. The time in elementary school a group of older boys pushed me out of the boys' bathroom and told me I could only use the girls' bathroom until my hair was short like theirs. The time in middle school a fan in the crowd yelled, "Knock that towel off the point guard's head. It's where he gets his power!"

When my older brother started middle school, some kids started calling him "Diaper Head." Harpreet tried to explain the reason for his turban, but those attempts didn't land and the bullying continued. That was the first time I realized that racism was about more than ignorance and that education would only take us so far.

My parents advised him to ignore their teasing: "You can't control how people treat you," I remember them saying over dinner one evening. "But you can always control how you respond."

This was my parents' general response to the racism we encountered: to ignore it, to let it go, to turn the other cheek, to be the bigger person. We talked often about the importance of maintaining our composure in these moments. This advice served me well for most of my youth. Walking away from conflict helped ensure that we didn't get baited into fights, sucked into negativity, or distracted from the things in life that truly matter.

Encouraging us to turn the other cheek doesn't mean my parents were passive. It means that when it came to their children's safety, they were risk averse. I didn't always agree with their approach, especially in moments when people yelled something hateful and it felt easy to yell something angry in response. But as a parent now, I understand why they insisted that we not respond with anger. It was a matter of strategy; they felt it would be safer for us to sidestep hate rather than confront it head-on.

I learned from my parents that we can be proactive in addressing hate without taking on much additional risk. We were one of the few Sikh families in all of South Texas, and well-meaning people often asked about our turbans, in restaurants, on playgrounds, and even at post offices. For my parents, every interaction was an opportunity to educate the people around us about our heritage. At the beginning of each school year, my mother would come to our schools to give presentations on Punjabi and Sikh culture. She would lead us in singing while playing the harmonium and tabla, share samples of home-cooked Punjabi food, and even show how we wrap our hair and our turbans. As we got older, we began leading these sessions with her, and eventually, on our own.

I felt a tinge of ambivalence with each presentation, and I feel the same even now as I deliver them for my own kids. When families like mine come in to offer cultural-awareness programs, it's a reminder that children would not learn about people like us unless we made the effort to open ourselves up. Presentations like these are a reflection of how much immigrants do to assuage xenophobia. My parents came to seek refuge in the U.S., and in a bid to ensure their children's safety, they go out of their way to share their culture, as if to say: *Please don't fear us or harm us. We're really very nice.*

These efforts are rarely seen for what they are, taken for granted both by the children of immigrants (including myself) and the onlookers for whose benefit we do this dance. This is not to say that we don't enjoy sharing aspects of our cultures or that we don't want the people around us to appreciate who we are and where we come from. The point is this: Instead of fearing difference, embrace it. And that means rewiring the culture that fuels fear in the first place. If that sounds far-fetched, then you haven't experienced society as a marginalized group, where changing the culture of fear is our only option.

At the same time, I'd be lying if I said these presentations felt like an important part of my childhood. I was never all that interested in discussing what made me different; I'd much rather enjoy the pastimes I shared with my friends: playing Ninja Turtles, admiring and trading our growing collections of basketball cards (which I still haven't been able to part with), and, most important, playing sports outside, whether real or made-up, organized or makeshift.

By middle school, my brothers and I had heard all the standard stereotypes and slurs. (Racists aren't all that creative, it turns out.) But we were bored with the tropes and started to shut down hate with humor, making a game of nailing quick, witty responses.

When an older kid came up to Darsh at a theme park and asked him if he was a genie, he said, "Yeah, and I'm going to make your racist ass disappear."

When a player on an opposing basketball team pushed Raj and called him a terrorist, he smiled and said, "Is that what you call everyone you can't guard?"

When a classmate announced that I would be better at math because "all Indian people are good at math," I rebutted, "It's not that we're all smart. It's just that you're not."

When someone outside a mall cursed at Harpreet and said he'd go to hell if he didn't convert, he responded, "Didn't Jesus say something about loving your neighbors?" (It amuses me when people try to convert us by threatening us with hell. It's an unconvincing argument, primarily because, as Sikhs, we don't believe in hell.)

In high school, my brothers and I found a new way to amuse ourselves. We would show up at a new basketball court where we didn't know anyone and play into people's assumptions that we were foreign, speaking to one another in Punjabi and hitching our shorts up so high that we gave ourselves wedgies. We would wait our turn to play, and then stun everyone by running circles around them. I'll never forget the time a guy watching us from the sideline announced out loud what we knew everyone was thinking: "Man, these dudes don't look like ballers—but they can BALL."

========

Being hated feels isolating. Having company makes it bearable. My brothers and I helped one another understand and move beyond the racism we faced, and I felt fortunate to have them by my side. We may not have had many people around who looked like us, but at least we had one another.

We also had the support of our friends, classmates, and teammates, many of whom showed up for us in moments when we really needed them and in ways we didn't always expect.

I was in middle school when our club soccer team began traveling for games around Texas. We were near Austin for a match, and just before halftime, the other team had a two-on-one breakaway. The forward on the ball took one too many touches, and I was able to slide tackle the ball away and clear it up the field to my teammates. The referee turned his head to follow the play, and I jogged along, too. Suddenly I felt a sharp pain in my back and thudded to the ground. Their forward stood over me, sputtering slurs, like "Saddam" and "Sand-Ni**er." I hopped up to defend myself. I gave him a hard shove, then landed my fist on his jaw. Apparently, my teammate Levi had been right behind me, because he grabbed my jersey from behind and said, "I saw that and heard that. I got this." Levi tackled the guy, and they wrestled on the ground for a few seconds before two of the referees pulled them apart. Levi and I both received red cards for our troubles and had to sit out the rest of the game. Levi also had a busted lip and the beginning of a black eye. Because we were disqualified, our team played the rest of the game down two players. We lost 3-1. But the rest of the match and the whole ride home, I felt a kind of comfort I had never felt before. My friends had my back.

It wasn't just our friends and teammates who stood with us and for us. Our teachers and coaches did, too. Just before his very first high school basketball game, Darsh saw Coach Maxwell arguing with referees and the other team's coach. The opposing coach was fuming and shouted loud enough for everyone to hear: "He can't play with that thing on his head! Show me in writing where it says he can play!"

After a few more minutes of arguing, Coach Maxwell walked over to the bench, pulled out his small whiteboard, and wrote on it furiously. He turned around to show the other coach, the referees, and anyone else who was looking. Written in all caps were the words: "HE CAN PLAY!!!"

This story makes me so happy. I loved seeing Coach Maxwell—a living stereotype of a high school basketball and football coach in Texas— showing up to defend this lanky, turban-wearing kid he had just met weeks before. This story also shows me the promise of standing up for one another. With Coach Maxwell's support, Darsh would go on to play basketball in college and break new ground: He would be the first tur- baned Sikh to play basketball in the NCAA, an achievement that the Smithsonian Institution in Washington, D.C., would recognize by dis- playing his jersey in its exhibits.

(As Darsh's brother, it's crucial I tell you he wasn't *that much* better at basketball than I was. I used to beat him in one-on-one all the time when we were kids. I sent the Smithsonian a letter saying as much, along with two of my old YMCA jerseys. I'm still waiting to hear back from them on that.)

As you may have discerned by now, our lives in Texas were both nor- mal and atypical. They were normal in the sense that we saw ourselves as conventional American teenagers. We loved nothing more than hanging out with our friends. School was fun because it was a vehicle for our so- cial lives. We cared more about sports than learning. And aside from Sundays, we didn't think too much about culture or religion. We were different, yes, but our differences didn't determine who we hung out with or how we spent our time.

At the same time, our teenage years were atypical in that we experienced ignorance and prejudice in ways that many people can't even imagine. We were cognizant of how people perceived us, and we had developed specific strategies to defuse tense situations. We didn't judge people who didn't share our experiences, nor did we think ourselves better for learning how to endure hate. Our lives were just different from our friends' lives in certain ways, and therefore our approach to living in the world varied in certain ways, too.

We had learned how to survive and thrive in the place we called home. And thank God that we did. Because in the next few years, racist hate would hit us harder than ever before.

Four

SEEING OURSELVES

A long with about three thousand other Texas teenagers, my brothers and I attended O'Connor High School, located just outside San Antonio in a town called Helotes. O'Connor was the premier agricultural magnet school for South Texas, which meant we had actual barns and pens on campus to house the cattle, sheep, pigs, and other livestock that students were raising (and endless jokes about our high school being full of shit). It also meant that in addition to the relatively diverse populations zoned for the school, O'Connor attracted students from across the region. To give a snapshot: The student parking lot had about three times as many pickup trucks as cars, and more than once I was surprised to learn that a friend had proudly pasted a Confederate-flag decal on the back window of their truck.

I made dozens of friends at O'Connor High School, many of whom I'm still close with today and visit frequently. My brothers and I made friends easily, and we had a good reputation among our classmates and teachers. Our parents' open-door policy certainly didn't hurt that cause; our friends had a standing invitation to join us for a meal or stay over anytime they wanted. Our front and back doors were always unlocked, and it wasn't uncommon for our friends to be at our home, unannounced, even when the rest of the family was away at work and school.

We weren't just well-liked because our parents were generous and cool. (At least that's what I tell myself.) Being involved in extracurriculars helped us make friends across cliques. Harpreet played basketball and led the marching band as its drum major; I ran cross-country and captained the soccer team; Darsh was class president while playing the saxophone and varsity basketball; and Raj would later become president of the National Honor Society and varsity soccer captain, too. We were connected in different circles, which meant we had support networks among students, teammates, teachers, and coaches.

Our deep relationships proved crucial my senior year at O'Connor when, at the outset of the school year, our country was shaken by the terrorist attacks of September 11, 2001. We stood together in Mrs. Strong's social studies classroom, silent in shock and grief as we watched the Twin Towers fall and saw the residue of the plane crash into the Pentagon. My heart sank further when the television networks showed pictures of Osama bin Laden and identified him as the likely perpetrator of the attacks. The brown skin. The long beard. The white turban. I trusted that my circle of friends knew that I had no connection to bin Laden or his beliefs. But I also knew that most Americans would not be so informed or understanding, and that if history was a guide, life for my family and me was about to become much more difficult.

Within a few hours, my mother arrived at our high school to take us home. My brothers and I rode home in silence, and after we walked through the front door, I watched her lock the door behind us for the first time. She didn't have to say anything. Each of us knew the stakes.

Like millions of Americans around the country, our eyes stayed glued to the news all day as we tried to learn what we could about the attacks.

That same day, we received the first death threats at our home. I answered the phone first. An angry voice shouted slurs and curse words and threats until I hung up, breathless. My brothers and I agreed not to tell our mom about it. We didn't want to worry her. Instead, we picked up the phone every time it rang that afternoon until she intercepted a call during dinner. Unlike us, she had the awareness to tell them she was calling the police. She then hung up, dialed 911, explained the threats, and came back to the dinner table as if nothing had happened. Once again, each of us knew the plan without anyone saying a word: No one would be leaving the house until it was safe.

I appreciated seeing my mother display courage in the face of death threats against her family. It also shook me. Since waking up that morning, we had been attacked twice: first as Americans, and now as Sikhs. It was hard to process, and even harder to imagine how life would change. All we knew was that life would never be the same.

As our family stayed home the next two weeks, we saw two different sides of America. The threatening phone calls continued, and some strangers even drove by our home yelling angry threats. But far more people checked in on us—neighbors, classmates, teammates, and even strangers. Some brought gifts of food, others brought flowers. All of them brought their love and support. I'll always remember my parents pointing out then, in that moment of extreme difficulty, how one finds hope in the face of adversity: Notice how much more love there is in the world than hate.

The death threats rattled me initially, but I didn't feel perturbed for long. Without follow-through, the harassment seemed empty and cowardly. Like many teenage boys, I also felt invincible.

What really got my attention, however, was seeing how communities all over the country, including my own, were being devastated by racist backlash and could only do so much to protect themselves.

Hate violence surged, targeting anyone and everyone who appeared to be linked with the perpetrators. The Sikh community recorded approximately ten attacks per day. A Sikh friend of ours in New York City, a doctor named Navinder, rushed to help the moment he learned about the attacks. He was at Ground Zero less than an hour after the Twin Towers had fallen, risking his own life to care for survivors. The very next day, when Navinder ventured out of his apartment, New Yorkers who had no idea who he was and what he'd been doing hurled racist slurs at him. The day after 9/11, our family watched the national news with horror as they showed SWAT teams surround an Amtrak train and arrest a Sikh man, Sher Singh. A fellow passenger reported him to the police because he looked suspicious. And on September 15, 2001, we learned about the murder of Balbir Singh Sodhi, a Sikh gas station owner in Mesa, Arizona. His killer, Frank Roque, saw Sodhi's turban and beard, presumed him to be responsible for the terrorist attacks, and shot him. Sodhi died instantly, becoming the first casualty of a hate crime after 9/11.

In America and elsewhere, hate violence was not a new experience for me, for my family, or for other Sikhs. It wasn't a new experience for others targeted in the post-9/11 backlash either, including Muslims, Arabs, and South Asians. Yet, as in previous moments, there are times when bigotry intensifies, revealing more about what's underneath the surface and how far we still have to go.

Over the next several days, we huddled around the TV, watching reports from Ground Zero and Washington, D.C. In the evenings, we would crowd around the telephone, joining a nightly conference call organized by Sikh activists from around the country. Community leaders from across the United States shared what was happening in their local communities, including information on bias attacks, what measures people were taking to ensure their safety, and how community members were feeling. We would then move into community strategy with our shared concern: How would we respond to the rising hate we were facing in ways that reflected our values and made us safer?

I heard Sikhs from around the country share their views. Listening to their perspectives reinforced my own belief that deflecting hate is never the right answer and that the best approach would be to stand with the Muslim community. It was the right thing to do, and it also ensured that we would confront hate rather than ignore or redirect it. The experience of learning how to put our values into practice in a critical moment was formative; observing that many in the Sikh community decided to take the same approach was heartening.

Witnessing the violent incidents the first week after 9/11 helped me see that our physical safety was truly in jeopardy and that my approach to dealing with racism was insufficient. Here I was, a young man preparing to leave my home and enter the real world, wondering if I would ever truly belong in this country, when a cutting realization changed the trajectory of my life. If I didn't start proactively confronting the racism all around me, people I knew and loved would be killed. We didn't have the luxury of waiting for conditions to improve or for someone else to give us a boost. We had to do this ourselves, with passion and urgency and sacrifice.

It wasn't enough to ignore racism, as I had learned from my parents. It wasn't enough to deflect the hate with witty jokes and sharp rebuttals, as I did with my brothers. It wasn't even enough to have strong relationships, as I had developed with my classmates, friends, and teammates. Taking on hate was more than a moral responsibility and more than a form of activism that we take up in our free time.

For myself and for my loved ones, taking on hate was no longer a choice. It was a matter of survival.

I now see this as the moment that moved me from being non-racist to being anti-racist. The difference between the two is substantial. Before, I would turn the other cheek in uncomfortable moments, disagreeing with the racism I saw but largely unwilling to do anything about it. I would walk away, without any sense of responsibility to hold people accountable.

But witnessing the surge in hate, I realized that I had to embrace the discomfort. I also realized the importance of proactively challenging racism wherever and whenever I encountered it. No longer could I let things slide, because to do so would be to help create the conditions for racist violence. Years later, I came across the words of Angela Davis that put into language what I'd felt so viscerally then: "In a racist society, it's not enough to be non-racist. We must be anti-racist."

My new resolution to challenge racism proactively did not mean that I would throw fists at anyone who said something hateful. It meant that I would try to be part of the solution, by proactively contributing in various creative ways.

While I had been dealing with racism since childhood, embracing this new approach as a seventeen-year-old in the immediate aftermath of 9/11 put me on a new path entirely. No longer would I be a passive observer of my own life. I would be its author.

Five

MOVING OUT
AND LOOKING IN

U p to my senior year of high school, I talked seriously about moving far from Texas after graduating. I loved my friends and family, but I also cherished my independence. My teammates and I talked often about skipping college and going to play semiprofessional soccer in Europe (and some of them did). Yet for a number of reasons, including my own uncertainty about what I wanted to do with my life, I ended up much closer to home than I had hoped—only twenty minutes away. I chose Trinity University because of its nationally ranked Division III soccer team and its stellar education program, though I nearly didn't go there. First, I wasn't the best student in high school, and I nearly failed to submit my application in time. I didn't even remember to ask Mrs. Strong to write my letter of recommendation until the afternoon it was due. Second, I was also being recruited by one of Trinity's nearby rivals, Southwestern University, where some of my friends from high school had gone to play. Being a ridiculous teenager, I staked my final decision on a soccer game between the two teams. I would go to the school that won the game. Trinity won in a close match, and that sealed the deal.

We weren't exactly shocked to learn that I'd be the first turbaned Sikh to attend Trinity University. There weren't many racial or religious

minorities on the entire campus—and I was both. Trinity was a historically Christian school, and at the time, admitting a diverse student body
was not a high priority. I felt out of place, especially after attending a
public high school with far more racial diversity and class diversity. At
the same time, I was used to being the only one of my kind, so I was
comfortable enough. Besides, my first-year roommate, Michael, was a
childhood friend. We had played soccer together for years, including all
four years in high school, and we made friends easily, especially through
sports.

As kind and welcoming as my new college friends were, I could tell
that they had no idea what it felt like to live in my skin. One of my closest friends from college, Jenn, had grown up in Abilene, a town in North
Texas. Years after graduating, she told me how uncomfortable she'd felt
when she first saw me on campus: "I'm embarrassed to admit it now, but
I'd never met anyone before who looks like you. I was nervous and scared
and really didn't know what to think."

I wasn't surprised to hear her say this, and I imagine you aren't either.
We all have biases.

No one at Trinity shared these biases with me openly when we were
students, and to be honest, I didn't really expect them to. It's just not
something we really did back then. But in retrospect, I wish we did, because even though I made friends, I still felt like an outsider. I missed
having my brothers around more than I'd anticipated.

In a new community and without my brothers' support, I often relied
on my old friend—humor—to cope with unfamiliar situations. Sometimes my humor would backfire on my friends and me.

At a conference for resident assistants, where the theme that year was
"Boot Camp," each of the RAs selected a nickname for the drill sergeant
to use. I chose "Turbanator," thinking the name would make people
laugh and soften their perceptions of me. (I also thought then that the
nickname was original. Over the years, I would learn that virtually every
turbaned Sikh had the same nickname during the 1990s.)

An adviser from another institution approached our adviser, Katie, and berated her: "How can you let that poor international student be called that name? He probably doesn't even know what the Terminator is." The other adviser assumed I wasn't from the U.S. and that Katie was inviting my peers to humiliate me. The woman thought she was doing the right thing by standing up for me. But as is often the case with hidden bias, she was actually making a mistake.

Katie wasn't sure how to respond to this woman berating her, but I was. I walked up, put my arm on Katie's shoulder, and turned on my Texas twang: "I appreciate your concern, ma'am, but I'm from good ol' Texas, born and raised, and I love the Terminator almost as much as my barbecue. Don't you be thinkin' I'm from anywhere else now, ya hear?"

"Oh," she replied, in soft surprise, then turned and walked away. Katie and I both exhaled with relief, and when the woman was out of earshot, we laughed for two minutes straight.

——

It felt validating when my new friends would see there was more to me than how I looked. My self-confidence didn't rely on their ability to see it, but still, I appreciated when they got a sense of what we went through: seeing how people stared at me when we went out to eat, hearing nasty remarks slung my way at games, or watching police officers racially profile me during the trips we took together.

During our second year in college, I went on a road trip with my roommate Dave. We were driving through rural Ohio, Dave behind the wheel, when a cop pulled us over. Instead of going to the driver's side, where Dave was sitting, he came straight to the passenger side and rapped on my window. He asked me where I was from. I told him Texas. He asked me again. And again. And again. And again. Five times in total. Each time I gave him the same answer. I knew what he was getting at. But I wasn't going to give him the satisfaction of letting him think I was foreign just because I looked different or that he had a right to treat me unfairly because of how he saw me. I was tired of giving away my power.

Yet when he demanded my driver's license to run a background check, I handed it to him without hesitation. I knew it wasn't safe for someone who looked like me to provoke or even question a police officer. The next ten minutes felt like an eternity, but then came the reprieve. The officer returned to our car, handed my license back to me, and told us we were free to go.

I was annoyed and embarrassed. Dave was furious. He said that he had figured it was hard to be me but he never imagined what I went through or what it felt like. He was curious and outraged, and we ended up discussing my experiences with racism for the remainder of our drive.

Feeling Dave's concern and empathy made me feel better—less alone—and it deepened our friendship. At the same time, being shown how little power I truly have in this country, being reminded that many see me as the image of this country's enemy—turban, beard, brown skin—and having seen how hate and violence claim lives and destroy families, I had no choice but to ask myself the same hard questions that my father had asked himself upon first moving to the United States at age twenty-one. Why did I choose to look this way? Was keeping my turban worth the inconveniences that came with it? And if so, what did I need to do so that I would feel proud and confident as I wrapped it around my head each morning?

═══

I'll share something that was difficult for me to acknowledge then, and that is still uncomfortable for me to disclose now. To this point in my life, I had dismissed religion generally and Sikhi in particular as a vestige of my ancestral lineage, a way of life that was outdated and out of touch. It was for my parents and grandparents and for people in Punjab, not for me or my brothers in America. We had learned the basic teachings that our parents imparted to us from early childhood, and we appreciated being part of the small but growing Sikh community in South Texas—and we had extracted value from both. But even then, Sikhi felt more like an identity that we inherited and maintained as a way to stay bonded with one another. Why did I really continue wearing my turban? Because to sever my ties to Sikhi would be to risk severing my ties with my family.

As I began to explore why I thought Sikhi had little practical value, I realized that I had internalized ideas that my own people and their traditions were outdated and inferior. To even begin giving Sikhi a fair shake, and to truly see if Sikh teachings might have practical applications for my daily life, I had to begin by confronting my biases.

This was not easy at first, but with practice I got better at it. Here's how I began:

Anytime I noticed myself making assumptions and value judgments about different communities, including my own, I would pause, take a breath, and ask myself where those ideas came from. I couldn't always pinpoint the origin, even with some reflection and research, but at least I was acknowledging my bias and asking myself the question. I was training myself to leave old assumptions behind and to think in new ways about what I saw.

For instance, I had long felt ashamed that Sikhi did not have a clear explanation for what happens to us after we die. Friends and strangers, mostly Christians, would often ask me what Sikhs believe about afterlife. When I said there was no clear explanation, some would ask how Sikhi could be a real religion without answering that question. Hearing this response consistently really bothered me, and I began digging for answers. When I didn't find a compelling answer, I began to internalize the same doubt: *Is Sikhi even a real religion?*

This question nagged at me for years, until I learned in college to ask myself a different order of question: *Where does this focus on afterlife come from? And why do I care so much?*

It was through taking this new question seriously that I was able to uncover my bias. I wasn't asking this question out of curiosity or because I saw an inconsistency within Sikh philosophy. I was asking because it was a central question in other people's worldviews. They expected my worldview to mirror theirs because it's what they knew—and I had unknowingly come to internalize their expectations, too.

Now that I could see this clearly, I could see the beauty of my own tradition. Sikhi places little emphasis on the afterlife because it's a question of speculation: If no one knows with certainty what happens after we die, then why dwell on it so much? Sikhi teaches us to do what we can in the world that we know, that by dwelling in the here and now we can achieve joy and love and enlightenment.

This outlook makes sense to me. It's sensible and satisfying. It was also staring me in the face all along. I just couldn't see it until I cleared my biases, clarifying my own vision through honest self-reflection.

Going through the process of challenging my assumptions was about more than the outcomes. Honest introspection helped me see the personal benefits of inner spiritual work. It also showed me that spiritual practice could be intellectual, too—that opening our hearts and our minds is to open up our humanity.

Becoming proficient at identifying and dealing with my own biases, slowly and intentionally, helped create a new openness in my life for learning. I began delving into Sikh teachings with a curiosity and earnestness I hadn't felt before, and I was captivated by what I uncovered. Here was a tradition that had been living in my blood all along and that could help answer some of my most pressing questions. What does it mean to feel connected to the world all around us? How do we find love and joy in our everyday lives? And how do we learn to serve others and ensure justice in a world filled with suffering and inequities? I had been passionate about these issues for years, and for the first time I found coherent, sensible, and compelling answers.

My desire to learn about religion and race was also driven by personal experience. Although I would have preferred to ignore it, the backlash following 9/11 made me realize that I no longer had a choice: I had to confront the racism our communities faced.

I figured the first step to dealing with racism would be to understand it as best I could: its formation, its history, its expressions in art and literature, its manifestations in politics. I devoured every book I could find on the topic and enrolled in any relevant course available to me in college. It became clear that we can't understand American racism without understanding its religious roots. Here are three reasons why.

First, historically speaking, religion is the parent of American racism. Just a year after Columbus arrived in North America, Pope Alexander VI issued what would come to be known as the Doctrine of Discovery, which announced that Christians were superior to Indigenous "heathens" everywhere and therefore had the right to colonize them. Religion laid the groundwork for American racism.

Second, religion has been weaponized to uphold American racism. For instance, white supremacy often cloaks itself in the disguise of religion. We see this clearly in how Christian slaveholders in the eighteenth and nineteenth centuries used the Bible to sanctify the enslavement of darker-skinned people.

Third, religious minorities experience racism because of how they look and what they believe. This racism has dire consequences for us all. For example, how we perceive religious groups and the threats they pose leads us to commit endless resources to combating foreign terrorism and hardly any to combat white nationalism, even when we've known for years that white domestic terrorism poses a greater threat to our national security than outside sources.

I felt this third point in my bones because I had long experienced firsthand how religious minorities are swept up by American racism. I had always seen "my people" as the people around me that I knew and loved—neighbors, teammates, classmates, friends. My circle of friends reflected the demographic makeup of San Antonio: Hispanic, Black, and white. But strangers view me differently, especially since 9/11, perceiving "my people" through the lens of race: anyone who "looks Muslim," including Arabs, Sikhs, South Asians, and, of course, Muslims.

These perceptions perplexed me. I hardly knew anyone who belonged to any of these groups. The only Muslims I could think of was my childhood babysitter and her family. I didn't think I knew any Arabs. And we only knew a handful of other South Asians at the time. There simply weren't that many people from these groups in San Antonio when I was growing up, so I had never considered any of these communities as part of my core group.

That changed slowly over time. I began to feel a kinship with people of these backgrounds, despite not knowing many of them. It was enough to know that we had some shared experiences, that we were all being misperceived and mistreated in similar ways, and that we would all be in it together for a long time to come.

To see these communities suffering, to feel their pain viscerally, and to see how little power they had to even tell their own stories really upset me. I saw their need for justice and yearned to help.

I majored in English and religion at Trinity, and when I told Dr. Brown, my adviser in the department of religion, that I wanted to devote my career to justice, he suggested that I apply to Harvard for graduate school in religion. I literally laughed out loud the first time he said that to me. As a son of immigrants who lived in San Antonio and who only really went to college to play soccer, I had given zero thought to graduate school, least of all to a place like Harvard. I only knew one other person who had gone there, my second-grade math nemesis Maria—and she had demolished me with her brilliance all those years ago.

(I remember it vividly. We were the last two standing. The other students watched with bated breath. Mrs. Gutierrez rolled through our multiplication table. Maria and I took turns answering, always with ease. Suddenly, Mrs. Gutierrez moved to the eights, which I had not yet learned and which we had not yet covered in class. To my astonishment, Maria had all those memorized, too. She crushed it—and me.)

I took Dr. Brown's advice to apply to Harvard, and I was equal parts shocked and thrilled the day my acceptance letter came in the mail. Then came the rush of disbelief. My friend Stevie's unfiltered response summed it up best: "What?! How did *you* get into Harvard? You barely even made it through high-school math!"

As much as I loved growing up and going to college in San Antonio, a part of me looked forward to moving away for graduate school. I hoped leaving Texas would mean leaving its racism behind. Perhaps moving to a city like Boston would mean finally living with people who saw me for who I was rather than who they perceived me to be.

Six

GROWING PAINS

C ompared to San Antonio, Boston felt like a big city, and I had no idea how to even begin looking for an apartment of my own. Fortunately, our family friends Narinder and Supreet invited me to stay with them for a few months until I found my own place. They refused to accept rent from me, so I made up my mind to get them a thank-you gift. One afternoon, I was out for a run when a pair of guys flagged me down to ask for help. They were moving several big boxes and needed a hand. They spoke slowly and demonstratively, as if I was a toddler, and their jaws dropped when I responded in the most basic English: "Sure, I'll help."

It wasn't uncommon in Texas to help a stranger, whether it was moving a couch or changing a flat tire, so I didn't think anything of it. They kept expressing gratitude, and as a gesture of their appreciation, they offered to sell me a stereo system for a massive discount. I realized this could be the perfect gift for my hosts, and I agreed to give them $500 in cash for the set. Forgetting everything I had learned about "stranger danger" and leaning hard into my Southern naivete, I hopped into their car, had them drive me to an ATM to get cash, and then asked them to help carry the boxes upstairs. Being a hospitable Punjabi, I served them glasses of water and sliced apples, and then gave them a tour of the place. About an hour after they left, it crossed my mind that I might have been conned.

I ran a quick Google search on the brand and item number of the speakers. Red letters screamed at me: SCAM ALERT! I read about the scam on a few websites, and the more I read, the dumber I felt. I had been so glad to dispel a stereotype that I never thought to check the type of stereo.

I felt even worse for bringing strangers into my friends' apartment. When I saw Narinder and Supreet that evening, I confessed to them immediately and apologized. Instead of being upset, they laughed at my lack of street smarts for a solid five minutes. Their laughing relieved my worry, and I began laughing too. Fifteen years have gone by since I was duped, and we haven't stopped laughing about it since.

(In case you're wondering, the speakers never worked, but Narinder and Supreet kept them anyway. They roll them out ceremonially every time we get together just to make fun of me.)

While living in Boston I met Gunisha, who is now my wife. She was in medical school in New York City at the time, and we met when she visited Boston to dance with her team at Boston Bhangra, a well-known competition that attracts traditional Punjabi dancers from all over North America. I wasn't cool enough to be in the bhangra scene (and I'm still not), but I knew about Gunisha because I had been following her work on human rights in India. Her research was thorough and innovative, so I felt a bit intimidated upon first meeting her. But almost as soon as we started talking, I found myself at ease. We quickly discovered how much we had in common and how much we enjoyed each other's company. Over the next two years, Gunisha and I spent most of our savings on the Fung Wah, a $15 bus that trekked between Boston and New York City. We spent as much time together as we could, playing in the Boston snow, studying in coffee shops, and skipping classes just to hang out. She even laughed at some of my jokes.

During this time, Ben, Gunisha's best friend from medical school, came out to her as gay. He told her before telling his own family. Ben implored Gunisha not to tell me. He came from a devout Catholic family that considered homosexuality a sin. Ben assumed that because I was religious and straight, I must be homophobic. Gunisha had to assure Ben that his assumption about me was flat-out wrong and that I would not judge his sexual orientation, not in spite of my beliefs as a Sikh but because of them. This was the first time I had to contend with being misperceived as anti-gay, and the experience opened my eyes to a different kind of assumption that people have about me. While many see my outward display of faith as a mark of conservatism, they often overlook the real me: an open-minded person of faith who aims to be affirming, doesn't judge others, and doesn't impose his views on anyone. I wish they could see that more clearly. While Ben and I have remained close since we first met in 2007 and though we can now laugh about his misapprehension, I have become sensitive to what others assume about my beliefs and worldviews.

Gunisha and I continued to grow closer through experiences like these, and as my master's program was finishing, we agreed that we wanted to marry. Although our relationship was more typical of American courtship than my parents' arranged marriage, it was still important to both Gunisha and me that our families approve of our choice in partner. In Sikh culture, as in many cultures, we often say that a marriage is not just about the union of two people but of two families.

That's why we were so ecstatic when our families—parents, siblings, grandparents, and cousins—gave their blessings. While our relationship was more in line with American norms, our wedding was a traditional Sikh ceremony with all the bustling excitement of a typical South Asian wedding. More than 750 people attended our wedding in Buffalo—and, it turns out, many of whom we didn't know personally. To this day, people still introduce themselves to me by saying, "By the way, beta, I was at your wedding."

So in the summer of 2008, I earned my master's with a focus on South Asian religions, married my best friend, and moved to New York City. My new wife would finish medical school and start her residency there, and I would pursue even more school through a PhD at Columbia.

I'm not sure what my parents dreamed when they left behind their established lives in India to pursue a better future for their children in the United States. I can't even imagine what my grandparents thought possible while sitting in Indian refugee camps during Partition in the mid-1900s. But even for a child who grew up in an upper-middle-class family in South Texas, living in New York City seemed beyond anything I'd imagined for myself. It was one of those places that I knew a lot about, though mostly through books, movies, and TV shows.

Our family had visited Manhattan once when we were young, and while I can vaguely recall some of the tourist sites we visited, I remember one experience vividly. My brothers and I had been elated to see fellow Sikh Americans for the first time—hustling to work in their suits, drinking tea while driving taxis, pushing their babies in strollers—many of them with their turbans tied neatly atop their heads. We would excitedly shout "Sat Sri Akal!" to greet them, ecstatic when some would look up and greet us with a "Sat Sri Akal!" in return. (Before I lived there, I didn't realize that saying hello to someone in New York City is a dead giveaway that you're not actually from there.)

I reflected on our family's visit to New York City all those years ago, incredulous that now I was coming to live in one of the world's biggest cities. Moving to New York was not something I had dreamed of before or ever imagined for myself. But now, I felt eager to enter into the next stage of my life, as a married man, as a PhD candidate, and as a Sikh.

Seven

MORE RUN-INS

I moved to Manhattan in 2008, and it wasn't long before I fell in love with the New York City Marathon. It's the world's largest marathon, with more than 50,000 runners from more than 140 different countries annually. I watched it each year, along with about one million other spectators, and I was thrilled in 2011 to finally register for the race. I joined through a charity spot with the Leukemia and Lymphoma Society's Team in Training, which meant I would raise money for cancer research and follow a regimented program of running, diet, and weight training.

I felt ready on the big day, November 6, 2011. I had so much adrenaline pumping through me that the first few miles flew by. As I rounded a corner in southern Brooklyn—wearing black running shorts, a light T-shirt, Asics sneakers, and a blue turban—a couple of young boys started running after me, throwing rocks as they yelled, "Taliban! Taliban!" I focused my eyes forward and kept running, though I could feel my euphoria draining. As someone who has dealt with plenty of racism, let me tell you this: Hateful comments from kids sting a bit more.

While running the New York City Marathon again a few years later, a marathon volunteer refused to serve me at the water station, calling me "a filthy Muslim." I was so taken aback that I didn't fully process what she'd said for several minutes. About eight miles later during that same race, a spectator saw me coming and shouted to the runners ahead of me: "Run faster! That guy from ISIS is chasing you." The crowd around him erupted in laughter. I was too tired to respond. But I was aware enough to note that not a single person in the crowd called out his racism.

These kinds of encounters are all too common for people who look like me. Most people form these judgments—biased, intolerant, violent judgments—without ever getting to know me. They see how I look and jump to conclusions about who I am and what I stand for. Being constantly judged by my appearance and knowing there is only so much I can do about it is a daily frustration I can't escape or ignore.

Couple how I look as a Sikh with the broad ignorance of my religious community in this country, and it's clear why Sikhs have been on the receiving end of sustained, gratuitous violence. In 1907, less than a decade after Sikhs arrived in the United States from Punjab, white supremacists led race riots in which they rounded up and detained Sikh laborers in Bellingham, Washington. In 2012, about a century later, a white supremacist walked into a gurdwara in Oak Creek, Wisconsin, and opened fire on the worshipping congregation, killing seven and injuring several others. In the race riots a century ago, the attackers misidentified Sikhs as "Hindoos." Today, we're often misidentified as Muslims. In many cases, people who attack us don't actually know who we are.

In many other cases, people who attack us know precisely who we are. Even when correctly identified as Sikhs, we're still the targets of hate. We experienced this before 9/11, and we've experienced it since 9/11, too. Here's what I have come to know: Whether people attack us or any other community, hate is never justified. No one should be attacked for how they look or what they believe.

My lived experience of being perceived as foreign—even as an American-born, Texas-raised, sports-loving, marathon-running straight man—is a consequence of our collective cultural ignorance. The racist attacks are painful enough as they are. It's salt in our wounds that people continually misunderstand us.

The problem is not that people don't see us. It's that, too often, when people see us, they are unable to see our shared humanity.

The irony—and perhaps the tragedy, too—is that the way many people view me is the exact opposite of how I see myself.

This is life as a Sikh in America. It's a constant interplay of being visibly distinct in how we look—which triggers people's fears, anxieties, and racism—and of being rendered invisible when it comes to inclusion, representation, and belonging. Both, in my experience, are dehumanizing. Sometimes I wonder if this is how it would feel to be a ghost, people seeing right through you, a mere apparition until someone's fear makes you noticeable. It's an experience and a position that we share with every group coming out from the margins of American life, and it brings forth shared lessons on how we can all safely move from darkness to light.

Eight

LIFE AND DEATH

Everyone in town loved Balbir Singh Sodhi. He had emigrated from Punjab to Mesa, Arizona, to seek a better life for his family, and he had become a pillar of the local community. People from all over would come to his Chevron gas station for his wholehearted generosity. All the kids knew that Balbir would give free candy to anyone who stopped by. All the adults knew that he let poorer customers fill their gas tanks for free.

Balbir had been married years before, but he had come to the U.S. on his own. Like many immigrants, he would work long hours to boost his earnings, then send most of what he'd earned to his wife and kids back home in Punjab. Balbir Sodhi saved up for years, hoping to earn enough that his loved ones could join him in Arizona. But just as he was about to reunite with his family, someone shattered Balbir's American dream.

On Saturday, September 15, 2001, Balbir went to a nearby Costco, searching for an American flag to display at his gas station. He was still devastated by the terrorist attacks just days before, so when he approached the Costco checkout line and saw a donation box for first responders at Ground Zero, Balbir didn't think twice. He took out his wallet and emptied all $75 dollars into the donation box.

Balbir returned to his store, and later that same day went outside to plant flowers with landscaper Luis Ledesma. A man drove up in his black pickup truck, pointed his gun at Balbir, and shot him at point-blank range, killing him instantly. Balbir Singh Sodhi's death was the first hate crime murder in post-9/11 America.

The killer, Frank Roque, described himself as an "American patriot" and explained his killing as an act of revenge for the 9/11 terrorist attacks. According to police reports, Roque had told his wife that "all Arabs should be shot" and that he wanted to "slit some Iranian throats." Eyewitnesses heard Roque threatening to "kill Middle Eastern people." At Roque's trial, his coworker testified that Roque had said: "We should round them all up and kill them. We should kill their children, too, because they'll grow up to be like their parents."

Roque's own words demonstrate how racism works. Ignorance causes unnecessary tragedy for others simply because people are not willing to look beyond their own prejudices and hatred.

Balbir Singh's murder rocked our family. I had just turned seventeen in the summer of 2001, and I saw a lesson in his murder. For communities that are largely overlooked in America and elsewhere, being seen can be a fight for survival. Had Frank Roque truly *seen* the man he murdered, perhaps both Sodhi and Roque would still be with their families today. I knew that Roque was responsible for his own hate and that he carried the blame for Sodhi's murder. But blaming Roque didn't feel helpful either. What mattered most was doing what I could to protect myself and the people I loved. This is how and why I committed myself to addressing this long-standing problem for marginalized people: to claim and express our existence in a way that truly brought forth our humanity.

At a time when we hear the constant refrain that representation matters, we must also acknowledge that representation in its own right is not enough. In his seminal book *Orientalism*, Edward Said reminds us that when outsiders tell our stories, their distorted representations come to be accepted as fact. (Some people think that because I'm a scholar trained at Columbia, I'm contractually obligated to mention Edward Said and Michel Foucault at least once anytime I write. I'm not, though I love to cite them when I can.)

Said's insight echoes the oft-quoted African proverb: "Until lions have their own historians, tales of the hunt will always glorify the hunter."

Until and unless we tell our own stories, we will remain misrepresented, if we are even represented at all. To create equity, people need opportunities to tell their own stories. This revelation framed my own trajectory: I entered the world of scholarship to acquire cultural authority as an expert storyteller. I wanted to share my stories and the stories of my communities. More than that, I wanted to empower others and create opportunities for them to tell their own stories, too.

This is not the only way to give voice, nor does it stand on its own; self-representation is one of many important avenues to advance justice. I speak about this path because it is the one I chose. I was awakened to this issue in the immediate aftermath of 9/11 violence, when already sidelined communities—my own and others—were further maligned and marginalized. We had little access to media platforms, and news outlets seemed uninterested in telling stories about the wave of violence washing over our communities. Some journalists and politicians were speaking about us and for us, yet very few listened as we tried to speak about the events from our points of view. Social media didn't exist as it does today, so disseminating our own stories wasn't as easy then as it is now. We experienced this moment as cultural assassination. It was more than overlooking and concealing our stories; these were judgments on the values of our lives in Western civilization.

Once I decided to follow the path of advocacy and justice, I began to look for examples of people who were doing it well. Whose work could I follow? How should I frame my approach? I found myself intrigued but dissatisfied by classic Western modes of research. I wanted to do more than write scholarly articles for limited, academic audiences, and I wanted to do more than share my personal opinions with the general public. I found a helpful perspective from within my own tradition: Intellectual study and public engagement are not at odds with each other. They go hand in hand. My challenge was to recognize this paradigm and re-create it for my own life.

Nine

From Locked
Out to Unlocking

H arvard was the first place where I saw people who served as mirrors, reflecting back how I saw myself. I was a scholar-activist, a historian, and a theologian, simultaneously committed to learning about the world around me and living into my Sikh faith. Despite its reputation and vast resources, the university had its limits. "We don't offer Sikhism here," my professors informed me when I arrived. "Your best path is to specialize in Hinduism and Islam, and then figure it out from there."

I was crushed. I had come to Harvard because people had told me that it was the university best equipped to accommodate my interests in studying Sikhi. And yet there was no real space for me here either. I remember sitting on the steps outside the historic Widener Library my first week there and asking myself: *What does it mean to be so marginalized that one remains outside the archive?*

Having lived on the outside for so much of my life, I had a sense of what it would take to make ourselves part of the archive. We have to disrupt our cultural norms. We have to help center people who have been pushed to the sidelines, waiting for a chance to play. We have to interrupt our typical ways of operating, so that we can bring awareness and empathy to the experiences of those rendered invisible. This commitment—of bringing light to places of darkness—is the work of love and justice.

Love and justice are at the core of Sikhi and how I try to live. Many of us talk about wanting to fight hate with love, but not many of us know what that means or how to do it. Loving our neighbors unconditionally is one of those aphorisms that's far easier to say out loud than it is to embody.

Yet we must learn to do that, because hate and anger swirl all around us every day, affecting our politics, our workplaces, our relationships, and even our inner selves. Everyone we know is affected. Everyone we know is infected.

So where can we look? Who can teach us about living with compassion?

As with any journey, the best guides are those who have gone before us and know the way. No one can take the steps for us, and identifying the destination only gets us so far. We are best served by following those who have made the trip.

This guidance, for me, has meant seeking out those who have found goodness in the moments that seem designed to bring out the worst in us. Those who, when faced with fight or flight, have chosen neither, finding that middle path of grace and compassion, even in the most extreme situations.

Fifteen years after Frank Roque murdered Balbir Sodhi in 2001, Roque spoke with Balbir's brother Rana over the phone. "I want you to know from my heart, I'm sorry for what I did to your brother," Roque said. This was the first time that Roque expressed remorse for taking Balbir's life. Believing Roque to be sincere, Rana received his apology with an open heart. He said to his brother's killer: "If I had the power to take you out from prison, I would do it right now." Hate may have taken his brother's life, but Rana felt that empathy was the best path to healing.

After Wade Michael Page massacred a Sikh congregation in Wisconsin in 2012, the local congregation responded in a similarly compassionate way. They didn't have to forgive the man who'd tormented them, but they didn't have to internalize his hate either. Rather than calling for blood or revenge, they shared with the world a core Sikh teaching: "No fear, No hate (Nirbhau, Nirvair)."

A year later, my friend Prabhjot was beaten brutally near his home in New York City by nearly two dozen teenagers of color, who shouted racial slurs as they assaulted him. Prabhjot was a physician and on the faculty at Columbia University, and his story made international headlines. At a press conference after he was released from the hospital—and mindful of the school-to-prison pipeline—he announced: "I care more that these kids are taught, not caught."

Each of these incidents played a powerful role in shaping my understanding of what it would truly look like to fight hate with love. But these were not the only examples. Through them, I could see that my own life was a case study in dealing with racist hate. We didn't look like or even live like the people we grew up with in Texas, and we faced discrimination often. It would have been so easy for me to internalize the hate, anger, and fear directed at our family. But having access to people who showed me a better way helped me deal with intolerance. I began to model my responses to align with those I admired, and through that, I developed a new method. When prejudice showed up, I would pause and ask myself what a compassionate, values-based response would look like—and then try to implement what I envisioned.

As time passed, something inside me began to change. I still felt a fiery passion for justice and fairness, and my body still tensed when racism showed its face. But now, the heat of discomfort that would flash through my body started to feel more like the warm glow of a fireplace. My bitterness has been replaced with a feeling of sweetness, for myself and for others. Sikh wisdom, it turns out, had transformed me.

Ten

FINDING ANSWERS

The new calm within revealed how valuable it can be to recognize the troubles of our world and to choose not to feel overwhelmed or disillusioned by them. While I still encountered the same racist hate, my experience of it had changed completely. Hate no longer governed my responses or dictated my emotional state in those moments. Instead, I was able to face hate, even if I did not understand it. I was at peace.

In the years since, I have discovered that although my experiences may have been unique, my feelings were not. Rage, anger, and fear afflict us all, no matter our backgrounds and situations. Whether at work or at home, on the highway or on the tennis court, there is so much out there that provokes us, afflicts us, and causes us pain. And while we often comfort ourselves by saying that this is just how people are, there is a simple truth that can set us free: We don't have to live this way. Living with calm and compassion can be learned and earned.

This is what Sikh wisdom has taught me. Liberation is not about what happens to us after we die; it's about the here and now. It is about unlocking our potential and unfettering ourselves from anything that keeps us from connection, love, and joy within this life. This is why Guru Nanak announces so defiantly, "Set fire to any practices that take you away from love." His message is clear and simple: *Let's focus on what really matters.*

Guru Nanak's emphasis on *what we do* also speaks to why I believe religious wisdom is about more than what it teaches. We can *believe* anything. We can *preach* anything. But what truly shapes our character is what we *practice*.

Sikh wisdom prioritizes disciplinary practices that help cultivate inner strength. French philosopher Michel Foucault (two for two!) calls these practices technologies of the self. Daily practice helps nurture our aspirational ideals into inner qualities. They are no longer just resolutions we declare to the world but values that we embody.

In the face of adversity and dehumanization, Sikh teachings have given me the tools to do the right thing unconditionally. This is not to say that I always make the right call at every decision point (just check my nutrition log). Yet I do believe that, through daily practice, I am better equipped to end the cycle of hate rather than perpetuate it or let it go unchecked. If my Sikh appearance has opened me up to the world and made me vulnerable to judgment and violence, Sikh wisdom has guarded my spirit and nourished my heart, planting roots so firmly that they are not shaken by the daily tumult of our lives.

My practice has taught me how to live with the paradoxes that hurt and frustrate us all: sharing what's in our hearts without worrying that they might be crushed; caring deeply for others without relying on their validation; enduring hate without returning it; seeking constant growth without feeling pressure to attain perfection.

I'm not perfect by any means, but I am getting better. I say this because learning to embrace these paradoxes has forced me to adjust how I view my life and how I engage with others. And as with anything, the more I've trained, the easier it has become to find relief. Just as physical exercise strengthens our bodies, practicing equanimity strengthens our inner balance.

Eleven

MOVING FORWARD

I may not have been the best student growing up, and I may have earned a reputation in high school for falling asleep in class. But even then, I found a degree of comfort with the type of knowledge we learned at school, the facts of science, math, history, and literature. Like many people, I grew up believing that education could cure the world's problems.

It was in the midst of the Great Recession in 2007–2008 that I first began to question if knowing *about* the world was enough. Here we were, in the wealthiest country in the world, and yet so many of us were deeply unhappy. Anger and rage and fear were all around us. Empirical knowledge offered no refuge. Technological innovations were being used as weapons. I lived in New York City then, too, and could see the emotional devastation wrought by people's greed and impropriety. It's not that they didn't know better; they just didn't care.

The apathy seems even more urgent and concerning today than it did in 2007. We are now the most educated society in human history. More people today have college degrees than ever before. We have access to more information at our fingertips than we know what to do with. And yet by nearly every available measure, from the statistical to the anecdotal, we know that hate is surging, that hate groups are growing rapidly, and that hate violence is skyrocketing.

Education alone cannot save us. Sheer knowledge is not the answer.

Feeling betrayed by these systems that had promised liberty and justice for us all—and having seen little of it—I find myself now asking different questions and seeking different answers. How do we find happiness in a world filled with agitation and turbulence? What does it mean to be a good person? And what should we teach our children so that they may live healthy, satisfying lives?

Through the process of answering these questions, I went from seeing Sikhi as a remnant of my ancestors' life in India to cherishing it as something of my own. I began to feel grateful to my parents for raising us in Texas because our experiences gave us opportunities to grow in ways that would not have been possible elsewhere. Then my brothers and I had to figure out how to negotiate our differences for ourselves and others. Now as a grown man, husband, and father, I see these as lessons for dealing constructively with the anger and rage of our world, including how to receive hate without internalizing it, how to challenge injustice without perpetuating it, and how to receive life's most strident blows and readily respond with my values.

⸻

For some, the solution to my problem seems simple: Why not just take off the turban and shave my beard? Wouldn't assimilating make my life easier?

I have had similar thoughts in my own life, at times wishing that I could blend in more easily and release some of the pressures: concerns over representing a diverse community, being mindful of potential attacks, or even just dealing with the loneliness that comes with looking different in a society that places immense value on appearances.

These questions return occasionally now that my wife and I are raising two young daughters of our own. And while I'd be lying if I said the idea of abandoning our Sikh identity has never crossed my mind, the truth is that I've never seriously entertained the idea of cutting my hair.

There are a few reasons why I wouldn't. One among them is my belief that the entire line of questioning rests on a false premise. Even if I tried to blend in by shaving and removing my turban, I'd still be perceived as a brown-skinned foreigner.

Racism always discriminates but rarely discerns.

———

Every morning as I wrap my turban around my head, I look in the mirror and reflect on the Sikh values that it represents. Oneness. Love. Justice. Service. Equality.

There was a time when I would try to explain myself to people who felt threatened by me. But I know now that we cannot explain our way into dignity, nor can we control how people choose to treat us—especially when they are operating out of fear. At first, realizing this made me feel disheartened and disempowered. If I couldn't change what people had in their hearts, what was the point of even trying?

I hear a version of this question from people all over the world: Why try to effect change without a guarantee of success? Why continue to engage when justice seems impossible and equity feels unreachable?

Here is the best answer I know. We may not be able to fix all the problems or make our world perfect, but we can help the people around us who are suffering. And through our efforts, we can change ourselves. Striving every day to live a life of love and service will ultimately make us kinder, calmer, and happier.

I draw this from advice my parents gave us years ago: "We cannot control how others treat us, but we can control how we respond." Endeavoring to live by this advice has been liberating because it shifts our focus. Instead of trying to reconfigure how other people perceive us, we can focus instead on transforming ourselves for the better. Responding to hate with grace is not just about turning the other cheek; it's also about turning inward and practicing those values we want to cultivate within ourselves.

Some might see this perspective as burdensome because it puts the onus on those who are targeted to react with grace and compassion. This is a valid and legitimate perspective, and I don't wish to belittle the truth of that experience. It's important to call out those who act on their racist ideas, and it's critical that we call on those who harm others to do better, including at the institutional and systemic levels. At the same time, my personal experience has shown me an additional possibility: Embracing difficult moments as opportunities for personal growth can be both empowering and liberating.

This approach has been empowering because it helps provide a level of control in moments when I have otherwise felt powerless. That inner confidence may not seem like much from the outside, but it has helped preserve my own humanity in the face of dehumanization. It has also been liberating because it is a reminder that the hate directed toward me is fueled by people's fear and ignorance. I can help resolve some of their inner confusion, but, ultimately, carrying their anger is neither my burden nor my responsibility.

Here's the upshot: What we encounter in this world is not the sole determinant of our happiness. We have agency, too, which means that we can choose how we experience each and every moment. It's the difference between running a 5K and running from a mountain lion. Our bodies might be doing the same actions in both, but our experiences of each can be entirely disparate; one is joy and freedom, the other fear and desperation. Our liberation comes in realizing that, no matter what's happening in our lives, we can always choose joy and freedom.

This is why I believe that Sikh wisdom has a precious gift to offer us all. Turning inward in a moment of difficulty is not an easy choice to make. But it *is* a choice, and it *can* make the difference between joy and suffering. And here's the best news: If we have the right framework and practice our core values, each of us can access that gift of joyfulness that awaits us all.

Part II

RADICAL CONNECTION

What would bother you more: a loved one being upset with you or a stranger saying something hateful to you? For many, the hate is more bothersome. It's more inflammatory, especially in a society rife with injustice. I see that, but my perspective has changed over time. Now I'm far more concerned when my wife is upset with me than I am with what someone on the street thinks about me. The reason for this is simple (and no, it's not because I'm scared of her). My wife cares for me and cares about me. I care for her and about her. Why should we concern ourselves with other people's bitterness?

My working thesis is that other people's hate is not actually about you or me. It's about an imagined sense of who we are based on bias and stereotypes. They don't truly know us, so their attacks aren't truly personal. When people say nasty things to me, I try to take in a deep breath, pause for a few seconds, and ask myself: Did I do something wrong? Did I cause this person harm? And if we replaced me with someone who looked like me, would this person attack them, too? By reflecting on these questions, I remind myself of one of the most powerful perspectives I've developed for dealing with hate—that, at its core, other people's hatred is not about us.

This is among the most difficult perspectives to grasp. In the moment, it's hard not to take other people's racism personally, because the threat is very much about your person: *your* body, *your* rights, *your* safety. The immediate consequences are highly personal, and so too are the long-term ramifications of how hate affects you and your communities, physically, emotionally, psychologically, and otherwise. And yet, when we ask ourselves why, it's often clear that one's animus is their own inner ugliness, not ours. Learning to remember this in the moment is both freeing and redemptive.

"I don't believe in enemies." "Respond to hate with love." "Love your neighbor." It's easy for us to say these words. And God knows we do, announcing them on our social media accounts for everyone to hear how virtuous we are. But not many of us live by our words. And fewer still even know what it takes to get there.

I have developed some answers through decades of practice, yet there's always more to learn. I've grown a lot the past few years, particularly through embracing a painstaking personal challenge: endeavoring to see the humanity in a white supremacist who hatefully massacred members of my community as they prayed. Not to forgive him for what he did, and not to forget what he did, but to see his humanity in spite of what he did.

I share my perspective with the hope that it may help you to see what I can now see: that there *is* a way for us to cherish and celebrate our differences, and in doing so to live in this world as one.

Twelve

THE MASSACRE

Gunisha and I had just sat down for fresh coffee and homemade brioche French toast at Bani and Gurpreet's place when we heard about the massacre. A gurdwara in Wisconsin was on lockdown. A gunman had gone on a killing rampage.

We were stunned into silence. Each of us had endured racism personally and had long ago accepted it as a sad part of our reality. Just that week, a parking attendant in Chicago had called the police on my friend Jasveer. They arrived within minutes, deploying a bomb squad to inspect his car. Someone reported that "a real-life terrorist had shown up." The officers were searching him "out of an abundance of caution."

Experiences like these are horrifying, but they are not uncommon for people who look like us. Yet, although we have grown accustomed to hate, Sikhs had never experienced violence in America on the scale of what was unfolding in Wisconsin. The killer, Wade Michael Page, would ultimately take seven innocent lives in addition to his own. At the time, it was the deadliest attack on a place of worship in the United States in nearly fifty years.

I worried for our family the day of the massacre because we had a personal connection there. My sister-in-law Lakhpreet was visiting her parents and siblings in Milwaukee that weekend. When we heard the news, we scrambled to get in touch with Lakhpreet and her family over the next several hours, but we couldn't get hold of them. We watched the news, by turns anxious and hopeful as reporters in Milwaukee shared the names of those counted safe. We tried to stay positive, but everyone in my family began to prepare inwardly for the worst. Only much later that evening did we learn that Lakhpreet and her family were okay. They had gone camping that day and didn't have any signal until they returned home. We were relieved to learn they were alright. They were horrified to learn their community had been massacred.

Two conflicting feelings rushed over me that day: I was shocked by the news and at the same time completely unsurprised. Unsurprised because I had been collecting anecdotal evidence of racist violence throughout my life, building a mental archive of all the worst memories I would have rather forgotten. Unsurprised because I had been working on the frontlines of hate, working with survivors, their families, and their communities to address their pain. Unsurprised because my research examining hate violence had taken me to the same white supremacist message boards and neo-Nazi discussion groups that Wade Michael Page used to frequent. I saw what he saw.

While we had found some comfort and friendship since settling in America, my family had also been made to feel invisible and inferior. Everyone saw us but few knew a thing about us—and fewer still cared enough to ask. This feeling surfaced again thirty years later as we watched reporters cover the Oak Creek massacre, stumbling through their descriptions of who Sikhs were and what was happening. I remember watching a prominent news anchor misinform millions of viewers that the gurdwara was a mosque and the murdered were Muslims. Ten minutes later, a journalist on another network misidentified the site as a Hindu temple. A third reporter described the Sikh religion as a sect of Islam, referring to us as "sheikhs" rather than "Sikhs."

Our community had been in the country for more than a century, struggling to be seen and heard. The national spotlight was finally on us—but this was not the kind of attention we had wanted. The hateful massacre magnified what we already knew to be true: that even when people saw us, they didn't actually *see* us. No one knew who we were. My stomach tightened in the same way it had more than a decade earlier in 2001, the day Balbir Singh Sodhi was murdered in Arizona—the same way my stomach would tighten nearly a decade later in 2021 when a gunman in Indiana would slaughter eight people, half of whom were Sikh. Even when we're targeted and killed, and even when we have people's sympathies, we *still* don't get the dignity of being acknowledged and understood for who we are.

This visceral feeling speaks to the difference between sympathy and empathy. In sympathy, I might feel bad that you're suffering, but that doesn't mean I care enough to help you. Sympathy might help see someone's pain, but we still see the world through our own eyes, still rooted in our own self-centeredness. Empathy, on the other hand, is rooted in our connection. Plenty of people expressed their sympathies after the Oak Creek massacre, but only a handful felt moved to action. The gap between the two is larger than it may seem: While sympathy *points* toward our shared humanity, empathy *honors* it with depth and fullness.

I was grateful for the outpouring of sympathy nevertheless, because even though it didn't carry the promise of social transformation or long-term justice, it reminded me that people were ultimately good and that they at least cared enough to reach out in crisis. Receiving this light in a moment of darkness saved me from falling into self-pity and mistrust.

At the same time, the sympathies sharpened my feeling of being unseen yet hypervisible. I felt more invisible now than I did growing up in Texas—a high bar. Until this point, I had clung to the hope that we might overcome racism during my lifetime. But now the doubt came in waves. Perhaps it didn't matter how we saw ourselves. Perhaps our humanity would always hang in the balance. Perhaps we would be perpetually foreign, aliens from another world, forever looking for a way in.

Perhaps, perhaps, perhaps. The United States was the only home my brothers and I had ever known, and I was finally ready to accept that we might never feel the certainty of belonging.

=====

In moments of overwhelming hardship, history has been a key source of support for me. Looking at the past helps. Placing my own experiences into a broader context provides much-needed perspective and prevents me from becoming too consumed with my own hurt. When someone scratches a racial slur on my car door or when a waiter refuses to serve me, it can be easy to get sucked into my own anger. Remembering the plight and enduring resilience of others has helped me come out of my pain in those moments. We don't have to minimize our pain, but we don't have to let it isolate us either. When done responsibly, locating ourselves in relationship with one another, feeling connected, can be a powerful antidote to our own suffering.

At the same time, we can't allow ourselves to fall into comparative suffering. It's easy to look at other people who are dealt a worse hand than us and to feel guilty for complaining about our own challenges. I have felt this most acutely when comparing my own experiences dealing with American racism to the state-sanctioned anti-Sikh violence in India that my family and community endured. When I put the two side by side, I have a feeling of disquiet, like my pain is fractional and therefore invalidated. In those moments, I have felt shame about my own hurt and have therefore buried it deep inside myself rather than try to address it in a healthy way.

An extreme analogy would be denying ourselves food because we feel guilty that others are hungrier than us. Or refusing to treat our cough because others have cancer. Just because others might be suffering more doesn't mean our own pain isn't real.

Nothing good comes from denying our own pain. Acknowledging our hurt doesn't take away from the hurt of others, nor does it diminish our own. Instead, we must learn to acknowledge our feelings while also keeping them in perspective. Connecting with the plight of others is not about numbing our pain or making us feel better about our own; connecting with others is about becoming more empathetic, reducing their suffering, and maintaining perspective. This is especially true in more difficult moments when our natural response is to become more self-absorbed.

When we can tap into history while remaining grounded in the now, we can live in the past and present simultaneously. Having a foot in both the world that was and the world that is can feel like an impossible balancing act—I've toiled with this as a historian and an activist. The trick is to recognize that the two are intertwined. The past resides within us in each moment because the past shapes each moment and shapes us all, individually and collectively. None of us lives outside of history, and none of us lives beyond the present.

James Baldwin put it like this: "The great force of history comes from the fact that we carry it within us, are unconsciously controlled by it in many ways, and history is literally present in all that we do. It could scarcely be otherwise, since it is to history that we owe our frames of reference, our identities, and our aspirations."

=====

As I sat there watching the news about the massacre in Oak Creek, my mind went into autopilot, whisking me back in time to one of the darkest moments of Sikh history. During the eighteenth century, Sikhs in Punjab banded together to resist political authorities who terrorized and oppressed minority communities. Because Sikhs staunchly insisted on standing up against injustice and inequalities, the rulers of the day focused on persecuting Sikhs such that their numbers dwindled into the low thousands. In fact, there were two separate periods in the 1700s that Sikhs remember as the Lesser Holocaust (Chota Ghallughara), which took place in 1740, and the Greater Holocaust (Vadda Ghallughara), which occurred in 1762.

Just before the Chota Ghallughara, the governor of Lahore, Zakaria Khan, announced that he would pay citizens who helped wipe out the entire community. He put a literal price on Sikh heads, offering ten rupees to anyone who informed on a Sikh's whereabouts and fifty rupees for anyone who brought the severed head of a Sikh to government officials.

According to Sikh memory, in 1739 the state issued an official declaration that the entire Sikh population had been exterminated. Wanting to register their resistance, two Sikhs—Bota Singh and Garja Singh—emerged from hiding, set up a tollbooth on the Grand Trunk Road near the city of Tarn Taran, and announced their sovereignty by collecting toll taxes from travelers. The two were eventually arrested and executed for their defiance, but their legacy lives on today. Even now, I think about this story often, grateful that I'm not being hunted down and inspired to live with fearlessness and resilience.

My brothers and I were in elementary school when our parents first shared accounts of past persecution like these with us. Then, I experienced them as breathtaking stories that captured my attention. They were so gruesome and evocative. In my teenage years, I thought of them as collective myths that religious educators used to instill pride in our heritage. As a young adult, I began to value these memories as offering models of courageous moral fortitude. And now, I see them differently still. While all of the above remains true, these stories now also anchor me. They are sources of grounding and perspective and human resilience, serving to remind us that, while we may be suffering, others have endured and survived worse—and that, therefore, so can we.

═══

These accounts of audacious resistance and moral courage remind me of another story that I love and that has inspired me over the years. During his tenure in the 1970s, former Alabama attorney general Bill Baxley prosecuted one of the men responsible for the 1963 hate-fueled bombing of the 16th Street Baptist Church in Birmingham, Alabama, which resulted in the death of four Black girls between the ages of eleven and fourteen. This infuriated the Ku Klux Klan, which issued a written threat to Baxley. Not to be deterred, the attorney general responded on official state letterhead as follows:

> *My response to your letter of February 19, 1976 is—kiss my ass.*

I see in his response the same fearless spirit that drove Bota Singh and Garja Singh to come out of hiding and announce their presence. They knew that coming forward as Sikhs would be to embrace death, and they did so anyway. Why? Because our tradition teaches us to always place a tax on hate.

I reflected on these stories as I watched the massacre unfold on the news that Sunday morning, remembering that then, as now, the turbans on our heads and the hair on our faces have meant that Sikhs would stand out wherever we are; that we would be easy targets of those ruled by fear and hatred of the unfamiliar; that by opting to be hypervisible, we were also choosing to put ourselves at risk. Courageous vulnerability. This, too, is part of our tradition. Our shared memory is that standing out in a crowd means we answer to a higher level of accountability; tying the turban is a daily promise—to myself and to the world—that I will live by the principles I proclaim.

Thirteen

ACTIVATING

Within an hour of the massacre in Wisconsin, my editor, Paul Raushenbush, an ordained Baptist minister, reached out to offer his condolences. I thanked him and asked if he had any guidance on what I could be doing to serve my community in this difficult moment. I'll never forget his words: "You have a voice and a platform that few others in your community do. If you're comfortable, consider sharing with the world how you're feeling right now. I think they'd like to hear from you."

At the time of the massacre in 2012, I was a PhD student in the Department of Religion at Columbia University and a contributor to *The Huffington Post*. I had been studying Sikh and South Asian history for years and had been developing educational materials and programs that would help Sikhs growing up outside of Punjab connect with their heritage. From the outside, I probably seemed like an ideal candidate to speak about the violence in Wisconsin and what it meant for the Sikh American community. But internally, I wasn't confident sharing my thoughts in public. Hell, I didn't even speak in my classes through college and graduate school because I worried what my peers might think of me.

As I paused on my own uncertainty, I recalled my mother's approach to hardship. While many would freeze, unsure what to do, she would take a step forward and help how she could. Her support was thoughtful and useful, immediate and caring, and her hopeful pragmatism shone through the darkness. I had tried emulating her example over the years and practiced stepping forward in moments of difficulty. This practice turned into a habit and gave me comfort over the decades, perhaps because it felt like I was helping, perhaps because it gave me a sense of control in situations where I had little, or perhaps both.

While I was still uneasy, I decided to push through that feeling because I knew that I was comfortable *enough* to embrace my discomfort. I sat down and wrote an essay from the heart and sent it to Paul without even rereading it. He wrote back to say he would publish it immediately and use a sentence from the text for its title: "As a Sikh American, I Refuse to Live in Fear and Negativity." He also offered another piece of advice: It wouldn't hurt to run spell-check next time.

Once live, the essay spread like wildfire, and within hours Paul had called me back to say Amy Goodman at Democracy Now wanted to interview me for her program the next morning. I wanted to tell him I was too scared, but how could I after writing an essay about not giving in to fear? I didn't want to do the interview, but I also knew that this was an important opportunity for our community. It never really felt like a choice to say no—not because it was a burden but a responsibility.

So I asked Paul to accept on my behalf, and then spent the next few hours preparing for my first television interview. At one point that evening, I called Paul to say I was feeling intimidated because there was no way I could capture the richness of our community and the depth of our experiences in ten minutes. I told him it didn't feel right for one person to represent a community that was so diverse. He assuaged my fear by giving me a simple goal: *Don't try to speak for every Sikh or even for your tradition. Instead, share your own perspective and experience, and as you do so, take the opportunity to introduce Americans to their Sikh neighbors.*

Paul's advice served me well then, and it continues to guide me years later.

As nervous as I was, and as awkward as it was to have someone put makeup on me for the first time, everyone was lovely and the interview went well. I also gained confidence through the interview, realizing that I had the lived experience and depth of knowledge to speak about who we are and what our lives are like in America. This is how I, along with a number of other Sikh Americans, ended up sharing our experiences on television and radio for the first time in 2012. It's also what moved me to start sharing stories of pain, survival, resilience, and hope from among those who were directly affected.

There was a lot more to do than simply tell stories, though, especially given that the nation was paying attention to our community for what felt like the first time. For instance, I supported an effort led by the community's largest civil rights organization, the Sikh Coalition, to push for policy changes, such as calling on the FBI to finally start tracking hate crimes against Sikhs and other marginalized groups. Despite facing hate violence for more than a century, the United States still did not track these statistics. We were able to help change that through our advocacy, for the Sikh community and other communities, too. I also began connecting with Sikhs around the country to learn how to best help people in our communities who felt traumatized by the attack.

Those of us doing this work quickly realized the importance of presenting a unifying message that would resonate across the country and help our community feel empowered. To do this, we called on Americans of all backgrounds to confront bigotry wherever they encountered it and to quash hate so that it could no longer fester. We condemned neo-Nazi and white supremacist ideologies, reminding Americans that we have always been stronger when we have stood together.

These were easy positions to take and even easier messages to share. We were here to challenge hate and bigotry in all its pernicious forms.

Everything sounded intuitive and uncontroversial. Everyone seemed to be on board.

But there was one problem. In public, I was saying all the right things—calling for peace and unity and kindness. I was showing up at vigils and on televisions screens, offering remarks on resilience and justice and our shared humanity. Yet I never shared the other, more complicated feelings in my heart. I couldn't. Because underneath the surface, I felt angry and upset. I was furious that innocent people were dead because one man couldn't control his own hatred. My heart ached as I watched people grieve their loved ones, taken from them too soon and for no good reason.

I knew my feelings were natural and legitimate. But I also knew it wouldn't be helpful or constructive to announce openly how I felt. If I have learned anything from being in a brown-skinned body in the United States of America, it's that we're not supposed to share our discontent with the people around us. To express anger is to come off as untamed and to feed into the stereotype of darker-skinned people being predisposed to violence. We have been taught, by our elders and through our experiences, not to show these characteristics to the world if we value our well-being.

Having to repress these feelings was onerous, but I'd been contorting myself for other people's comfort for so much of my life that it hardly bothered me. What really bothered me, though, was realizing the chasm between what I practiced and what I preached. Hypocrisy had always irritated me, and I worked hard to avoid it when I could. Yet here I was, living that same double life, guiding people with lofty ideals without embodying them myself. The inner dissonance was tearing me apart.

Once I acknowledged my own hypocrisy, I felt overcome by uncertainty. I was no longer sure if I believed the ideas of unity and love and justice that I was sharing with the world. These ideas had been at the core of how I understood myself and my worldview for years, calcifying into convictions that had been rock-solid for as long as I could remember. And in one single moment of white supremacist hate, it no longer felt so solid. The ground had crumbled beneath me, leaving me with nowhere to stand and nowhere to step.

I also felt betrayed, as if someone had taken advantage of me during one of my most vulnerable moments, entering into my home and taking what they wanted. If you've ever been robbed, you know that your sense of loss extends far beyond the objects taken from you. A robbery also takes from us emotionally, breaking trust and compromising the assurance of being safe in one's own home.

This is how I felt, and these feelings of betrayal and distrust stayed with me for more than a year after the massacre. To be clear, it wasn't that these emotions stymied me into inaction. I was still stepping forward, working with the Sikh Coalition to create more awareness about Sikhs and to advocate for better hate crime policies for all marginalized groups. But the feelings inside took a toll on me every single day. I was angry and confused and overwhelmed. I needed emotional comfort. I needed answers.

Fourteen

INSIGHTS

A s with so much in our lives, the answers I was searching for didn't come quickly. It took me several months of intense soul-searching to reach a place of emotional comfort following the Oak Creek massacre. During that period, I tapped deep into my inner nerd and read voraciously, gathering all the spiritual and psychological wisdom that I could find.

Some of the wisdom was helpful: *Being with community can give us solace. Recalling past tragedies can help us maintain perspective and build resilience.* Some of the wisdom was less helpful: *Life is a fleeting illusion. Numb your pain and let time wash it away.*

The unexpected takeaway from this exercise was that feeling better didn't require perfect resolution. Simply acknowledging my hurt and making the conscious decision to try to heal made me feel lighter and more hopeful. As I began to put the wisdom I had collected into practice, I noticed myself growing more emotionally resilient. And over time, I discovered a joy deeper and longer lasting than any I had experienced before. Light came from darkness.

Looking back on that difficult time now, I can see that there were broadly three steps in my quest toward finding inner peace. Each was formidable, and it would have been far easier to simply sit back. Yet each step brought insights that changed my life and continue to guide me every single day. The conclusion I came to at the end of this endeavor, blandly stated, is seemingly quite obvious: that finding inner peace and working for justice go hand in hand, and that to get there, we have to uncover what connects us—but the journey to get there, one on which I hope you'll accompany me, is illuminating, filled with uncertainty, and hopeful in unexpected ways. In the pages ahead I will show you exactly how, but here it is in a nutshell. My initial step in this journey seemed impossible when I first began. In the days and weeks after the massacre, I found myself going through emotional ups and downs. At times angry with the killer and everyone who enabled the climate of hate in our country; at times sad for the families who'd lost their loved ones; at times grateful for all who came to support; and at times all three at once. My feelings were natural, but also exhausting, and I wanted to channel them in a healthy and productive way. I found wisdom through the survivors, who found ways to live with courage, resilience, and optimism. I watched them cut through their grief to access and sustain joy. I also saw them discover how to live within this world and enjoy its richness without becoming attached to it. I'll call this the insight of how we feel.

Once I felt emotionally sturdy, I was ready for my next challenge: to see the humanity in someone who hated us and hurt us. Rather than focusing on the rage in his heart, I wanted to cleanse the residue of anger from my own. This was one of the toughest and most demanding tasks I've ever taken on, but on the other side of it, I radically expanded my capacity to empathize with others. Undergoing this process showed me that we all have the power to change how we see the world, and that doing so can enhance our lives and bring us more happiness. That there is more to life than living as a passive spectator and that we can define ourselves by more than what we have and what we do. I'll call this the insight of how we see.

The third stage came in trying to figure out how to connect with people of all backgrounds, not in spite of our differences and not by ignoring them—but *because* of our differences and by honoring them, by finding connection across boundaries and identities. This is why loving our enemies is about more than just helping the people who oppose us. It's also about helping ourselves. Learning to love everyone we encounter is an approach for breaking the seemingly endless cycles of negativity that ensnare us and a way for us to find the happiness we seek. And I'll call this the insight of how we connect.

How we feel. How we see. How we connect.

Each of these three insights stands on its own as transformative wisdom. Yet, like Harry Potter, Ron Weasley, and Hermione Granger, the trio is most powerful when they come together. They build on and reinforce one another, creating an interlocking system to facilitate growth and challenge the darkness.

I offer my journey into each of these three insights, with the hope that sharing my experiences might help you grow and challenge the darkness, too.

Fifteen

INSIGHT 1: HOW WE FEEL

I n the days and weeks following the Oak Creek massacre, I began asking myself what it would take to feel happy again. It bothered me that Page had taken so much from us. I couldn't let him rob me of my happiness, too.

I began asking others, too, and soon found all sorts of answers from various sources. Unfortunately, though, I tried their suggestions and none felt truly satisfying.

For instance, some well-intentioned people encouraged the Sikh community to forgive Page. They said doing so would relieve our pain and anger. I tried my best to forgive, and, honestly, it felt good to release some of my rage. But something about it also felt forced and empty. Page had killed himself at the end of his rampage. He was cowardly and hateful and unapologetic. Could I really forgive someone who never felt remorse for the harm he caused? Wouldn't sweeping his hate under the rug prevent us from healing? Forcing or feigning forgiveness didn't seem like the right answer to me.

Some of my journalist and academic friends thought it might help to study Page's life to see where his hate came from. They said that understanding his rationale would help us make sense of our hurt. I tried that, too, and reading neo-Nazi message boards was both gripping and soul-crushing. But even then, rationalizing his hate with my brain didn't do much to soothe the pain in my heart. Sure, it helps to study history, and analyze racism, and investigate white nationalism; we can learn much about their beginnings and their mechanics. But I have experienced enough racism and collected enough knowledge to know that understanding his hate intellectually would not bring emotional comfort.

My activist friends told me the best way to find happiness would be to channel my anger into fighting white supremacy. They said that taking down racist institutions and helping other people become less racist always helped them feel better. I knew there was truth to what they said. I had been there before, and it *does* feel good to know you've made the world more fair. But I also knew that challenging racism wasn't enough on its own either. I had been doing racial justice work for years and still felt an internal disconnect that I needed to address.

I had also been an activist long enough to know that cultural change doesn't happen overnight and that we will never convince everyone to carry all the same beliefs that we do. Tying our happiness to changing other people's minds is a recipe for disappointment. The various suggestions for dealing with the pain and stress were helpful in the short term. But they were also shortsighted, each in its own way.

It had been weeks since the massacre. I had developed some clarity and coping mechanisms by this point. Yet I still felt myself sinking into negativity and wasn't sure how to pull myself out of it.

Just as my confusion started to tip into desperation, I found wisdom in a place I least expected it—the very congregation that survived the massacre.

The Oak Creek Sikh community had every right to be bitter and demoralized after the attack. And yet its members showed a kind of resilience I had never seen before. One theme rang consistently throughout my dozens of conversations with the survivors: Each and every person I spoke to referred to the Sikh teaching of chardi kala, a phrase that translates roughly to "everlasting optimism."

Every day, as Sikhs pray for the uplifting of all humanity (sarbat da bhala), they speak of chardi kala in the same breath. I had heard this phrase since childhood and had learned about it as a concept. I even knew many people who thought of chardi kala as a way of life. Yet I had never witnessed it in the face of intense trauma. Seeing the community's resilience and hearing their commitment to this idea led me to ask the question: Is chardi kala powerful enough to withstand deep human suffering?

The answer to this question was in the survivors of the massacre. Chardi kala became the community's unofficial slogan, a rallying cry that boomed from their gurdwara and echoed all around the globe. Everything and everyone said chardi kala. It came from the mouths of survivors as they shared their stories with the world. It was literally emblazoned on their chests, a motto printed on the shirts worn by the Sikh community of Oak Creek and all across the country.

The spirit of chardi kala animated the community engagement and activism following the attack. In his testimony before the U.S. Senate, Harpreet Singh Saini, whose mother, Kamaljit Kaur Saini, was murdered by Page, spoke about the Sikh spirit of chardi kala that his mother embodied and how this idea continued to give him hope in the midst of crushing pain.

Mandeep Kaur, a woman whose family survived the massacre, wanted to honor the survivors and worked with local youth to create an annual community walk/run in Oak Creek, which they named the Chardhi Kala 6K.

Pardeep Kaleka, who lost his father that day, says now that the idea of chardi kala saved his life. The teaching helped transform the pain and anger he felt after the attack and led him to the most unlikely of friendships—a deep and sincere friendship with former white supremacist kingpin Arno Michaelis, who has since renounced his hate and works now to deradicalize white supremacists through his nonprofit organization Life After Hate. When Kaleka reached out to Michaelis to try to understand the hate that motivated his father's killer, they forged a friendship that helped both of them deal with difficulty. The two have remained close since.

I was also struck by a growing trend. On the one hand, many Americans called on Sikhs to abandon their turbans. They suggested that doing so would help them blend into mainstream society, and therefore guarantee their safety. This fits into a larger pattern of Americans asking the marginalized to change themselves rather than demanding change from those who enact the violence.

Rather than giving in to these recommendations, some young Sikh women across the country did the opposite: They decided to start wearing a turban daily as an act of defiance and resistance, and as a way of asserting their voices as Sikh women. One of the many who did this was Harleen Kaur, a young woman who lived in the Milwaukee area and knew firsthand the risks of looking different.

I share these examples because they show us what fierce optimism can do for us. If it can give light to folks enduring the most extreme pain and violence, then just imagine how powerful chardi kala can be for us in our everyday dealings with fear and frustration, whether at home, at work, at school, or in public.

———

We have all experienced happiness in fleeting moments. It could be the most mundane of experiences such as eating your favorite ice cream, or something that runs deeper such as going for a walk with a loved one, or an event that is profound and life-changing such as witnessing the birth of a child. Our challenge is not that we don't experience happiness; our challenge is that we can't sustain that feeling over time.

We know happiness well enough to know that we want it, but not well enough to know how to nurture it. So what can we do to bring the kind of joy into our lives that is both sustained and sustaining? How do we cultivate and internalize this idea of chardi kala?

I posed this question to some of the Oak Creek survivors, and I noticed a theme echo across their responses. Happiness and optimism are sustained when we root them in the firmament of connectedness. Here's how.

If we see people as evil, then we will be drawn to anger and pessimism. No matter where we come from or what we do, we are susceptible to negativity: negative thoughts, feelings, actions. It can be easy for us to dwell on the problems around us, especially when the world feels as if it's constantly in crisis. But getting lost in negativity leaves us with nothing but delusion, doubt, and dissatisfaction. This is how I had felt since the massacre, too. The negative ideas were feeding off one another, making me feel worse about myself and worse about the world.

I expected the survivors of Oak Creek to feel similarly disconsolate and angry, but in spending time with some of them, I saw that their capacity to see the best in others and to feel connection with them had given them a deep-seated hope that overshadowed despair. Chardi kala nourished their souls and nourished their communities, and their compassionate actions speak to the beauty and power of this worldview: When we feel connected with our surroundings, no one can take our optimism away from us.

Through my conversations with the survivors, I also gleaned another lesson that many of us have learned repeatedly throughout our lives: that closing the gap between what we believe and how we live can make all the difference. I had intellectually accepted the idea of divine connectedness years earlier, but I didn't yet feel it. This showed me a stark difference between myself and the Sikhs in Oak Creek. While I was thinking about ik oankar, they were embodying it. While I was finding happiness in short bursts, they were living in chardi kala. The tragedy struck much closer to them than it did me, but somehow they were able to tap into optimism in a way I hadn't. I wanted to know how.

Sixteen

ENHANCING HOW WE FEEL

I had the opportunity to ask a few of the massacre survivors how they were able to find happiness in the midst of such pain, and their responses were consistent. They all pointed to the idea of ik oankar: "Everything is divine," the survivors would say. "Of course we're in pain. But how could we be unhappy when God lives in our pain, too? Everything in life is beautiful, even the hard parts."

Their answers reflected the story my grandmother used to tell us as children about how, as he was being publicly tortured and executed, Guru Arjan sang: "Your Will is so sweet to me."

I had long regarded this story as stirring and inspiring but unattainable for everyday people. Having grown up with three brothers who thought professional wrestling was real and who liked to "practice" our body slams on one another, I sensed that feeling joy even while in extreme pain was an ideal that only enlightened people could achieve.

Yet here I was, sitting face-to-face with everyday people who'd felt deep human pain in the wake of a traumatic massacre and at the same time exuded the spirit of chardi kala.

Seeing the power of this outlook made me want to know how I could embrace it for myself. The more I learned about their responses, the more admiration I felt for them; the more my admiration grew, the more I desired to find practical steps to apply in my own life.

In my check-ins with the survivors, they would often talk about chardi kala in some form, and I typically found myself asking two specific questions:

At what moments do you find yourself most at peace?

And are there specific practices that help you cultivate this feeling?

As I expected, people shared a diversity of practices and moments that they felt instilled optimism and happiness. Some referred to the power of prayer, others identified a reconnection with loved ones, and others still identified a renewed sense of purpose in their community service. Despite their different perspectives, there was one practice that every survivor mentioned: gratitude.

It confused me that, after watching their loved ones murdered in cold blood, a community would lean into gratitude as a response. I must have done a poor job of masking my confusion, because when I would ask the survivors what specifically they might have to be grateful for, they would respond as if surprised by my question.

"We have so much to be thankful for," a young Wisconsin woman in her thirties told me. "I have my life. So many people I love are safe. It could have been so much worse. Someone was looking out for us that day."

I was struck by this perspective, both because I hadn't thought about it that way and because I knew she was right. We had learned so much in the past months about various factors that had limited the death toll to seven. The good fortune that Page never opened a door into the kitchen, where nearly a dozen congregants were hiding. The courage of congregation members, including gurdwara president Satwant Kaleka, who'd lunged at Page as he opened fire on the worshippers. Lieutenant Brian Murphy, the first officer on the scene, who somehow kept the killer at bay, despite being struck by more than fifteen rounds of gunfire.

I had heard about the many factors that helped limit the death toll. But I had never really thought about this as something to be grateful for. I was so focused on the pain that I hadn't seen the blessings. Perhaps they weren't visible to me because I wasn't looking for them.

I learned through my conversations with survivors that gratitude is not something that happens by accident but rather is cultivated through intention and practice. The more we bring it into our lives, the stronger it becomes. Adopting gratitude as a practice enables us to find the blessings and silver linings all around us, changing forever how we see the world and experience our lives.

I learned about the immense power of gratitude from these survivors—that it *can* be an attitude, but only if we choose to adopt it as such and practice it every day. In this way, being thankful is a source of inner light in even the darkest moments we encounter.

Gratitude, I learned, is not about changing the world around us, although it absolutely carries that potential when enacted collectively. Instead, it is about helping us find happiness and connection, and about helping us feel ik oankar and chardi kala.

I learned all this from the Sikh survivors, and I learned it from Lieutenant Murphy as well. I interviewed him a few months after the massacre, just before President Obama recognized him in his 2013 State of the Union address. Lieutenant Murphy still had bullets lodged in his head, back, and shoulder, and he still experienced sharp bursts of pain where the bullets had ripped through his flesh. Despite this, he felt grateful to be alive and attributed his positive attitude to the concept of chardi kala that he'd learned from the Oak Creek Sikh community.

"I realize how fortunate I am to be alive. I don't know why and I don't think I'll ever know why I'm alive," he told me. "But I've come to terms with the fact that I'm extremely lucky and just so happy to be here. Even being in pain is okay because it means that at least I'm still alive."

Once again, I heard echoes of Guru Arjan in his graceful reflection: "Your Will is so sweet to me."

These words carried new meaning for me now, and I decided it was time to make gratitude a daily practice. I started simply, spending five minutes each evening reflecting on three things from that day for which I was grateful. What I identified each evening varied widely. Sometimes

I would recall more ordinary items, like a new pair of running shoes or an enjoyable meal. Sometimes I would think about less tangible gifts, like a meaningful relationship or some wisdom I had gained. And sometimes I would reflect on more exciting experiences, like going to a fun concert or a basketball game with a friend.

Within weeks, this daily practice began transforming me. Because I knew that I would be reflecting on my blessings each evening, I began identifying experiences during the day that I wanted to write about that evening. I began to notice that I had much more to be grateful for than I had realized, from the mundane to the spectacular. I also realized that my life hadn't suddenly changed, nor did I have more to be thankful about. The change happened inside me. I was recognizing life's beauty because I had enacted a practice of gratitude.

Counting my blessings became a self-fulfilling loop—the more I looked for them, the more apparent they became. And the more apparent they became, the more I found myself looking for more.

I can say this for certain: Adopting gratitude as a daily practice meant that I had never felt happier. I had never felt more connected. I had never experienced such joy.

This is not to say that everything was going right in my life at the time. Just because I was happier didn't mean that life no longer threw challenges my way. But life felt easier, because I was able to feel joy through my hardships, just as the Sikhs in Oak Creek were able to find joy in facing theirs. This was my first step toward feeling chardi kala. I was starting to understand that chardi kala was not just for enlightened people. It's for all of us.

We all know that true happiness comes from within us. What we may not realize, though, is that it doesn't come on its own; we create joy by making it a daily, intentional practice.

Hopefulness brings us happiness in the present, and it also plants seeds of happiness for our futures. When we feel optimism, we will continue investing in ourselves and in our relationships. It's easy to remember that negativity is a self-perpetuating cycle—it's even easier to forget that positivity is a self-perpetuating cycle, too.

I have gained so much personally in experiencing the world in this way. It's not intuitive—I had to learn it. And it's not easy—I've met my own challenges and I continue to meet more. But I know this much to be true: Seeking to live in chardi kala is worth the effort.

Seventeen

INSIGHT 2: HOW WE SEE

The next flash of insight following the Oak Creek massacre came when I least expected it, a reminder that sometimes our most profound lessons can come from the hearts of young children.

It was a crisp morning in late August. It had been about three weeks since the attack. Gunisha and I were at a picturesque summer camp in upstate New York, and I had been given the unenviable task of speaking with Sikh children about the massacre.

The kids sat at picnic tables overlooking a lake at sunset, and I stood in front of them trying to compose my thoughts. I stroked my beard nervously, looked around at the group of forty children, and decided to find out what the kids already knew.

"Today we're going to talk about something very important. Who knows what happened in Wisconsin a few weeks ago?"

Dozens of hands darted to the sky. Each of the kids had heard about the shooting. I asked for volunteers to share, and forty eager hands shot up again. A young boy in a powder blue patka stated that someone went into the gurdwara and started shooting people. A girl in a green tank top said that she was "scared to go to gurdwara now because people might try to hurt us." A third young girl, who had just lost her first tooth that day, waited patiently for me to call on her. I finally pointed in her direction.

"A bad, bad man came and killed a bunch of us. He was evil."

I nodded my head in agreement and saw the other kids nodding as well. I then tried to determine where to take our conversation next and found myself feeling unsure. I was familiar with this feeling, having experienced it in teaching college students. In those situations, I pause, close my eyes, and reflect on the most recent comment. And as I played her words again in my head, I realized something was off. Her words were the same, but the voice was mine.

Here's what was bothering me. This young girl had echoed what so many of us had been expressing in the days since the massacre: that Wade Michael Page was evil. On the one hand, I preferred this framing because it helped make sense of a seemingly senseless massacre. But on the other hand, hearing a child say these words out loud revealed a truth that upset me. I took comfort in seeing him as evil. But I don't believe in evil as a reality of our world, and I certainly don't believe that people are evil. Damaged and destructive, yes. But evil, no.

When I first started discussing Page, I used the terms "racist," "white supremacist," and "neo-Nazi" to describe him. I wanted people to see how he saw the world and the hateful ideologies he espoused. Over time, however, I began to use them as euphemisms to say that Page was rotten to the soul. That's how I had come to see him, and that's how I had been describing him whenever and wherever I discussed the Oak Creek massacre. *Evil. Bad. Rotten.*

This young girl's comment helped me realize that I had taken it too far. I could condemn his bigotry and hatred without condemning him as a person. I could denounce the toxic ideology Page espoused while also seeing him as a human being. The truth, though, is that I did not make this distinction. This was the source of my inner conflict. Seeing him as evil was not just foreign to my worldview as a Sikh. It was antithetical to it.

Sikhi teaches us to see every human being as equally divine and to reject the good-evil binary. I *believed* that we are all inherently good and embodiments of God, but I wasn't *living* my beliefs. I was betraying my own convictions. It was emotionally easier to dismiss someone as evil because they caused me pain. My rage and despair had subsumed my identity and beliefs—I was becoming the opposite of who I was and who I aspired to be.

My anger for Wade Michael Page had kept me from seeing his divinity. "Of course, I'm better than a white supremacist," I would tell myself. I started to see him as inferior to me, and this feeling grew and grew. I began to take comfort in dehumanizing someone who had dehumanized us. Without knowing it, I had started drinking the poison of hate.

We can criticize and denounce someone's behavior without judging their humanity. But that's not what I was doing here. Instead, I was reproducing the very supremacy I was trying to condemn. And in doing so, I was compromising my own humanity. My feelings of anger and despair would have no impact on Page's life. He was already dead. But not being able to fully control these feelings was already having a negative impact on my life.

I didn't want Page to hurt me anymore, and I didn't want him to have any more power over us than he already did.

That was the moment, standing in front of those children at summer camp, that I decided to let my hate go. I wasn't ready to forgive him, nor would I give him a free pass for the suffering he'd wrought. I wasn't even sure what my next step would be. All I knew was that, having fallen, I wanted to get up.

Falling can be important and instructive. I know because I make mistakes often. Falling can remind us of our imperfections and instill humility in us. Falling can show us what we need to do to lift ourselves up. Having stumbled, I tried to learn from my misstep, reminding myself that none of us are immune from falling into the clutches of hate. Remaining upright takes more constant vigilance than we expect.

This is what I saw in this young girl's comment: It was bad enough that I had begun internalizing hate and anger unconsciously. Far worse was that I had unknowingly transmitted these messages to our own children, through my teaching, my interviews, and otherwise. After devoting so much of my life and soul to fighting hate with love, I was devastated to realize that I had fallen into hate's clutches and had dragged these young children along with me.

═══

I had never considered these thoughts before in my life, let alone since the massacre. I certainly hadn't prepared for these reflections prior to standing before these children. But here I was, tasked with the responsibility to help guide them, and suddenly the most pivotal question could not have been any clearer:

What can we do to protect ourselves—and our kids—from being contaminated by the poisonous ideas that swirl all around us?

Answering this question is a lifelong journey. My life is a testament to that. I've been a father long enough to know that parenting is just one long series of trials and errors (emphasis on errors). But that summer, standing in front of those children, I realized I didn't have a whole lifetime. These children needed guidance. Someone needed to help direct them through their hurt and suffering. I also wanted the same for myself.

It had been nearly a month since the massacre. I felt ready to find alignment and to overcome the toxicity that had found its way inside me. I felt ready to recalibrate my mind.

I looked at the kids and dug deep into myself, trying to remember what it was that had protected me from giving in to the racist hate we had endured since childhood. It took a few beats of searching before the generational wisdom I had internalized began rising to the surface.

Once I found my footing, the most basic lessons from Sikh wisdom began pouring out.

"In Sikhi, we believe that Vahiguru (divinity) is in everyone and everything. Has anyone heard this before?"

All the kids nodded their heads. I asked them to give me examples of where Vahiguru is present, and they chorused: "In our hearts!"

I was not surprised to hear them all on the same page. This is typically the first concept Sikh children learn. One of the older boys raised his hand to share that his parents had discussed this idea with him the week before and said there was a line in scripture they had read together: "I can't remember it exactly, but it's something like God lives in the universe and the universe lives in God."

There are many such lines in the Guru Granth Sahib, the foundational text of Sikhi, and I shared one with them that I loved, a simple statement that brought me clarity at their age.

> *Loga bharam na bhoolo bhai khaalak khalak khalak mai khaalak pur rahio sabh thaai.*
>
> *Hey, people! Hey, siblings! Don't be deluded. The Creator is in the Creation and the Creation in the Creator—completely permeating all spaces.*

This wisdom comes from Bhagat Kabir, a fifteenth-century poet-saint claimed by Sikhs, Muslims, Hindus, and those who disavowed religion alike. His writings were so compelling that the Sikh gurus included a number of them in the Guru Granth Sahib.

The simple and direct style of Bhagat Kabir's words make it a wonderful choice for reaching and teaching young children. The ideas are basic enough to grasp as a child, yet subversive enough to challenge the ways we all view the world.

I asked the kids to explain what it meant for the Creation and the Creator to be residing within each other, and a number of them offered their interpretations. One suggested that we should respect the environment better by treating the world as if it was Vahiguru. A couple of kids followed that up by saying God is in every human being so we should treat everyone equally. One child's exact phrasing stuck with me: "It means there's no difference between us and Vahiguru."

Satisfied that they'd understood the point, I pressed forward. When I asked if they knew where we could find Vahiguru outside of our bodies, they shouted out aspects of the natural world: "Trees! Lakes! Ducks!" They then offered up more mundane objects: "Benches! Pencils! Plastic cups!" One added softly, "Vahiguru is in those things, too, because Vahiguru is everywhere."

It was a deeply reaffirming moment. For the first time in a long time, I felt rejuvenated, confident again in beliefs that had sustained me all my life and beliefs I had almost abandoned when I needed them most—beliefs informed by the fundamental idea that the Creator and Creation are inextricably intertwined. Mutually reinforcing. An invisible force that permeates every aspect of our world.

Another way to think about this idea is to view divinity as light. Light is something we can see all around us. Light is illuminating, ever present, and connective. It brings clarity in moments of obscurity and uncertainty. The light is always there. The nature of the light doesn't change. The sun is always shining; our ability to see it depends on our position and perspective. Not surprisingly, Bhagat Kabir has something to say about that too:

> *Aval allah nur upaaiaa kudrat ke sabh bande. Ek nur te sabh jag upajaia kaun bhalay ko mande.*
>
> *First, the Divine created the light and then all the people of the world. If the entire world is born from just one light, how can we call anyone good or bad?*

The children nodded in agreement.

We all come from and share the same light. Therefore, we are all equal.

It seemed simple enough.

As we got to the end of the conversation, I remember feeling satisfied. Not only had I done my job in guiding these kids, but also, after weeks of confusion, I was finally feeling a bit of clarity.

Before I could nestle into my newfound comfort, an arm shot up. It was one of the older boys, his eyebrows furrowed in thought.

"I'm confused. If we say that Vahiguru's light is in everybody, does that mean Vahiguru's light was also in the guy who hated us and killed us? Or did he not have the light and that's why he killed innocent people?"

I loved the question as much as I hated it. I loved it because it made me feel less alone, like I had company in my darkness. I had been grappling with this same uncertainty for weeks. Investigating that question on my own had made me feel as though there was no one else in the world who could understand my inner conflict.

I hated it at the same time because it had finally felt like the fog was starting to clear and now his question catapulted me back into confusion. Is a hateful killer just as divine as the innocent people he murders?

Before I could even say anything, a girl wearing a sky blue chunni (headscarf) lifted her hand shyly as she adjusted her pink-framed glasses. "I think the killer had Vahiguru inside of him, but he chose to ignore God and so he did a bad thing. He didn't see that light in himself or in other people. That's why he could hurt them."

The fog began to clear again. This girl was speaking directly to my soul. She had articulated my understanding of Sikh wisdom more simply and precisely than I had been able to in the weeks since the Oak Creek massacre. She also helped me process something I knew deep down but didn't want to admit: While dehumanizing someone we dislike is an easy perspective to hold, it's a heavy and useless burden to carry.

Eighteen

REFINING HOW WE SEE

W hat I learned through my conversations with these young children led me to a critical question: *How could I overcome my anger for Page without dismissing it?*

Sikh wisdom teaches that the only way to find happiness is to free ourselves from the burden of anger and to do the more difficult work of seeing our shared light. Fighting through my anger to connect with Page was a herculean task that I wanted no part of. But then again, nothing else had worked. If I truly wanted to be happy, this seemed like a necessary step.

I wanted to begin this process immediately and wanted to bring the children along with me. I asked the class to close their eyes and take their classmate's wisdom to heart. "We all have the divine light within us. When we don't see this, then we are willing to hurt ourselves and others." We sat in silence for a moment, breathing together, as I tried to instill this gentle reminder in my soul. This man may have carried hate in his heart, but I don't need to carry hate in mine. Neither did these children.

The weight of anger started to rise out from within me. The resentment that had been simmering in my blood for weeks finally started cooling down. The simple meditation was cathartic, and it was also more than that. The young girl's wisdom had helped to heal me. Her words helped start the process of cleansing my soul of the hate that had crept inside me. I still had a lot of unanswered questions and unresolved feelings, but after weeks of trying everything else, this simple shift in perspective finally brought with it a semblance of peace.

I had spent years of my life guarding against the toxicity of hate. I had dealt with hate for decades and had made a commitment to never be its cause. But even letting my guard down for just a few weeks had enabled those feelings to infiltrate my heart. In a moment of weakness and uncertainty, in a moment of not knowing how to deal with this white supremacist's massacre of Sikhs in Wisconsin, I had fallen into its trap.

That little girl's insight helped lift me out of my anger, and clarified and strengthened my own understanding of how vulnerable we all are to its allure. In this sense, her wisdom was as preventive as it was liberating. I was heart-whole again, and also more conscious about protecting my heart in sensitive moments.

If simply embracing these ideas could have such a life-changing impact in the wake of a deadly killing spree, imagine how powerful it can be for us in our everyday interactions. We all struggle in our relationships to honor the full humanity of the people we care about. We struggle even more with people we don't care for or don't know personally.

We have each experienced firsthand how our inability to navigate the minefields of hate has broken up relationships at various levels—families, marriages, friendships, partnerships. I have countless friends and colleagues who have said they don't feel like going home for Thanksgiving or other holidays anymore, that they can't face the inevitable tension of being confronted with those whose views they find repulsive. Ultimately, the most burdensome cost of not knowing how to navigate hate is that it prevents us from experiencing true inner contentment and happiness.

How different would our lives be—and how much happier—if we were able to see the divine light in everyone we encountered? How much more would we enjoy time with our families if instead of focusing on the aspects that annoyed us, we were able to focus on the aspects that we love?

A step in this direction can come through a perceptual shift: how we see the world all around us, how we see one another, and how we see ourselves. We can begin by finding connections in the things that feel most familiar to us, such as loved ones or nature. Over time, we can expand our connections to include aspects of this world that feel more disparate or disconnected, such as political opponents we've learned to fear or places we've been taught to despise, or—perhaps most difficult for me—those insufferable Lakers fans.

The Sikh kids I taught that day were able to process this insight with a degree of ease because it was a foundational concept with which they were already familiar. This foundational concept, ik oankar, is a vision of radical connectedness in which everything and everyone is bound together by a singular force.

The first component of the term, *ik*, is the numeral one. *Ik* refers to the oneness of the world, the connectedness of reality, the intermingling of creator and creation, the integration of all we know, the wholeness of our being. The second component, *oankar*, refers to a dynamic, divine force that permeates every aspect of our world. One way of understanding this concept is to consider it on an atomic level. If everything we know in our physical world is composed of atoms, then think of each atom as being infused with the same divinity. There's no escaping this force because it's infused into everything we encounter and experience.

Ik oankar is the very first term to appear in the Guru Granth Sahib, and many say that the entirety of Sikh wisdom derives from this single concept. For generations, ik oankar has been the first concept most Sikh kids learn. It's the first concept my parents and their siblings learned while growing up in Punjab, the first concept my brothers and I learned growing up in Texas, and the first concept Gunisha and I taught our two daughters while raising them in New York City.

Ik oankar is radical connectedness, and this simple idea—something that even elementary school students can understand—has the potential to change our world for the better.

I speak frequently with college students around the country, and at a recent event a young woman of color asked me an incredibly difficult question. "I work at a high-end coffee shop near campus, and I just find myself angry at the customers all the time. They're all so unaware of their privilege that I can't even look them in the eyes. I feel like I'm being eaten alive by my own rage. How can I stop being so angry?"

What she described encapsulated a tension I see people around the world struggling with. How do we deal with inequity without becoming constantly outraged? How can we deal with the disease of hate without becoming infected by it ourselves?

If we embrace the notion that we all share the same light, then we can also see that the various forms of social oppression and hierarchy—racism, sexism, homophobia, to name just a few—are not inherent in us as human beings. We are not born with these ideas. We learn them. This can be empowering to realize, because when we accept that these behaviors are learned, we also accept that they can be unlearned. This outlook comes with the promise of possibility.

For instance, recognizing that racist ideas are learned helps us see how they become embedded within each of us. It can be difficult and painful to admit to ourselves that we are influenced by racist messages. Trust me, I've been there. It took deep, sustained introspection to acknowledge that, to whatever extent, racist ideas reside with me, too.

It was also difficult to accept because I always saw myself as a recipient of racism, not a perpetrator. But once I saw the truth, the payoff was invaluable: Confronting my inner biases and questioning my assumptions went a long way toward fostering understanding within myself and with others. By acknowledging that racist ideas exist inside me, it became possible to empathize with other people who harbor and act on racist feelings. I still disagree with them, and I still want them to do better. But at least now I can empathize with them rather than judge and look down on them. Their imperfections are my imperfections, too.

The young woman at the coffee shop is all of us. We each struggle with anger in our own ways. The problem is, we don't know how to deal with it proactively or constructively. Even when we make a conscious effort to channel our anger, we end up burying it rather than directing it.

I offer radical introspection as a tool that can keep us grounded in an age of rage. Acknowledging my own biases and imperfections has helped me see the humanity in those I might otherwise see as enemies or adversaries (even if at times their humanity seems deeply buried). Recognizing that I have biases, too, and that they, too, have been socially produced and internalized, creates space for me to humanize those who have biases of their own. As we learn from Oprah Winfrey and Dr. Bruce D. Perry, this self-awareness is the difference between asking, "What's wrong with you?" and asking the more empathetic and generative question, "What happened to you?" Radical introspection enables me to see myself in them—and that simple connection can help us go from a place of intense resentment and anger to a place of sincere connection, inner peace, and in some cases perhaps the ability to change how people feel about us.

Radical connectedness is not exclusive to the Sikh tradition, nor is it only applicable to those who identify as religious. The logic of oneness is universal in its scope; it works for believers and nonbelievers, people of faith and people of no faith alike. Any of us and all of us can benefit from this straightforward worldview.

Ik oankar has universal value; it is a way of seeing and experiencing the world that evokes compassion, equity, justice, self-worth, and joy. In our world that feels increasingly polarized, in our communities that feel increasingly divided, and in our own lives that feel increasingly fragmented—radical connectedness is a response for our unanswered questions. It also lays the groundwork for an ethic of activism rooted in those same values, one that seeks to serve all rather than just the self.

Guru Nanak's vision of ik oankar offers a unique way of thinking and lays the groundwork for us to *feel* interconnected. Adopting this outlook can transform our life experiences from disconnected and dissatisfied to connected and joyous. Once you understand it intellectually, the benefits are obvious. The challenge comes in truly living by it.

Nineteen

A FRESH PERSPECTIVE

The question of seeing humanity in our adversaries is a timeless one that touches all our lives. We all have difficult relationships, whether at home or at work or at school, and we can all picture people who challenge us. (For me, it's that woman in my fitness class who floats through the workouts with such ease that she doesn't even break a sweat while I lie on the mat gasping for breath.) It can be easy to give in to our annoyance and begin to feel negative about that person we dislike. It's also easy for this dislike to snowball into distaste—the next thing we know, we begin seeing the people we dislike as inferior to us. We're all guilty of doing this to varying degrees, and we have all seen the horrific violence that ensues when we allow dehumanization to be normalized.

We each know from personal experience, too, that feeling animosity for others never does us any good. Hating others doesn't just inflict pain and unhappiness on them. It also brings pain and unhappiness into our own lives.

As I grappled with anger and discontent in the months following the Oak Creek massacre, I found myself wondering if it was even possible for us to truly love our enemies. I also wondered if we could take the next step and feel compassion for them, even when they actively seek to harm us.

Dr. Martin Luther King speaks to this in his sermon "Loving Your Enemies."

To our most bitter opponents we say: "We shall match your capacity to inflict suffering by our capacity to endure suffering. We shall meet your physical force with soul force. Do to us what you will, and we shall continue to love you. We cannot in all good conscience obey your unjust laws, because noncooperation with evil is as much a moral obligation as is cooperation with good. Throw us in jail, and we shall still love you. Bomb our homes and threaten our children, and we shall still love you. Send your hooded perpetrators of violence into our community at the midnight hour and beat us and leave us half dead, and we shall still love you. But be ye assured that we will wear you down by our capacity to suffer. One day we shall win freedom, but not only for ourselves. We shall so appeal to your heart and conscience that we shall win you in the process, and our victory will be a double victory."

I recalled Dr. King's powerful words when I saw the spirit of chardi kala in the survivors of the Oak Creek massacre. Seeing them put love into action helped me understand that any of us can live with love. Their example also made me want to find more examples of people who loved in the face of hate.

My quest led me to the story of Bhai Ghanaiya. I had heard his story since childhood, but perhaps because it felt far in the past and far from where I was spiritually, I had never connected with it on a personal level. Now, though, in my current state of questioning, the story couldn't have felt any closer.

It was the early 1700s and the Sikh army was locked in an intense battle with soldiers of the Mughal Empire. Some of the Sikh warriors observed one of their own walking through the field, attending to those who were hurt. As they looked closer, they noticed something strange. Bhai Ghanaiya was not just attending to the injured Sikhs; he was serving water and dressing wounds for the injured Mughals as well.

The Sikh warriors were outraged. They seized Bhai Ghanaiya and angrily brought him to the court of their leader, Guru Gobind Singh. When Guru Gobind Singh asked him to explain, Bhai Ghanaiya said: *You taught us that we all share the same light. I don't see enemies among those who are injured. I just see people who need our help. So that's what I'm doing.*

The warriors waited for their leader to admonish Bhai Ghanaiya. Instead, traditions recall that Guru Gobind Singh praised him: *Ghanaiya, you have learned the true meaning of ik oankar. Please go back into the battlefield and continue your good work. And everyone else here—please learn from the example of your brother Ghanaiya.*

Despite having taken place several centuries ago, Bhai Ghanaiya's example resonates today. At a time when it feels so easy to dismiss people different from us as "wrong" or "evil," his story gives us another way of looking at the world. Bhai Ghanaiya shows us how we can maintain our convictions and stay connected with humanity without becoming blinded by the identity politics that dominate our landscape. He exemplifies the principle of radical connectedness in its purest form. Bhai Ghanaiya was able to see those who opposed him as divine, to the extent that he traversed a literal battlefield and nursed back to health the very people who sought to kill him.

If he could do that in the face of violence, then surely we can bring this practice into our daily interactions and relationships.

What we learn from his example is that the power of radical connectedness is not just in the idea, or even the feeling it inspires. Believing in oneness is not enough on its own. Bhai Ghanaiya had put the idea of radical connectedness into practice. He truly lived it.

Bhai Ghanaiya's embodiment of ik oankar reminds us of something we already know yet often forget: We unlock the power of our ideals when we put them into action.

The story of Bhai Ghanaiya reveals another reward of radical connectedness. Once we experience the world as being inextricably connected, compassion will become our natural state.

When we truly feel connected to those around us, witnessing their suffering causes us to feel pain. When we truly feel connected to humanity, it is no longer possible to remain complacent. When we truly feel connected, we are moved to action.

Your pain is my pain. And my pain is yours.

Your joy is my joy. And my joy is yours.

Bhai Ghanaiya's example is powerful because it reminds us that, however implausible it might sometimes feel, it really is possible to see the humanity of those who annoy us, those who dislike us, and even those who try to hurt us. His embodiment of radical connectedness helps us transcend the very ideas of evil and enmity. When you see everyone as being connected, you stop seeing enemies entirely. Everyone is equally divine, an extension of your own divine self.

I found his story hopeful and reassuring, especially during a time when I was struggling to connect with the white supremacist who murdered people I love.

Bhai Ghanaiya's example can feel distant. He lived a few centuries ago, and his spiritual achievement may seem far from where we are personally. That's why it feels so jolting when we witness it before our eyes. I would see a beautiful example of this years later, in 2020. When the Indian government passed three new agricultural laws that would benefit large corporations and significantly harm small farmers, Punjabi Sikh farmers began a demonstration—the Indian farmers' protests—that would soon bring in millions of supporters from all over the country and around the world. In November 2020, protesters marched toward India's capital city in a campaign called Dilli Challo (Let's go to Delhi). Protesters were met by Indian law enforcement who used violence to deter them. Videos circulated on social media of police officers brutally beating peaceful protesters and unleashing tear gas and water cannons on them. While some videos showed protesters standing their ground and continuing their resistance, other videos caught something remarkable: The protesters were giving water to the very police officers who had attacked them. Why? Because they were thirsty. And because the Sikhs who served the officers did not see them as their enemies.

Seeing the compassion of the protesting farmers gave me inspiration and insight, and it also reminded me that it truly is possible to see everyone's inner light.

Years earlier, as I grappled with Page's massacre and reflected on Bhai Ghanaiya's example, I wasn't quite sure I could get there. I certainly wasn't sure how. I still felt overwhelmed, unsure of how to achieve this state. The ideal still felt far from where I was spiritually and emotionally.

I decided to start at a more basic level by asking two fundamental questions:

What is my goal in this moment?

And what is my first step toward that goal?

Reflecting on these two questions helped discern my intentions. In reflecting on the account of Bhai Ghanaiya and my own feelings for Wade Michael Page, I determined that my goal was to find more compassion within my own life. This brought me back to my own long-standing conviction that compassion is born from connection.

I knew right away that I was taking on a challenge and an opportunity. It was a challenge because I knew that to get there would require serious internal work. It was also a challenge because I still felt intense anger for Page.

And yet, it was an opportunity because I saw this as a chance to grow my inner strength, to tap into my own potential, and to bring more healing and joy into my life. This wasn't just about resolving my anger for Page; he had become a test case for me. If I could solve my anger for him, I could enter into a new world of empathetic connection.

Once again, I found myself unsure of how to begin. I knew what quality I wanted to nurture (compassion) and who I aspired to emulate (Bhai Ghanaiya). Now I had to figure out the next step on my path.

Twenty

BUILDING EMPATHY

I struggled for weeks trying to figure out how to take a first step toward cultivating empathy. I was about to give up on it when I stumbled into some helpful guidance.

My wife and I were hosting some of our Sikh friends for dinner in our New York City apartment. The one-year anniversary of the Oak Creek massacre was a month away, and we wanted to get together with our friends to hang out and check in on one another.

The conversation was light and upbeat until we finally started talking about the massacre. Many of our friends shared their stories of how they'd found out and the people they knew who were directly affected. My heart quickened when a woman I didn't know very well, Jaskiran, opened up about how hard the year had been for her emotionally and how she had found spiritual solace in two core concepts of Sikhi: nirbhau (without fear) and nirvair (without hate).

She explained that her own catalyst was simple: that Sikhs are taught to recognize Vahiguru's presence everywhere and therefore to love everything and everyone equally. Everyone in the room nodded their heads in agreement. I nodded, too, recalling my conversation with those children at summer camp all those months back. And then someone in the group posed the same question I had been struggling with: "So how do we actually grow that all-encompassing love?"

Jaskiran explained that she wasn't a spiritual expert, but that she had made progress by just trying to see the inner light of those she already cared for. "That was easy," she said, "because I already loved them and already felt connected to them. My younger brother has bothered me since we were kids. But I've always known deep down that I loved him. Our love made it so much easier to see our connection, and we've gotten really close ever since."

The harder part, she explained, came in trying to connect with those she didn't know as well. How could she feel a deep connection with people she had never even met?

Jaskiran had a persuasive answer. She said that the more she worked on connecting with those she already loved, the easier it became to see the humanity of those she didn't know as well. "It's a way for us to grow our capacity to care for others," she told us. "And it helps us to live into the teaching of nirvair (without hate)."

Her explanation reminded me of what I experienced in practicing gratitude, that the simplest of daily practices could have a profound impact on my outlook. I was just starting to think of how I might bring this into my daily practice when her excited voice broke into my contemplation.

"Can we try an exercise that helped get me onto this track? I want each of you to pick a partner, look into their eyes, and see Vahiguru within them."

I accidentally groaned out loud, and when everyone turned to look at me, I maintained that this was going to be awkward.

Jaskiran laughed knowingly. "Of course it's going to be awkward! But trust me, it's worth it."

I partnered with Sartaj and we smiled uncomfortably. We looked into each other's eyes for less than ten seconds, and as I stared deeper into his, I felt a deep sense of admiration and contentment well up within me. *I see it*, I thought. *I see his inner light.*

I had always been told that we all share the same inner light. Every day of my life since childhood, I had repeated Guru Nanak's words in my nightly prayer: "The same Divine light resides in all beings." But I had never actually seen it. I had always thought "Divine light" was strictly a metaphor.

Now, however, I saw it for the first time, in Sartaj's eyes. I looked around the room and started seeing it in other people's eyes as well. I wasn't sure why I hadn't seen it before. I'm not even sure how to describe it. The only truth I was sure of in my heart was that I never wanted to stop seeing the light in the people around me.

I had trouble falling asleep that night. My spirit was rising and my mind was racing. I finally had a sense of how to nurture more compassion. I needed to connect with people on a deeper, more personal level. And I needed to do it in a way that would enable me to see our shared divinity.

I lay in bed that night thinking of how to adapt Jaskiran's exercise in a way that would work best for me. I recalled my success in cultivating gratitude through sustained daily practice, and I determined to do something similar to practice connectedness. I decided to start simple. In one interaction each day, I would try to see and connect with the shared humanity of another person. There were only two rules that I set for myself:

1. Superficial commonalities don't count. It isn't enough to notice someone wearing the same brand of shoes as me or someone who follows the same sports team I do. To see someone's light means making an intentional and meaningful connection with them.

2. Interactions can't be repeated. I have to go beyond deepening my connections with my best friends. I'm challenging myself to find a new person to connect with every single day.

The first few days of the exercise felt easy. I started with people I already knew and cared for—my partner Gunisha, my parents in Texas, my brothers and cousins and close friends from school. But after a few weeks,

I had already counted all the people I connected with on a daily basis. I had to begin connecting with people who I didn't know as well—neighbors, shopkeepers, bus drivers, and yes, even people who eat pizza with a fork. The more I practiced seeing humanity in the people I met each day, the more I began to notice humanity all around me. It only took a couple of months before I started seeing the divine light in people all around me, including strangers. My daily practice had begun forming into a habit that deepened my own feeling of connection.

I didn't even realize how much this connective practice had transformed me until I had an unexpected encounter with racism.

One of the perks of being a marathon runner in New York City is that it can be easy to double up your daily commute with your daily workout. This might not sound exciting to you, but here's the truth: There's only one thing a New Yorker appreciates more than avoiding the subway during rush hour—and that's efficiency.

I was running home from my office at NYU when I heard someone shouting: "Fucking Osama! Fucking Osama!" I looked over and saw three teenagers of color looking at me and laughing. I'd dealt with situations like this all my life, and my standard response is to ignore the hate and move along. But because I had been working on connecting with the people around me—including those I didn't know—and because the person yelling at me looked about the same age as the students I taught every day, I couldn't help but see him as one of my own. In the same moment that he denigrated me, I felt compassion and saw his humanity.

I stopped running and slowly approached the young man who had shouted at me. He averted his eyes as I approached him, and when he realized I was coming his way, he put out his hand and looked up at me. He offered a quick apology, trying to defuse any anger. But I wasn't angry.

"No," I said calmly but firmly. "It's not that easy."

"I'm sorry, man. I was just joking."

I told him that it wasn't funny and that he had to listen to me for a minute. I wanted him to see my humanity, just as I saw his.

"It hurts," I told him. "It hurts when people say racist stuff toward me. It hurts when people see me and assume I'm the enemy. And it hurts even more because I'm guessing you know how that feels. You know how messed up that is?"

He responded, "Yeah, that's true."

I saw his eyes soften a bit, but I wanted empathy, not sympathy. I wanted a real connection.

"You ever think the stuff you learn about in school is not just history? Slavery. Internment. The Holocaust. You know that stuff comes from this same kind of hate, right?"

Now his eyes widened as he connected the dots. This wasn't about me versus him. This was about me and him together. It was about us.

"Shit, man," he said, this time with sincerity in his voice. "I'm really sorry."

And that's all it took. The difference between recognizing his error and continuing in his ways? We can be that difference. All it takes is growing our capacity to see one another's humanity and giving people the chance to connect with us.

I extended my hand and he reciprocated. We shook hands, I thanked him for listening, and then I turned around and jogged away.

I'm not sharing this story because I think every encounter with racism could or even should go this way. If I have learned anything in all my run-ins over the years, it's that prejudice is complex and manifests itself in various ways, and that therefore each incident requires its own response.

I'm sharing this story because it shows how the insight of compassion completely transformed how I thought about the person yelling slurs at me. Weeks earlier, I wouldn't have given this young man a second thought. I would have continued with my run, trying to shut out my own emotions while letting him continue to live with racism and prejudice. Both of us would have gone along feeling more angry and more upset.

But now, after working to see the inner light of those I knew, my gut response was to connect with this young man who saw me as a stereotype.

As I ran home, I realized from this brief interaction that my capacity for empathy had grown. My compassionate response took us down a different path entirely, one that broke the cycle of hate and took us both in the direction of happiness, healing, and humanity.

This experience was instructive for me, and it was for others, too. I published an essay about the run-in for NBC, and a number of outlets reached out to cover the story. I think they were interested because we are so used to seeing stories like this ending poorly and causing more damage. There's something refreshing about a positive outcome.

At the same time, while the situation turned out positively, I still wasn't where I wanted to be eventually. I could see the humanity in the young man who'd yelled at me, but I still didn't see it in Wade Michael Page. I knew that I had a long way to go, but I also felt reassured, knowing that I was on the right track.

Twenty-one

INSIGHT 3:
HOW WE CONNECT

I was starting to make progress in seeing people's inner light. I felt that I was getting closer to seeing humanity in people—even in people who didn't see me as fully human. Yet I still felt that I was stagnating. While I believed Page was a vessel of divine light like everyone else, I didn't feel that in my heart. My goal of recognizing our shared humanity still seemed far out of reach.

So I decided to take small steps. I began rereading all the writing I could find about him, including articles written about his rampage, features examining his life and outlooks, and the white supremacist message boards he frequented. It had been more than a year since I had examined these message boards, and this time I was studying them less as research material and more for personal reasons. I thought that understanding Page's life and psychological makeup might bring me more clarity about who he was as a person, which in turn would help me see his humanity.

But the more I read about Page, the more distant he felt from me. It was a problem of opposition. Everything about Page felt like the antithesis of my values, aspirations, and lived experiences.

Because I couldn't find common ground between us, I had trouble connecting with him. Because I couldn't see his inner light, I had difficulty feeling compassion for him.

Speaking with friends had helped me in the past, so I reached out to a few folks I considered especially wise. The first was a good friend and Lutheran minister I had met on the interfaith circuit. (Yes, the interfaith circuit is a real thing, and yes, we're as dorky as we sound.) My friend encouraged me to remember that, however different we may be, there's nothing that distinguishes the humanity at our core. Looking deeper, he told me, would help us overcome our judgments of difference and help us focus instead on what we share.

His words sounded familiar. This is what Guru Nanak meant by ik oankar; that while we divide ourselves up on the basis of different aspects that make up who we are—ethnicities, nationalities, religions, genders, sexual orientations—we are still all pots of the same divine potter. We may each be molded differently, but the clay is still the same. I had grasped this idea as a child and had been trying to apply it throughout my life.

My minister friend went on, however, to offer an opinion that didn't feel so resonant. He explained that our differences don't matter and that we're all essentially the same. I'd heard this refrain frequently over the years in various settings, from interfaith gatherings and racial justice workshops to diversity trainings and classes on inclusion, and it never sat quite right with me. Such statements rub me the wrong way because they oversimplify the reality of our experiences and overlook the complexity of our shared humanity. To me, our differences *do* matter and we're *not* all the same.

What we've experienced in life shapes who we are as individuals and how we see the world. For instance, a study by researchers at the University of Western Australia and the University of Aberdeen in Scotland found that people's impressions of trustworthiness are based on their past interactions. We each interact with different people daily, which means that who we see as trustworthy is entirely personal and subjective. This is just one example of how our differences make up an important part of who we are.

When someone dismisses our differences by saying, "We're all the same," they signal that they don't care about us. If they cared, they wouldn't overlook aspects of our identities that we cherish and consider significant. They might say they care about diversity, but what they really care about is sameness.

Part of what makes life so beautiful is that each of us is unique. And those aspects that make us that way play important roles in shaping who we are, how we experience the world, and how we see ourselves and one another. In my view, ignoring our differences is more harmful than helpful. We can hold enough complexity to see one another's humanity without erasing one another's cultures and histories.

I appreciated my friend's advice because it was well intentioned. I also realized in talking to him that dismissing our differences as insignificant creates more problems than it solves. In the words of Audre Lorde, "It is not our differences that divide us. It is our inability to recognize, accept, and celebrate those differences." I want everyone—friends and strangers— to see my turban and beard, not ignore them. Truly understanding what they mean to me can bring us closer together.

Guru Nanak's teaching on ik oankar can help us appreciate human differences while also creating meaningful connections across them. Ik oankar does not call on us to erase or ignore what makes us different; ik oankar does the opposite, calling on us to celebrate the diverse manifestations of our shared essence. In Guru Nanak's view, there is a oneness in our plurality.

Seeing oneness in diversity is central to Sikh teachings. If the core teaching is that divinity permeates every aspect of our world, the corollary is that divinity is within those differences, too. Diversity is to be honored and celebrated, not ignored and denigrated. Everything and everyone is divine. The world is created in the image of God because the world *is* God.

According to Guru Nanak, all of creation is interconnected, and the divinity that binds it all together presents itself in myriad ways. This is why Sikhs say that God is without form and yet has infinite forms.

I had never really thought about ik oankar in this way, though these ideas were not entirely new to me either. Guru Nanak speaks to the idea of oneness in plurality in one of his best-known compositions. The closing stanza reads: "There are countless seconds, minutes, hours, days, weeks, and months. There is one sun, yet many seasons. O Nanak, the Creator has countless forms!" Guru Nanak uses increments of time here as an analogy, reminding us that while we can break down time into increasingly smaller units, ultimately they are each different forms of the same order.

We don't have to look through diversity to find our oneness; rather, we can see oneness through our diversity. The difference is subtle, but it's critical. We don't appreciate one another *despite* our differences. We appreciate one another *because* of them.

Before finding this wisdom, I had thought connection and compassion were born through commonality. We can see the humanity in someone when we see ourselves in them. This belief had driven my practice for growing my compassion: connect with people through how we're alike and then feel empathy through that connection.

Now I realized that there is more to it than that. It's not just that we all come from and share a single divine light. It's also that our differences are expressions of that one light.

Walking this fine line can move us from tolerating our differences to celebrating them. When tolerance is our goal, we prevent ourselves from releasing something far more powerful—a model of pluralism that sees our differences as beautiful and does not feel threatened by them. Until and unless we are able to embrace such a model, we'll remain unable to tap into the richness of our humanity.

This is how Sikhi teaches us to see coherence in our worlds. We can honor our diversity and oneness at the same time. The two are not mutually exclusive.

This is the insight of connection.

———

It took some effort to wrap my brain around this idea, but after some mental grappling, I developed a new appreciation for ik oankar. I was beginning to get a clear vision for how to connect with someone like Wade Michael Page, a man who seemed like my polar opposite. We could be wholly different, yet still be connected. We didn't need to have anything in common for me to see his humanity. What I needed to do was to embrace the idea that all forms—whether they are like us or not—are equally divine.

Accepting this teaching was humbling. It required me to stop looking for myself in others in order to feel connected to them. It reminded me that the world was not created in *my* image and that the world was not of value because it was a reflection of me in some way. Rather, the world is beautiful for the opposite reason: it's about more than me. When experienced through the lens of ik oankar, the expansive diversity all around us can remind us how small we are and, at the same time, how we are part of something greater.

This teaching has so much to offer all of us. Today we are not taught to see oneness across our differences. We are taught to view difference as a threat and to accept that "we fear what we do not know." We create boundaries between ourselves and others, positioning ourselves as superior and others as inferior. This is the same practice that contributes to the formation of supremacies and the same logic that fuels and sustains colonialism.

Thinking we're better than others harms us individually and spiritually because it reinforces our egocentrism. When we feed our egos daily, we build a wall between ourselves and the world. As these walls thicken, it becomes easier to feel isolated and disconnected. It also becomes harder to see our interconnectedness.

Viewing ourselves as superior also harms us socially and politically, because it creates inequities and incites violence around our world. We have seen this play out repeatedly, both in the past and the present. When we believe we are better than others, or more privileged, or more deserving, we justify giving ourselves advantages at the expense of those we deem inferior. Until we can acknowledge and overcome our supremacist mindsets, we will be stuck in our cycles of suffering.

Oppression. Repression. Depression. Repeat.

Seeing oneness in difference. Connecting through diversity. Ik oankar. This is Guru Nanak's answer. Radical connectedness is a powerful and progressive solution for our deep-rooted problems of ego, inequality, and injustice.

We find a helpful idea in the wisdom of Guru Arjan: "I see no strangers. I see no enemies. Wherever I look, I see my people."

Does this mean that Guru Arjan knew every human being personally? Of course not. Nor does it mean that everyone loved the guru. In fact, some hated him. He met his end in 1606 when a political opponent had him arrested, tortured, and executed.

What Guru Arjan taught, and what he believed, is that experiencing the world as being interconnected means no longer having to perceive others as adversaries or enemies. In fact, we no longer have to see "others" at all.

This is the transformative potential of a unified worldview. Seeing ourselves as connected—rather than constantly isolated and divided—creates a substantively different way of relating to the people in our lives, *including* those responsible for the pain we endure.

When we can witness our diversity as unique forms of divinity, and when we see ourselves and others as equally divine, we will transform how we treat one another. We will no longer oppress or hurt one another because we will know that harming others is harming ourselves; that stripping others of their humanity is stripping ourselves of our own humanity; that devaluing others and seeing them as inferior is to move away from love, not toward it.

For several months after he attacked the Sikh congregation, I had not been able to see the humanity in Wade Michael Page. I made significant progress in my healing over that time, but my pain and anger still prevented my connecting with him. It frustrated me to know that he still had power over me, despite the time that had passed and despite that he had long been dead.

But now, nearly a year removed from the massacre as I began to implement Guru Arjan's teaching, I finally felt fully liberated from my pain and anger. The answer did not come from a false sense of forgiveness, nor did it come from giving in to hate. The answer came from finding oneness *through* our differences. Wade Michael Page and I are vastly different but we are also one. This is how the insight of radical connection gave me the lens to see his humanity. In this instance, I was living into the doctrine of ik oankar.

As a result of this new thinking, I felt better within, feeling more happiness and less hurt than I had in a long time. It felt good to break the cycle of hate.

Twenty-two

ADVANCING
HOW WE CONNECT

Air travel is a privilege, and I'm lucky to be able to enjoy it. But it doesn't always feel like a privilege. While few people these days enjoy flying, I think it's fair to say that flying is even more painful for people like me than most others. I'm racially profiled by airport security across the country—pulled from lines, patted down, and questioned. And it's obvious how uncomfortable fellow passengers are around me—the stares, comments, and requests to change seats.

On one flight, an older white man came to my row, saw he was sitting next to me, and sighed heavily. He jammed his bag into the overhead bin, crumpling my suit bag in the process, and then harrumphed at me, ignoring the gentle hello I had offered him. I stood up to smooth out my suit bag and move it to another bin. As I did, the woman sitting in the row behind me made eye contact and mouthed *Sorry* while rolling her eyes.

I sat back down and saw that my neighbor was already watching a right-wing news channel, shaking his head furiously every time it showed images of refugees in camps and detention centers. The concern and discomfort bubbled up within a minute of his sitting down: What might he think of me? Was he going to confront me during the flight? Would I be safe?

I faced my discomfort with a strategy honed over years of similar experiences: I struck up a conversation.

"Where are you headed?" I asked, gently again.

He removed his headphones with a soft tug. "Back to Detroit."

"Work or family?" I asked.

"Heading home," he told me through his frown. "But not from work."

I resisted the urge to parrot the cheesy Hallmark greetings that flashed through my mind. *There's no place like home! Home is where the heart is!* Instead, I nodded, as if to invite him to share more if he wanted to, and to my surprise, he accepted willingly. Within minutes of small talk, he shared that he was returning to Detroit from a chemo treatment and that he felt utterly defeated by cancer. My heart sank. He may have had a stereotype about me. But I also had a stereotype about him. We had both let each other down.

We began to talk about family and friends who had dealt with cancer, and then we began a deeper conversation that reflected on life and death: what we believed and how we wanted to live. Bit by bit, in cramped airline seats, a sick, frightened white man and a bearded, turban-wearing Sikh had forged a connection.

Perhaps our connection changed something inside him. Maybe talking to me challenged his stereotypes or his views on the humanity of immigrants and refugees—or anyone who looked different than he did. It's hard to be certain of that, and it didn't feel appropriate for me to ask. But questioning him didn't feel all that important to me either. It takes a lot more than a single conversation to move people, and changing people's views isn't my goal in moments like these. If I've learned anything on this quest, it's that tying our happiness to other people's behaviors and outlooks will only leave us disappointed and dissatisfied. Instead, we must search for the common ground between us, the space where we are both one.

What I do know is that conversing with him changed *my* entire experience. By my willingness to forge a simple connection and by making the effort, my feelings of discomfort and concern turned into feelings of comfort and ease. Connecting with this man—a scared, unhappy stranger—was not about changing his politics. It was about preserving my own happiness. If he has marginally better opinions about people who look like me at the end of the flight than he did at the beginning, then that's icing on the cake.

Simple connections like these can save us hours, days, even lifetimes of pain. This is how applying connection as a practice can decrease our unhappiness and bring us more joy.

There is so much we can gain from bringing ik oankar into our lives. It helps us see the humanity of everyone around us, live with compassion, treat people equally, celebrate the differences we encounter, and see ourselves within the context of universal connectedness.

Guru Nanak's doctrine of ik oankar has transformed how I see the world. It has also transformed how I see myself. For years, my tendency had been to underestimate and underrate myself. Study after study has shown that this is not uncommon for people who belong to marginalized groups, including women and people of color. It's not that I was self-loathing or even pessimistic. I was generally happy and content. Yet I had been taught that to succeed meant being twice as good and working twice as hard. I measured myself against the highest standards in every regard, and while that may have helped me strive for excellence, it also created the feeling within me that I was never good enough. I was good at school, but I didn't always have straight A's. (After all, I was the kid who almost didn't go to college!) I was good at soccer and basketball, but I wasn't always the star player on my team. I helped serve meals at the local food shelter, but many of my friends volunteered more consistently than me.

In every aspect, I felt I could be better. I sought validation externally, measuring my value based on how I compared with others. I constantly felt as if I was coming up short, and this led me to devalue myself. This outlook, to state the obvious, was not healthy.

But in examining the wisdom of my tradition, I came across a line in Sikh scripture that caught me by surprise. In the words of Guru Amardas, the third Sikh guru: "O my heart-mind, you are an embodiment of divine light (joti). Recognize your origin!"

I had goosebumps the first time I heard this insight. The words wrapped around my chest and hugged me tightly. I had heard all my life that Vahiguru resided within everyone and that we should treat everyone as divine. Yet I had never really considered what that meant for me. It never crossed my mind that I was as much a part of ik oankar as everyone and everything around me.

In the original Punjabi, the word for "origin" is "mul," which literally means "root." It's a powerful choice of words, reminding us that we are each divine to our core. The light already exists in us. It *is* us. Which means we *are* it. We just have to learn to see the light we carry and the light we give.

To see ourselves as being part of the divine light is a profound shift. Adopting this outlook would elevate our own feelings of self-worth. We would no longer rely on external validation through verbal compliments or clicks on social media. We would feel confidence internally, knowing that, whatever our imperfections, we are all embodiments of the most beautiful and powerful force in this world. We would see the light within ourselves, and that alone would transform us.

This perspective has changed me because I now understand that my value as a human being resides within me. What I do is important, and I can always improve in every facet of my life—so can everyone. Yet nothing I do changes the fact that I, at my core, am divine. No one can take this from me, and I don't need anyone to validate my worth.

Embracing such a perspective is self-care for the soul. It can shift our entire understanding of who we are as individuals. Our shortcomings are a part of us, but they do not define us, because we are sufficient as we are. We don't even have to do anything superhuman to access this light, because it already resides within us all. In a world overrun by arrogance, selfishness, loneliness, and depression, seeing ourselves as part of the divine light offers us a way out of our suffering.

This is the transformative power of ik oankar.

I highlight this because one of the biggest challenges in speaking about ik oankar is trying to communicate the extent of its power. A second challenge is that actually living by its teachings can feel so far from where we are currently that it seems unattainable. I've had to deal with both of these challenges in my own journey. In that spirit, let me share a true story that has been profoundly helpful to me in understanding and internalizing the power of ik oankar.

⟨⎯⎯⎯⎯⎯⎯⎯⟩

Twenty-three

THE POWER OF CONNECTION

S atpal Singh was thirty-three years old when supremacist hate nearly claimed his life. On October 31, 1984, just a few hours before he was scheduled to return home by train from Hyderabad in the southern part of India to Amritsar, Punjab, the young scientist heard the shocking news: Indian Prime Minister Indira Gandhi had been assassinated by her Sikh bodyguards.

It crossed Satpal's mind that violence might break out in response to Ms. Gandhi's assassination, and he briefly considered delaying his trip. But he thought it unlikely, and he wanted to get home to his young family: his wife, Narinder, four-year-old son, Amandeep, and nine-month-old daughter, Gunisha. He boarded the train with hope in his heart and prayers on his lips.

What Satpal Singh didn't know was that violence had already broken out, that angry mobs were roving the streets of the capital city, New Delhi, looking to avenge the murder of Ms. Gandhi. The mobs blamed the entire Sikh community, and therefore initiated a large-scale massacre, killing Sikh children, raping Sikh women, and "garlanding" Sikh men—a torturous way of murdering people by placing a rubber tire around their necks, dousing them with kerosene, then burning them alive. If Satpal had known what was happening, he likely would not have boarded his train, which was scheduled to pass through India's capital city the next day.

The train was tense yet uneventful and calm enough at first that Satpal was able to sleep the first few hours of his trip. As the trip continued, passengers heard more and more reports of mob violence in the capital city. They also began hearing about mobs storming trains around New Delhi and brutally murdering any Sikhs they found.

Satpal's concern heightened when the train made an unscheduled stop at a small railway station near the city of Bhopal. Passengers in his car climbed down to see what was happening, then clambered back in to report that small groups of men were going from car to car looking for Sikh passengers to kill.

Satpal had nowhere to go. He lay on his berth and placed a bedsheet over his head, knowing full well that he was hiding in plain sight. A mob of about twenty-five men burst into his compartment and found him almost immediately. They rushed toward him and one of them yanked off the sheet. Satpal was now face-to-face with his would-be killers. They wasted no time whisking him to his feet, unleashing a fury of punches to his head and midsection. The young scientist crumpled to the ground. But the men didn't slow down. They kicked him repeatedly until his body went limp. Presuming him to be dead, they grabbed hold of his ankles and wrists, dragged his body to the train car's exit, and hurled him off onto the tracks. He had just enough energy to plead with a police officer nearby to help him before he passed out.

Satpal regained consciousness not long after. When he opened his eyes, he saw a stranger standing over him and that his train was still at the station. The man helped Satpal to his feet and urged him to get back on the train before he was stoned to death. Satpal looked up at the platform to see a crowd of people shouting and holding large stones in their hands. He crawled back onto his train car and was relieved to see that the mob had left his car.

Satpal had several more near-death experiences over the next ten heart-wrenching days. But he survived those, too. By the time he made it back to his wife in Amritsar, she was ready to give up hope that their young children would ever see their father again. Narinder hadn't said a word about his absence to their two children, both of whom were too young to realize that something was amiss.

While Satpal's survival is itself remarkable, it's not even the most remarkable part of this story.

The most remarkable moment took place when the mob first entered his train car. Satpal made eye contact with his killers and knew it was time to say goodbye. He bowed his head, closed his eyes, and recited Ardas, a common prayer that Sikhs around the world recite daily.

He asked Vahiguru to take care of his wife, whom he would be leaving a widow. He requested love and support for his young toddler, Amandeep, and his baby girl, Gunisha. And then, most remarkably, Satpal asked God to give peace to those who were about to attack him.

He felt concern for the very men who had no concern for him. He saw humanity in his own would-be murderers. In the face of death, he had the capacity to respond to hate with love.

I first heard this extraordinary story from my father-in-law—for he is the man in the story. He is Satpal Singh.

When he first shared his account with me in 2007, I wasn't sure how to react. It was a stunning, moving story. After composing myself, I asked the first question that came to mind: "What gave you the strength and clarity to respond with such grace?"

Without hesitation, he replied with the most fundamental and central of all Sikh teachings: ik oankar.

"In that moment, I truly saw those men who tried to kill me as my own brothers," he said. "I saw the anger and hate in their eyes—but I didn't feel anger or hate for them because I also saw the light in their eyes. I saw ik oankar. That's why I prayed for them, just as I prayed for my own family."

In Satpal's view, his killers deserved his prayers just as much as his own beloved family. He saw them as equally human, no matter the harm they sought to inflict on him. This is the power of radical connectedness.

Satpal Singh forgave his would-be killers. How could he? They never apologized for what they did to him. But he was still able to see their humanity and feel compassion for them. Doing so helped him find inner peace—not because he was retreating from the world and ignoring his pain, but because he embraced it and, in doing so, harnessed a more productive way of achieving his goals. I say this because I have witnessed firsthand how Satpal Singh has retained his practice of ik oankar in the years since. Decades later, he remains devoted to justice work, including efforts to build bridges across religious divides and to address violence against women. Moreover, he remains one of the most carefree and joyful people I know. Even now, he wears his boyish grin just above his long gray beard. He's unlocked that rare combination of love for self *and* love for others.

Years after hearing his story, I remain in awe of the grace he maintained in the face of extreme adversity. His story reminds me of Guru Arjan singing while being tortured: "Your Will is so sweet to me." Both of them were exemplars in their own way, and yet both of their examples felt unattainable to me. Did I have it within me to achieve a similar spiritual state?

For weeks after Satpal told me his story, my mind's answer was no. I was just a regular person. Sure, I had learned to ignore and confront racism that came my way, but that didn't make me superhuman. I just didn't have it in me to love in the face of such extreme hate.

———

I had come to terms with my own limitations when something happened to change my thinking. I was at a Knicks game in Madison Square Garden with a friend in 2017. We were walking to get popcorn for the second half when we crossed paths with a young woman. Her eyes flickered with recognition and she pivoted abruptly to grab me by the shoulder.

"Are you Simran, by any chance?" she asked, only slightly mispronouncing my name. "The running professor at NYU?"

At the time, I was a postdoctoral fellow in NYU's Center for Religion and Media and a chaplain for Sikh students there. I wasn't teaching classes then, but I nodded anyway, trying not to laugh at being identified as "the running professor."

"I just want to tell you that I saw your story on NBC about stopping to talk with the young man who yelled hateful slurs at you. I wanted to thank you because it has helped me deal with my own anger after Trump's election. I had stopped talking to one of my best friends due to political differences. I had felt like just being friends with her made me complicit in all her political views, and the guilt from that made me feel like it was morally wrong to be friends with her or even respect her. Your example and advice helped me patch up our friendship. We still disagree about politics, but I can see her humanity and respect her again. That relationship is really important to me, and I'm so glad to have salvaged it."

This interaction has stuck with me—not just because it speaks to the power of this worldview, but also because it made me realize something new about myself: I actually did have the capacity to maintain grace in the face of hate. I had not seen my previous encounters with racism as meaningful to anyone else, because they seemed far smaller in magnitude than the merciless beating Satpal Singh endured; they seemed minuscule in comparison to the brutal torture that preceded Guru Arjan's execution. This woman's comments opened my eyes to the truth: I *did* have it within me to respond to hate with love. And what's more, I had even tapped into it recently.

Before, I had felt doubtful I could ever achieve such a state. Now, I felt the opposite—motivated, empowered, and energized to nurture these qualities, knowing that if I worked at it, I might one day achieve the state of radical connectedness that my father-in-law had unlocked.

Satpal Singh's response illustrates the force of ik oankar at its best. It's a way of living and experiencing the world that brings compassion and connection, even in the most challenging of situations. It's a force that resides within each of us, waiting to be unlocked and released. It's an antidote for the divisions and supremacies that plague our world today. This is the universal power of ik oankar. It's a spiritual, ethical, personal, and collective balm for our times, all wrapped up into one. And it's already in each and every one of us, waiting to be acknowledged and nurtured, ready to help us through hard times.

Part III

FROM CONNECTION TO LOVE

We weren't allowed to curse in our home growing up. Once, when my brothers and I were playing basketball in the backyard, Harpreet missed a shot and said, "Damn." I dropped the ball and sprinted inside to tell on him. Not because I felt offended, but because I was petty and loved getting him in trouble.

As we grew older, more four-letter words entered our vocabulary. But there's one four-letter word we would never say to one another: *love*.

It's one of the strangest traits of our family. We talked daily about love, we treated one another with love, and I knew without a doubt that we loved one another through thick and thin. Yet, even to this day, we don't actually voice our love to one another. And while sometimes I wish we would, to an extent saying it out loud doesn't seem necessary. My confidence in our love for one another resides deep within me.

Journeying into ourselves is a necessary step in preparing us to journey into our worlds. Our great wisdom traditions teach us that to be one with the world, we must be one with ourselves. *As above, so below. As within, so without. As the universe, so the soul.* Guru Nanak tells us that when we conquer our minds, we conquer the world.

But living in this world is not a solitary practice. We live alongside one another and in community with one another. We cannot retreat into ourselves and ignore the people around us. This is where Guru Nanak's teaching of ik oankar comes in. Ik oankar calls on us to see we are all interconnected, and that therefore we are all in relationship with one another—even with those who live across the world and those we have never met. Forging these connections lays the groundwork for a different kind of love than we typically know, a love that is deep and abiding and that we feel viscerally within ourselves and through everyone we meet.

Truly feeling connected with others unlocks what we all aspire to but remains too hard to reach: the capacity to love our neighbors *and* ourselves. This is not an easy state to achieve, and it's rare to find people who live by this commitment. But it is not impossible. The capability resides in each of us. The challenge comes in laying a strong foundation for ourselves (ik oankar), and then building up from there, brick by brick, with rightful values, outlooks, and practices.

This is the way into living with love, my favorite four-letter word.

Twenty-four

EXPANDING OUR LOVE

Our first daughter was born in the winter of 2016. The moment my baby girl came into my arms, I understood what everyone had been saying all along about parenthood. This was a different kind of feeling, unlike anything I had experienced before. The word "love" no longer felt sufficient.

I thought a lot about my parents that day, finally understanding why they gave up everything they had in India to chase a better life in the United States for their future rambunctious, ridiculous turban-wearing boys. Viewing the world through their eyes for the first time, I realized that love is an unstoppable force, one that gives life to hope and inspires rightful action, no matter how hard it is or what the consequences might be.

It made sense now why my friends' descriptions of this moment felt like platitudes and why they said things like, "We can't describe the feeling to you. You just have to experience it yourself." I know now that there are not enough words in this world to articulate that all-consuming, life-changing emotion that knocked me off balance.

The experience of becoming a father changed me forever in many positive ways. And not just because it legitimized the terrible dad jokes I'd been telling all my life. Part of my growth has come through being challenged to revise some basic things I thought about the world and about myself.

For instance, I had always thought of myself as a loving person, as someone who had a complete experience and knowledge of love. My joyous memories and scars of heartbreak testified to my *experiences* of love. My years of studying the most profound devotional poetry ever composed bore witness to my *knowledge* of love.

Yet here I was, a lover of love, accepting with reluctance what must be true: there was more to love than I knew. I didn't fully *know* love—a stunning realization that made me wonder if I had ever really known love at all.

While this thought dizzied me, the discomfort of uncertainty had positive effects, too. It pushed me to find answers wherever possible, a process of self-discovery that led to incredible insight and growth.

My first step in this journey, and perhaps the simplest one, was to recognize that none of this is as simple as it may seem. Love, as most of us experience it, is complicated.

Even the word "love" itself is complicated. It's impossible to put that feeling into human language. No matter what we do or how hard we try, we will always come up short in trying to speak about love.

This is not just true about love. Language cannot fully capture the depth of human emotions. Words can help us approximate what we mean in terms of common experiences, but they will never carry the full force of the feeling. Humans create language to help signify reality; but language is not reality itself. Talking about love is different than living with it.

Because we each have different life experiences, we all use and understand language differently. The word "turban" may mean something different to me than it does to you. I have worn one every day since my childhood, and for me as a Sikh, the word "turban" connotes royalty, dignity, equality, and justice. On the other hand, most Westerners hear the word "turban" and immediately think of terrorism, violence, extremism, and hate. Language is not uniform; how we understand words is informed by our own perspectives, perceptions, and yes, prejudices.

If language is a reflection of our experiences, then how we understand certain words can change as we have new experiences. Here is an example of how I have seen that happen in my own life.

The greatest losses I had ever felt in my privileged childhood were in sports; the most soul-crushing loss in my memory was when our high school soccer team lost in the Texas state playoffs. As the starting sweeper, I felt as if my world had been taken from me, and as a cocaptain I felt responsible for my teammates' sadness, too.

(As sad as I felt, I have a great memory from this loss, too. We were playing in Austin against Westlake High School, or as our coach called them, "The Evil Empire." I was a bit taken aback when their fans started shouting at me to go back to where I came from. I felt a bit unnerved, until suddenly I heard a familiar voice above the noise. My mama bear stood up angrily and shouted: "Why?! Why should he?!" Hearing her was all I needed to compose myself and return my focus to the match.)

I don't mean to trivialize the feeling—our grief was real, and it hurt. But because this was the worst loss I had endured, this was what grief meant to me.

Due to my limited experience, I struggled to fully empathize with my high school friend Chris when his mother died unexpectedly around this time. Chris was using those same terms that I knew—"grief" and "loss" and "heartache"—but his feelings were so much deeper and more painful, his loss so much more final than mine.

Sharing a deeply personal feeling with someone who has never experienced it is like trying to describe the colors of the rainbow to someone who has never seen color. How can someone truly relate to a feeling they've never felt?

The grief of losing a soccer game is not even in the same realm as losing a parent. Yet we use the same words to describe both feelings. This is how the same language that serves us can also deceive us.

Words like "loss" and "grief"—and "love"—can be useful for communicating our shared emotions, but our experiences of them are not universal truths. My understanding of grief as a teenager was different from how others understood the term because we had different life experiences. My understandings have also changed with new experiences; "loss" and "grief" mean something different to me now that I have witnessed loved ones die before my eyes. We all understand this because we've all been there. Part of being human is learning and growing as we move through life.

It is also a shortcoming of the English language that we reserve one word, "love," to capture one of the most profound and complex human experiences. Many languages—including Persian, Arabic, Sanskrit, Punjabi, Urdu, and Hindi—can accommodate a much richer spectrum of this concept, with multiple words to relay the experiences and intricacies of love.

In Punjabi, we use multiple words (muhabbat, prem, pyaar, sneh, ishq, preet, bhau), each of which carries its own nuance. For instance, the term "bhau" indicates a level of reverence, admiration, and awe, whereas "pyaar" connotes a more interpersonal sort of love reciprocated between equals. Both words derive from Sanskrit and both refer to feelings of love. Yet each has its own valence. In English we wouldn't distinguish between the two, let alone any of the others. In English, all the complexities of love are flattened into a single word.

It can be challenging, confusing, and frustrating to express this complex feeling through a single word. When I recognized this limitation, I decided to stop trying to define what "love" means literally and to start thinking of love as a spectrum. This single word has a range of meanings, some of which carry tremendous weight—*I love my spouse*—and some of which carry less weight—*I love mangoes* (though as a South Asian, the mango love runs deep). Love, as we all know from personal experience, is not one single thing.

When we only have one word to capture the range of feelings that we describe as love, then we can easily fall into the trap of arguing whether or not something is "true love." I found myself in that quandary after my older daughter was born, wondering if I had ever actually known love at all.

The truth is, I did know love before my daughter was born, but it was qualitatively different from what I experienced the day she came into our lives. The love struck me with such force on that day that it felt entirely fresh. And yet it was also familiar because it was the same core feeling alive in so many of my relationships: love for my wife, love for my brothers, love for my parents, love for my teachers.

They were all different forms of love, experienced and expressed in different ways. That one felt more powerful did not invalidate the love in my other relationships. They could all coexist. They could all grow.

Love, like any human emotion, is not all-or-nothing. We experience it to different degrees. The English language does not help us access these degrees of love conceptually; instead, it obscures them and, therefore, limits what we are able to conceptualize.

How do we get beyond that? Looking inward to our own experiences and looking outward to other cultures and languages can help us embrace a richer understanding of what love means and what it could look like in our own lives.

Experiencing my daughter's birth showed me that love is far more expansive and powerful than I had ever imagined, and it's led me to ask a number of follow-up questions: Might there be more to love than what I was feeling for my daughter? Could we potentially expand love to every relationship we have in this world? And what might our world look like if we could love one another the way we love our children?

Twenty-five

LIMITLESS LOVE

One Sikh memory recalls that during his travels across Asia in the sixteenth century, Guru Nanak comes to a town filled with spiritual teachers. A group of leaders meet him at the edge of the town, and one hands the young guru a bowl of milk filled to the brim. *Just like there's no room for more milk in this bowl, there's no room for you in our community.*

Without batting an eye, Guru Nanak plucks a flower from the ground and places it on top of the milk. His wordless message comes through clearly: *When we open ourselves up, there's always room for more.*

(Pro tip: This spiritual lesson also provides a good justification for eating dessert even when you're full from dinner.)

I heard this account as a child and hadn't thought of it for years. I must have filed it in my memory bank, though, because it came back to consciousness unexpectedly in 2017 while I was teaching at Trinity University in Texas.

One of my students, Miguel, had started visiting my office hours to discuss course material when he was a sophomore, and his visits grew into a weekly tradition of discussing life over coffee and cookies. One afternoon Miguel walked into my office as I was finishing a phone call. When I hung up, he smiled: "Getting flowers for the wife? So smooth, Dr. Singh!"

I laughed and corrected him, explaining that I was anything but smooth and that the flowers were for a student whose mother had just had a heart attack.

Miguel said he had just heard about a classmate, Andy, whose mother had had a heart attack. When I confirmed that I was speaking about Andy, too, his eyes widened in outrage.

"Are you joking, Dr. Singh? You know Andy hates you, right? He's the one who wrote that anonymous note telling you that you're not welcome here! And he's one of the students who got you on the Professor Watchlist and tried to get you fired! You know that, right?!"

I appreciated Miguel's protectiveness and reflected on the strife I had already been through that year. Death threats credible enough to warrant police and FBI involvement. Calls to the university president's office demanding that I be fired. Right-wing outlets including Campus Reform, Breitbart, and Turning Point USA harassing me incessantly.

I would have been naive not to expect abuse teaching Islamic studies at a university in Texas, especially given how I looked. It was 2017, after all, a time of heightened polarization when attacks on academic freedom were rampant and anti-Muslim bias was high. I prepared myself for attacks from right-wingers the day I signed the contract to teach at Trinity, and there were a handful of students, like Andy, who seemed to make it their mission to make my life difficult. It was not that their hatred for me caught me by surprise; it was that the attacks came more swiftly and vigorously than I had anticipated. It also saddened me to realize that students like Andy would come after me without ever getting to know me.

Dealing with each of those issues had been difficult, but the Professor Watchlist was probably the most challenging. At the time, it was a new and highly publicized right-wing website that claimed to hold professors with liberal agendas accountable. I hadn't done or said anything controversial—aside from condemning racism and hate—but the bar is often lower for people who look like me. It was a photo that ultimately landed me on the list, though the irony is that the photo wasn't even of me. The site managers found a photo I had tweeted of my younger brother flicking off the Trump Tower building in New York City and confused him for me—a shock given that he's not nearly as good-looking as me. Our friends were infuriated by the implicit racism and the negative implications for our lives, and they petitioned the website to take down the absurd and inaccurate post.

The site owners refused, though even if they had complied, it likely wouldn't have mattered much. The damage had already been done. Being featured on the site came with a daily barrage of harassment. My scholar friends discussed how making the Professor Watchlist was a badge of honor, and I appreciated that to an extent. But as someone who had seen racist vitriol spill into hateful violence, I was not thrilled about being a target for right-wingers, especially at a time when the American president was stoking the flames of racist hate. Moreover, as a young scholar just starting his career, I was concerned that being singled out might threaten my job security or future opportunities.

Miguel had been one of the few students who followed what I had gone through that year, and I appreciated his passion and concern. I told Miguel that I knew Andy had made my life hard, but he was still a student who deserved my care, especially in a moment like this. I explained that sending flowers to his mother's hospital room was the least I could do.

Miguel's stance softened. "How do you do it, Dr. Singh? How are you able to show love to those who make your life so hard?"

I recalled Guru Nanak's powerful teaching with the bowl full of milk and reflected on how to share that message with my student. Then I had an idea.

"Close your eyes, Miguel. At the count of three, breathe in as deeply as you can. And hold that breath in."

He complied.

After three seconds, I asked him to take in more air and hold it in.

Miguel complied again.

After three more seconds, I asked him to take in even more breath and hold it in.

He did, holding it in as long as he could before expelling it all out.

"Nice breathing exercise, Dr. Singh. I feel way calmer. Thank you."

"I'm glad, Miguel. Now let me ask you a question. How did you have room to take in more air with each breath? Weren't your lungs at capacity the first time I asked you?"

This wasn't just a breathing exercise. It's a lesson about how we understand our own limits and put boundaries on what we experience. Here's the real problem with the arbitrary restrictions we place on ourselves: If we don't even know what lies beyond our limits, how will we ever know what we're missing?

We all have capacity for more than we think.

This story is about challenging ourselves to grow by pushing our limits. It's also a message about love. Because if we restrict our ideas of love to our everyday encounters, we will only ever scratch the surface of what love has to offer.

Once you have a taste of a greater joy than you thought was possible, you might feel that you've been shortchanged all along. This realization might raise similar questions to those I asked myself after the birth of our first daughter: If love is more expansive than we ever imagined, was there still even more to uncover? What might we be missing? And what is the ultimate human capacity for love?

These are not just questions of curiosity. They are practical questions that emerge from a desire to stretch and expand the best feelings we have ever known. What would it take to make this transient feeling more permanent? How could we transform our most joyful moments into an entire lifetime filled with love?

I began examining everything that might help me answer these questions, from classical Sanskrit shlokas on viraha (yearning) and Sufi ghazals on ishq (love) to the lives of people I admired most, such as civil rights activist Dolores Huerta and humanitarian Bhagat Puran Singh. I even absorbed popular culture, listening to love songs (thank you, Alicia Keys and John Legend) and watching a range of sentimental films, from Hollywood to Bollywood.

After all this exploration, it turned out that my grandmother had shared with me, dozens of times, the greatest love story ever told. I had just never known to understand it as a love story.

Twenty-six

LOVE IN ACTION

During a period of violent persecution in South Asia in the early seventeenth century, a group of Kashmiri Brahmins came to Guru Tegh Bahadur's court for help. The ninth Sikh guru was not Hindu, and his community of Sikhs was not being persecuted at the time. Yet they came to the guru for help because he was known for serving anyone and everyone in need.

Guru Tegh Bahadur agreed to speak out on their behalf and journeyed with a band of Sikhs toward the imperial capital of Delhi. The emperor Aurangzeb was furious with Guru Tegh Bahadur's audacity. He imprisoned the guru and his Sikhs and, to make an example of them, publicly tortured and executed them, one by one.

This was how Guru Tegh Bahadur came to give his life defending the principle of religious liberty. Neither he nor his community was being targeted. He did not need to speak up, let alone risk his life. Yet he felt the pain of the persecuted Kashmiri Hindus. In living by the ethical commitment Sikhs make in their daily prayers—the uplifting of all humanity (sarbat da bhala)—Guru Tegh Bahadur made the ultimate sacrifice for a group of people he had never even met before.

Guru Tegh Bahadur was able to see beyond the boundaries of difference through a worldview rooted in ik oankar. I had aspired to live up to his example since I was a boy in San Antonio. I even carried a small paper in my wallet through high school inscribed with one of his teachings: "Nanak says: O my mind, recognize that a truly liberated person is someone who isn't affected by pleasure or pain and looks upon friends and foes as the same."

I had heard Guru Tegh Bahadur's story dozens of times since my childhood and had extracted several important lessons from it over the years, including what it means to remain steadfastly committed to one's principles, the courage that comes with conviction, and what authentic solidarity looks like.

It wasn't until I was an adult that it finally struck me that Guru Tegh Bahadur's life was a love story. He showed us what it truly means to love— to love oneself, to love one's people, and to love the stranger.

Guru Tegh Bahadur did what was best for the Kashmiri Hindus without regard for how it might affect him. If he had acted in self-interest, he wouldn't have endangered his own life to protect theirs. He was moved by a selflessness rooted in unconditional love. Observing this reveals something critical about the various accounts of love that we remember and retell. The greatest love stories are the ones where lovers make consequential sacrifices without regard for the consequences.

Love is unconditional, not contingent.

Love is selfless, not self-centered.

Love is ever giving, not transactional.

We all know this about love because we have each experienced it to some degree. For me, this experience came through the birth of our first daughter.

Before she was born, I would measure the pros and cons of every decision, even in relationships of love and even with my own parents. When my parents would ask me to come home from college and spend the weekend with them—a whopping twelve miles away—I would run an internal cost-benefit analysis, weighing the pros and cons before deciding if the twenty-minute trip was worth the effort. Sometimes I would agree to visit and sometimes I wouldn't. But the final decision is not the point here, nor is how much effort it entailed. What matters is that I was both rooted in and driven by my own self-centeredness. I wasn't deciding based on what was best for them or even what was best for all of us. I was deciding based on what was best for me.

My love was a calculated and selfish love. It was still love (at least in terms of how we define it in English). But it was far lower on the spectrum of love than what we have the potential to experience. It was certainly a lower form of love than the unconditional love my parents have always shown me, and the love that I feel for my own children now.

The new, higher form of love that came with my first daughter's arrival showed itself differently. My love was no longer just about me. When she was sick, my wife and I would stay up all night together because we couldn't sleep anyway. When she broke her foot and cried, tears rolled down my cheeks, too. When professional opportunities demanded that I choose between work and her, my heart led the way: She came first every time. I would continue caring for her even when I was exhausted or ill or even after breaking my arm and in extreme discomfort—solely because my baby girl's happiness came before my own.

This form of love continued uninterrupted when our second daughter was born, and all this has remained true with her, too. Both of our daughters are still quite young as I write this, so it may be the sheer lack of sleep talking, but becoming a parent launched me into a new realm of love.

The selfless love that came with my daughters' births enabled me to see the selfless love in the story of Guru Tegh Bahadur. His love was far deeper than mine, and for people he didn't even know. My newfound selflessness as a parent made me feel like his state was finally comprehensible and perhaps even within reach.

I thought of the people whose lives and words testify to this deeper, extraordinary love. Activists like Heather Heyer, a young white woman who gave her life standing against white supremacy in Charlottesville, Virginia, in 2017. Humanitarians like Ravi Singh of Khalsa Aid, who runs toward a crisis while most are fleeing it, routinely putting his life on the line to serve refugees all around the world. Advocates like Malala Yousafzai, who continued fighting for equal rights even after being shot in the head in 2012 by the Taliban for having the nerve to advocate for women's education.

I reflected on the courage of these real-life superheroes and asked myself: If they could tap into their potential to love, then why couldn't I? Why couldn't all of us?

Each of us *can* enter into the life-changing realm of selfless, unconditional love. We all carry a greater capacity for love than we realize. And what's more, that love is already inside us, waiting to be unlocked. All we have to do is open ourselves up to it.

The first step is perhaps the easiest. It entails nothing more than accepting that this potential resides within you. It's placing that flower atop the full cup of milk. It's breathing in as deeply as you can, and then taking in one more breath. It's opening yourself up to the possibility that we all have the capacity for more.

Once we accept this truth, the next step is for us to understand what consummate love looks like in practice. Achieving an elevated form of love is not something that we fall into or that suddenly falls into our hearts. Love is like any other quality or behavior; we cultivate it through regular and sustained practice. It is hard to be intentional when we define our goal generally as "living a life of love." We need practical steps that we can take every day.

The best way to begin is to articulate a clear understanding of our goal, identify some of its key aspects, and then develop specific practices that will help us achieve that goal. So let's focus on these for a moment. We can start by considering two interrelated features of love in its highest form and asking ourselves the question: *How might we proactively nurture connection and selflessness in our lives?*

Twenty-seven

LOVE IS CONNECTION

I t wasn't long after meeting her that I found myself enchanted. Gunisha, the woman who is now my wife, embodied so many admirable qualities and shared so many of my interests—justice, sports, literature, politics, Sikhi. She is funny, curious, and passionate about human rights and medicine. And although she grew up in Buffalo in the 1990s, and though it was nearly a dealbreaker, Gunisha was even willing to overlook that I was a Dallas Cowboys fan at the time.

We connected immediately, and as our bond deepened over the following weeks and months, she lived in my thoughts more and more. It seemed as if everything existed to remind me of her. Playing soccer with my friends in Cambridge Common reminded me that her favorite smell is fresh-cut grass. Eating Italian food reminded me of the time I dared her to drink olive oil with a straw—and then watched with disgust and delight as she did. Grocery stores reminded me of the time we borrowed a shopping cart from such a store and ran around Cambridge—I pushed as she sat inside the cart—until we crashed and she came tumbling out. When we were apart, everything I ate or read or heard reminded me of her. And all of these reminders made me want to be in her presence. Through my relationship with Gunisha, I learned that love is connection.

While she and I feel that our relationship is special, neither of us thinks our ability to access connection is unique. We have all experienced connection because we have all experienced love.

Raising children with Gunisha has revealed to me even more about the relationship between love and connection. I have never felt more connected to anything or anyone in this world than my two baby girls. I'm constantly thinking about them and carrying them in my heart. Even when I'm fast asleep in the middle of the night, I pop right up when I hear either of them struggling or crying. Love doesn't have a "snooze" button (though we might sometimes wish it did).

I used to imagine love between two beings as a single point of connection, almost like two metal rods fused together. The place where the two meet is the location of their bond. The two bodies remain distinct, and yet they have become so much a part of each other that it's not possible to simply pull one apart from the other. They have become attached, and to break that connection would be as traumatic as it would be difficult. This explained why it hurts so much when relationships are severed. It's a severing of a deeply rooted connection, a part of us being taken away from ourselves.

Now I see that a deeper kind of love requires a different kind of metaphor. I feel so connected with my daughters that our bond can never be severed. My own identity has become so bound up with their existence that it feels less like a fusing together or attachment and more like a merging or infusion.

It's as if someone took two glasses of water, poured them into a pitcher, and then poured the water back into the glasses. The contents are back in the same two containers, yet they're intermingled in such a way that there is no way of separating them back out.

Our connection can never be severed because I am them and they are me.

The deeper the love, the deeper the connection.

That love sparks joy is not just a personal realization. Research confirms this, too.

In 2013, researchers at Harvard completed a seventy-five-year study on happiness, one of the longest and most comprehensive studies of human development. The study found overwhelmingly that loving relationships were the largest single determinant for health and happiness later in life. George Vaillant, the lead director of the study, offered a concise summary of his research findings: "Happiness is love. Full stop."

Love makes us feel alive. It's enlivening and life-giving, and it is still more than all that. Love is the point of life itself.

As Guru Arjan writes: "I don't care about salvation, and I don't even care about power. All I really want is to be in love with the Divine."

According to Guru Arjan, our liberation comes through accessing love. It's such an empowering and profound idea. Unlike the pursuit of power or salvation, love doesn't require external recognition or validation. It all comes from within ourselves. If we can learn to love, we can achieve everlasting and unconditional bliss (anand). This is a markedly different approach to happiness from what we find in many worldviews, religious or otherwise, and it's an intuitive one, too.

This outlook resonates because it matches up with our life experiences. How often have we sacrificed happiness today for the promise of happiness tomorrow—and then never fulfilled that promise? How many times have we told ourselves that we can relax and enjoy life once we finish the tasks ahead of us, only to realize at the finish line that we've forgotten how to relax and we still have more to do?

We all know it is possible to enjoy the journey, yet too often we're laser-focused on the destination. We find ourselves envious of those who are happy, wishing we could be the same. What we fail to realize is that we can have happiness right now—especially if we stop tying our happiness to what might happen later. That's what love can do for us, because love is about the here and now.

In addition to deprioritizing the promise of future salvation, Guru Arjan also dismisses power as an avenue for long-term happiness. No person in history has chased power for its own sake and found lasting joy within it. They may have been successful in gaining influence, and they may have felt momentary gladness. But none have come out fulfilled.

We all find ourselves enticed by the allure of power. This is normal, a part of our social conditioning. Influence is billed as a measure of success and a source of happiness, especially in our current era—and yet we know this is a false promise. If fame really gave us happiness, then wouldn't we see less anxiety and depression among the world's most well-known celebrities, politicians, and athletes?

We've learned this from the world's sages and through our own lives: Material wealth will not bring us contentment. Joy comes from living in the moment.

My college roommate Dave is a good example of this. With a Catholic mother and a Jewish father, Dave grew up in a religiously devout family in Omaha, Nebraska. We met while playing soccer as first-year students at Trinity, and we became instant friends. In the first few months of knowing him, it became apparent to me that Dave was one of the smartest and hardest-working students in our class. Dave would graduate in three years with honors, have his pick of medical schools, and select a program in Omaha to spend more time with his family. At the end of medical school, he had his choice of medical fields and chose pediatrics because he loves serving children. He decided to work at a clinic that served immigrant families, and he took a significant pay cut to set aside time for his greatest passion—volunteering in Nepal and India to help improve maternal and child health. Areas in these countries where he has worked have long suffered from a lack of health-care access, and Dave has felt drawn to serve there—even when it has meant paying out of his own pocket to do so.

What I have learned through my friendship with Dave is that happiness is not something to be saved for later, nor is it something to achieve through prestige or fame. Choosing happiness is a decision we make every single day. When faced with the choice between chasing ambition and cultivating love, he has consistently chosen love—love for his family, love for children, love for the most vulnerable and least resourced.

No wonder Dave is one of the happiest people I know. And no wonder people love being in his presence. He consistently chooses to live with love.

Dave is not a Sikh, yet he brings to life the vision of Guru Arjan, who tells us that the pinnacle of human achievement comes down to a single experience: love. Guru Arjan believed that it's possible to take the deep, interpersonal love we feel for one another and expand that into a love that permeates our lives and informs all our actions.

The key, Guru Arjan taught, is that we plant this love in the flowerbed of ik oankar. Every day is an opportunity to connect with the world all around us. The gurus describe the state of perpetual connection as love, the ultimate goal in the Sikh tradition.

How does one achieve this goal? How do we bring more love into our lives?

In Sikh teachings, the goal of life is the same as its practice: We achieve love by trying to live with love, day in and day out.

We realize love by growing it with care. The ends don't justify the means because the two are one and the same. The process *is* the result. Compromising the process is compromising the goal itself.

———

Nurturing love through interconnectedness is the secret to releasing a love so all-consuming that it produces everlasting joy. This is what it means to be one with everything. It's spiritual, mental, and emotional liberation. It's unconditional happiness, a love so deeply infused in our being that it can never be broken.

Guru Arjan's teachings on love are not just empty words or romantic ideas. He lived by these teachings, modeling for us how achieving a state of unconditional love could spark a life of immutable joy. It was he who, upon being tortured and executed, sang the famous words: "*Tera keea meethaa laagay.* Your Will is so sweet to me."

Sikh memory recalls that Sain Mian Mir, a prominent Sufi Muslim saint, overheard his friend Guru Arjan utter these words while being tortured. The saint asked the guru how he could possibly experience torture as anything other than suffering. *What could be sweet in this?* Guru Arjan replied simply that, in love, everything is beautiful. The guru had a different perspective on his own torture because he experienced it all as love. Yes, he felt pain. And yes, his body was traumatized. But his heart and mind were not suffering because they remained connected. Love had become so entrenched within him—and he within it—that the physical pain his body underwent was no match for the love he felt in his heart.

This is what we mean when we say, "Love endures" and "Love conquers all" and "Love wins." These are not empty platitudes. They are forceful convictions derived from extraordinary moments. They come from witnessing love withstand extreme duress.

This is the power of a broader kind of love, one that goes beyond personal relationships and moves into any kind of experience we have in this world. When we truly recognize the world as being interconnected, we can overcome suffering, even in the most extreme circumstances.

It can feel both affirming and invigorating to believe that this extraordinary potential resides within you and within each of us. What's even more powerful, though, is to begin tapping into it.

Twenty-eight

CULTIVATING CONNECTION

U ltimately, we all want the same thing. No, I'm not talking about tickets to the World Cup or a perfectly poured latte (though I wouldn't mind those either). I'm talking about happiness, joy, and love.

The question is: How do we access these experiences so that we, like Guru Arjan, can taste the sweetness of life in all situations? How do we cultivate a connection so strong that it becomes unbreakable? And what can we do to feel connected to everyone around us—not just those who already love us, but even those who might despise us?

I asked myself these questions for months, unsure of what specific, practical steps I could take to enhance my own life. I tried different approaches, including goal setting, leadership training, and attending spiritual transformation workshops. And while I noticed progress in certain areas, true satisfaction still eluded me. I felt like a hamster on a wheel (or like a human on a treadmill), running frantically yet stuck in the same place. Rather than feeling happier, I felt frustrated.

My breakthrough came by taking a step back from it all. I was reading a verse from Guru Nanak that, for centuries, Sikhs have read every evening as part of their daily prayers. Our family had sung this line each evening for as long as I could remember, but for some reason it hit differently one night:

"*Aakhaa jeevaa visrai mar jau*. In remembering, I live. In forgetting, I die."

I had always understood this verse as a simple remark on the value of meditation. This time, though, it occurred to me that Guru Nanak meant more than that. He wasn't just talking about the act of remembering. He was talking about a relationship, about connection, about *love*.

From the perspective of a lover, life and death have little to do with our physical bodies. Lovers feel most alive when they're connected with those they love and suffer most when they're disconnected. Guru Nanak understood this, which is why he likens forgetfulness and emotional disconnection to death. These are the stakes.

Guru Nanak's reframing of life and death resonated because I had experienced it before in my own relationships—we all have. We feel alive in the presence of people we love and feel pain when our love is somehow broken.

Guru Nanak's perspective also helps to explain why so many of us feel like we're cycling through our own heaven and hell from moment to moment and day to day. In oscillating between brief moments of connection and longer periods of disconnection, we're riding a never-ending rollercoaster of living and dying that leaves us feeling disenchanted, disillusioned, and dissatisfied.

Perhaps the greatest irony of our time is that while humans are more connected than ever before—by our phones, emails, and social media—we actually *feel* less connected. Loneliness is at its highest recorded rate in human history. Researchers of social isolation predict that the loneliness epidemic will become a public health crisis by 2030. To me, one of the most startling revelations of the coronavirus pandemic came through the practice of physical isolation and social distancing: We are social beings who crave social connection. Feeling connected makes us happy and gives us life.

A groundbreaking 2015 study by psychologist Julianne Holt-Lunstad of Brigham Young University found that in a worldwide sample of 3.4 million people, people who have strong social connections are 50 percent less likely to die. She explained the significance of her pioneering research in 2017. "Being connected to others socially is widely considered a fundamental human need. It is crucial to well-being and survival. Extreme examples show infants in custodial care who lack human contact fail to thrive and often die, and indeed, social isolation or solitary confinement has been used as a form of punishment."

My big takeaway from her conclusions is this: Feeling connected brings meaning and joy to our lives, and achieving that is the difference between life and death.

Connection is life. Disconnection is death.

Connection is joy. Disconnection is pain.

This brings us to a larger question. If we know this intellectually and have experienced it personally, why are we unable to sustain it?

Viewing Guru Nanak's wisdom from a fresh perspective opened my eyes to the simplicity of it all. When we understand that the journey and goal are inseparable, then our practices and processes become self-evident. And like anything else, the more we put these ideas into practice, the more impact they can have on us.

If you want to live a life of love, then practice love every day.

If you want to feel more connected, then practice feeling connected.

If you want to remember those you love, then practice remembering.

The beauty of Guru Nanak's teaching is that there is no magic potion or silver bullet. It all lines right up with our everyday life experiences. Any quality requires sustained practice and cultivation; everything is earned.

You don't have to be a rocket scientist to understand that what we do informs who we become and how happy we are. We make decisions every single day that shape our being. This is what philosophers and behavioral scientists mean when they say that we are what we repeatedly do.

If we eat well and exercise regularly, we will be fit.

If we do our homework and study hard, we will be prepared.

If we think positively, we will be optimistic.

And if we practice love every single day, we will be loving.

On the other hand, if an idea sits in our head but we never put it into practice, it has little impact on our lives and never becomes a part of who we are.

If we think about eating well but continue to eat junk food, we won't be healthy.

If we discuss business ideas but never execute them, we won't be entrepreneurs.

If we plan to take our medicine but it just sits in the cabinet, we won't feel better.

It's foolish to think that we might become more loving without bringing love into our lives as a daily practice. So the question we must ask ourselves is straightforward: *What can we do to cultivate love in our lives?*

Twenty-nine

CONNECTING
THROUGH MEDITATION

S eeking to cultivate love sparked a radical transformation in my life. When I accepted the importance of daily practice, I decided to take the first step prescribed in Sikh wisdom: traditional meditative practices, most commonly known as "nam japna" or "simran" (my name, for those of you paying attention!). To be clear, these were not new concepts or practices for me. They are at the core of Sikh teachings and some of the earliest lessons I received from my parents, grandparents, and other elders in our community. I used to practice meditation more regularly as a child and as a teenager but meditated less frequently during college.

I had come to see meditation and prayer as an empty ritual that carried little value. I appreciated the goodwill of friends and neighbors who offered to pray for me, but aside from their kind intentions, I took little comfort in their prayers, presuming they would have little impact on my life. I felt the same as our team knelt to pray before each game. I would join them out of respect, but every time I bowed my head, the same cynical questions flashed through my mind: *Am I really supposed to believe that an all-powerful being cares about the outcome of a high school soccer match? And what if the other team prays to God just as hard?*

Navjot Bhainji is like a spiritual sister to me, and one of the only disagreements I ever had with her was on this topic. I met Navjot Bhainji at a weeklong Sikh camp in Chicago in my early teens, and we had kept in touch since. She was only six years older than me, but she's one of the most thoughtful and insightful people I have known. I was a junior in college when she asked about my discipline in reciting my daily prayers, and although I still recited them regularly, I saw an opportunity to push back against the practice. Within those same daily prayers, Guru Nanak announces that even if everyone got together to talk about Vahiguru, what they said wouldn't make Vahiguru any greater or any worse. So what did our prayers effect? That was what I wanted Navjot Bhainji to tell me.

Would God even notice if I stopped praying every day? How does any of this matter?

Without flinching, she shrugged, flashed her signature smile, and said: "You're right. God probably doesn't care."

That she just let my comments pass unsettled me. I had expected her to react with hurt feelings or, at the very least, offer a counterargument. But her mellow response left me with a number of other questions.

Is Navjot secretly upset? Does she agree with me? And if so, then why does she still pray every day?

I pressed her for more information, but in her typical mysterious fashion, she responded: "The meaning is for you to discover for yourself. You'll figure it out when you're ready." At that, I knew it was best to let the conversation go.

Our discussion had slowly faded from my memory, but it returned years later when I began exploring meditation practices again. *Would I find myself in the same place again? Was this a treasure hunt with no treasure?*

I pushed these questions to the back of my mind, determined to focus on my new commitment. For the first time in years, I was open to the idea that meditation could be beneficial. I began by setting aside fifteen minutes every morning and evening. For a total of thirty minutes a day, I would put down my phone, stop thinking about work, and sit down to meditate. I would wait until Gunisha left for work and then would sit with my eyes closed, legs crossed, and back straight, just as I had learned from Sikh discipline when I was a boy. Meditating was hard at first. It had been years since I had tried it, and sitting quietly felt unfamiliar to my mind and uncomfortable to my body. But the discomfort faded in a matter of weeks, and within two months I could see that my capacity to pray and meditate had grown considerably. Whereas thirty minutes once felt like an eternity, it had now begun to feel like a quick reprieve that I looked forward to every day.

To be clear, the increased capacity is just a measure of the practice; it is not itself the reward. The real fruit of the practice was how it transformed my inner being. This sustained practice of remembrance made me feel more connected. And the more I felt connected, the more I felt alive and joyful.

What I did not expect (though I perhaps should have) was that there was even more to it. The happier I felt, the more I found myself in loving remembrance, simran. It had become a self-feeding cycle, one that has faltered from time to time but has continued to whir ever since.

This positive loop lines right up with what we know about love. We all know firsthand that when you love someone, you remember them constantly—and as your love deepens, the more entrenched they become in your thoughts. I know now that our love doesn't just grow by accident; it's actually something we can work on and grow actively. The more we practice remembrance and grow our capacity to remember, the more connected and loving and satisfied we feel.

Practicing meditation didn't just help me feel more peaceful; it also gave me practical answers for how to expand moments of calm into extended blocks of time. This practice has also helped me live in and enjoy the present rather than worry about what might happen in the future or perseverate over what happened in the past.

When feeling overwhelmed by the onslaught of negative news constantly swirling all around us, I recalibrate by pausing, turning inward, and reflecting. Without fail, it takes less than a few seconds before a feeling of calm washes over me, restoring my perspective through a feeling of broader connection. The situation may not have changed, but my mindset has. And this makes all the difference between a positive and negative experience.

We see this embodied by Guru Arjan, who tasted sweetness while being tortured. We learn from him that achieving a state of perpetual connectedness can lead us to taste the sweetness of love constantly, no matter the conditions or challenges we encounter. If he can find joy in the most extreme of situations, imagine how this wisdom could prepare us to deal with the frustrations of our daily lives—from being stuck in traffic to dealing with gossiping aunties or overly competitive colleagues.

Engaging a basic regimen of daily meditation serves as a first step on this path to internal peace. It's a simple practice that each of us can incorporate in a variety of ways, and it's one that carries immense transformative potential. To paraphrase Guru Arjan, this is the path to overcoming fear and finding joy in all we do, whether we are sitting or standing, sleeping or awake, inside our homes or outside them.

Reflecting on how meditation transformed my life revealed the answer to a question I had sought desperately years ago but had abandoned as a lost cause. I finally understood what Navjot Bhainji had meant all along. Meditation and prayer are not about changing God or directing certain outcomes; they are channels for transforming ourselves. The true force of prayer and meditation is its potential to shape us as people. This is why prayer and meditation receive such purchase today.

The first time the force of meditation struck me came as a teenager while sitting with Sikh friends in the woods just outside Houston one night. We had just finished dinner and began singing a nightly prayer (sohila) by a campfire. I looked up at the sky, and the stars seemed to shine brighter than ever before. We moved into Guru Nanak's composition about the entire world being in worship to divinity when I truly felt it for the first time. I was a part of it all, connected to the sky and the stars and the fire and the trees all around us.

I had been awed by the grandeur of nature before, but this was different. Before, I felt overwhelmed by how much more powerful it was than me. Now, I felt joy in realizing that the world was no different from me. For the first time, I was truly feeling connected with the world around me. This must be how Guru Nanak felt when he looked at the beauty of the creation and saw it all as an offering to the Creator; this must be what Guru Arjan felt when he said it all seems so sweet to him.

By no means am I claiming to have attained enlightenment in this moment, or even to have harnessed the full potential of ik oankar. But I have had glimpses of this experience—both then and in the years since—and I know this to be true: practicing meditation daily helped prepare me for this extraordinary experience.

A major challenge to finding such equanimity is that religious ideologies often tend to present worlds that are bifurcated and oppositional: good vs. evil, pure vs. polluted, heaven vs. hell, them vs. us. This kind of dichotomous thinking is dangerous for a number of reasons, perhaps none more so than that it leads to extremist outlooks that pit groups against one another. Even our politics are polarized, positioning one side against the other and leading people to judge one another based on how they identify politically.

None of this nurtures interconnectedness and remembrance. Rather, these outlooks foster division—the opposite of what we need. No wonder we live in such a fractured world. Our very way of looking at ourselves and at one another is destructive.

Examining myself and the world around me has helped me see how entrenched divisiveness has become within us. In the same way that workshops have helped shed light on my underlying biases, practicing mindfulness has inspired me to seek wholeness again.

I realized upon reaching this point that adopting love and oneness as mindfulness practices helped transform me in two related ways: They have helped me understand and *take apart* divisive ways of thinking that have become entrenched within me, and they have helped me *construct* a new way of viewing the world, an outlook that has cultivated in me a feeling of connection and joy that extends beyond personal relationships.

This resulting transformation led me to experience connection in a way that I never had before.

Our current way of viewing the world is overly simplistic and results in immense isolation and suffering. We have learned to understand our lives and experiences through the logic of division, defining ourselves in certain ways and pitting ourselves against a perceived enemy—including those we're convinced are wrong about politics and those who practice religions other than ours. As we continue living this way, and as long as we remain detached from our roots, we will never feel whole or connected.

Sikh teachings give us practical and effective guidance on cultivating oneness and love. When realized in their highest forms, these two precepts are one and the same. To experience oneness is to live with love. To experience love is to live with oneness. According to Sikh wisdom, this is what it truly means to be alive, to transcend suffering, to achieve liberation, to be in a state of perpetual joy, to be in love.

Thirty

LOVE AND SOCCER

I love sports. I always have. My brothers and I grew up playing every sport we could: soccer, basketball, baseball, football. You name it, we played it in our Texas neighborhood, on competitive club teams, and throughout our years in school.

We had to choose a sport to focus on in high school, and I begrudgingly let go of the others to focus on soccer. I soon became obsessed with the game. In the rare moments I wasn't playing soccer for my club or high school teams, I was watching it, talking about it, or daydreaming about it. My parents encouraged me not to be so singularly focused and to find balance, but I had a pretty solid counterargument: *Of all the things teenagers get addicted to, isn't this a pretty healthy one?*

I joined the cross-country team to supplement my fitness, which meant that most weekdays I would wake up early to run several miles before school, have soccer practice right after school, and then scarf down dinner on my way to club soccer practice in the evening. I even got my first job in high school as a youth soccer referee.

Playing soccer made me happier than anything else. It's hard to describe fully, but I feel safer and more carefree on a soccer field than anywhere else in the world.

Playing soccer also brought me some of the most crushing pain I had felt in my life. My sophomore year of high school, I tried out for the regional Olympic Development Program, a program designed to identify and prepare youth talent for professional soccer. Being selected for the team was one of the highest honors, so I was thrilled when one of my club coaches who served on the selection committee told me unofficially that I had made it. But the next week, when the roster was announced, my name wasn't on it. I was crushed and confused, and later that evening my coach called my parents and me to say that the committee's decision to take me off the Olympic Development team was discriminatory. He encouraged us to file a grievance and offered to support us in the process. My parents left the decision to me, but I was so hurt by what happened that I didn't want to pursue it. If the committee and team didn't want me, I didn't want them either. That experience made me more determined to prove them wrong and excel at soccer without their support.

Because of experiences like that, it felt even more rewarding when others began to validate my progress: being named team captain for my club and high school teams; being selected by peers and sportswriters for all-district and all-city teams; being noticed and recruited by college scouts and coaches.

I had never seen a professional athlete in any sport wear a turban, so I was never sure my dream of becoming the first turbaned Sikh to play college and professional soccer was realistic. Yet here I was, in spite of my doubt, preparing to fulfill my dream.

While I was open to playing anywhere and talked to scouts from all over, I began to set my sights on playing for Trinity University, a top college program in my hometown of San Antonio. The team had been nationally ranked for years and had sent several players to professional leagues around the world. So when the Trinity coach saw me at a couple of tournaments and invited me to come play for him, I couldn't have been more thrilled. I was still considering a few other programs, but would eventually decide on Trinity in spite of my admittedly dodgy approach to decision-making.

While most of our friends relaxed and celebrated the summer after graduating high school and before they went off to college or a job, my friend Bethany and I spent our days training through the blistering South Texas heat. Bethany had been recruited to play college soccer, too, so she was the perfect training partner. We ran and did drills early each morning to avoid the extreme heat, we lifted weights and studied professional games on film in the afternoons, and we played in pickup matches in the evenings. We felt ourselves getting better and faster and stronger every week, and by the time Trinity's preseason training camp rolled around, I was in better physical condition than ever. I could run two miles in under eleven minutes (in the Texas heat!), a prerequisite for joining the Trinity soccer team. I was ready and excited to live my dream.

Training camp was intense and grueling in the fun way that sports are. I felt challenged and sore, but more than anything else, I just felt happy to be there. It was everything I had hoped for.

Near the end of our training camp, it all fell apart.

The Trinity soccer team had a preseason friendly match against the University of the Incarnate Word, a nearby San Antonio team where some of my high school friends played. I subbed into the game about twenty minutes into the first half, appearing for the first time in my Trinity uniform. I had been in the game for just a few minutes when I raced an opponent to a pass headed his way. I reached my leg out just as he did, and our legs tangled up with each other's. We crashed to the ground and, as we did, the side of his body fell onto my right ankle.

I felt a flash of pain, but I had injured my ankle plenty of times before. In fact, I sat out much of my first year of high school soccer due to ankle injuries. It didn't feel that much worse than a serious sprain, so I limped off the field thinking it would be just fine. More than anything, I was irritated by what felt like a minor setback in my first match.

The trainer who examined me on the sideline worried that it might be more serious. He said it seemed okay but that the swelling was just bad enough to merit X-rays. My friend drove me to the hospital after the game, and the doctor confirmed what the trainer and I had feared: there was a small fracture in my ankle. I would have to sit out at least three months. The season would be over by the time I returned, which meant my season was already over. A season-ending injury before the season even began.

I was so gutted that I couldn't bear to stay with the team—crushed that I couldn't play with them the game that I loved. I was still friends with the players, but I avoided interacting with them if I could. I also avoided going to the games. I just couldn't handle the disappointment.

While the soccer team dominated their opponents, I rehabbed on my own, committed to being at full health for the spring season. The recovery was grueling, but even more painful was watching the team complete a dream season. The Trinity soccer team swept through the playoffs and clinched the national championship. I had to turn off the game as the referee blew the final whistle of their final game. I felt happy for my friends on the team, for the university, and for the city of San Antonio, but I couldn't bear the sight of them celebrating without me.

When the spring season finally rolled around, I was back to full health and, once again, in the best shape of my life. I left our first team meeting with a rush of excitement, bounding down the stairs to attend a lecture on the other side of campus. I didn't even realize I had missed a step until I was already tumbling down the stairs. I felt a familiar hollow pain in my ankle and knew before I even got to the hospital that my dreams had fallen with me.

I wouldn't recover this time. I didn't have it in me to start all over again. It was time to quit soccer.

Leaving the sport I loved so much was one of the hardest things I ever did. It was also one of the most illuminating. I never could have imagined that my love for soccer could be broken. Yet here I sat, ready to let it go entirely. I learned that, although I cared so much about the sport, my feelings for it were entirely conditional. I was only invested in it so long as it gave me gratification; the moment I stopped finding joy in it, I was willing to dispose of it.

At first, I thought this experience revealed something about the nature of love—that love is fleeting and deceptive, a crush that presents itself as a soul mate for eternity but fades with time and distance. It took me a while to realize that my experience was less a commentary on love itself and more a reflection on one particular relationship; while it was undoubtedly the deepest love I had felt to this point, I can see now that it was superficial.

Calling it superficial is not a denigration of how I related to the sport, nor is it a value judgment of my own devotion. I say it was superficial because I can see now that my love for soccer was nothing more than a love for myself. The joy I derived from it was rooted in my own ego and self-centeredness. The English language might still refer to this as "love," but there are other forms of love that reach higher and run deeper. If we think of love as a spectrum, selfish love remains relatively low.

I couldn't see this reality all the years that this selfish love consumed me—or that I consumed it. But now, with a bit of distance, it's clear. So long as we limit our love to objects and experiences that bring us pleasure, how will we ever go beyond our own self-centeredness?

There's nothing wrong with enjoying life or finding gratification in its abundant gifts. Food, activities, travel, sports. These all make up important aspects of our lives, and by no means am I saying we should resist them. The problem is when we—like I did with soccer—allow these experiences to consume us entirely. So long as they exclusively make up our understanding of love, we will remain entangled in our own self-centeredness, constantly looking for a way out of the webs into which we have woven ourselves. It's only once we expand our hearts that we can experience the fullness that life has to offer.

Thirty-one

LOVE IS SELFLESS

Many who espouse the practice of self-care draw their ideas from Audre Lorde's 1988 essay "A Burst of Light," in which she writes: "Caring for myself is not self-indulgence, it is self-preservation, and that is an act of political warfare."

Lorde's reflection on self-care has been both culturally significant and influential. Many people, including me, have benefited from her insights in dealing with social injustices and internalized oppressions.

At the same time, her ideas can also be misleading and misused when taken out of context. I say this because Audre Lorde wrote her essay as a Black lesbian woman who was battling liver cancer in the 1980s. No doubt she faced a host of challenges, including racism, misogyny, and homophobia, and no doubt that, given her context, any act of self-care was an act of political resistance and self-preservation.

Yet I imagine that if she could see how people were deploying her idea of self-care today, she would be surprised by how it's been twisted to justify an ethos of individualistic and materialistic self-gratification. As she herself stated, there's a difference between self-care and self-indulgence.

While Lorde's vision of self-care is beautiful and powerful, our current distortion of it shoulders a serious risk. If seeking love for ourselves through gratification becomes the *only* form of love we engage in, then we will quickly lose all perspective and fall into the trap of superficiality and self-centeredness—just as I did with soccer. This is not to say that we don't indulge in things that make us happy. Of course we do, and there's nothing wrong with that. I love an evening of binge-watching TV and eating popcorn as much as anyone else. But when gratifying ourselves becomes our only means of happiness, we quickly find ourselves unsatisfied and out of balance. Rather than distracting ourselves with transient moments of pleasure, we need to balance our momentary needs with our long-term pursuit of a deeper, sustained joy.

To discover a deeper kind of happiness, we must seek a deeper kind of love.

Guru Angad says as much when he proclaims: "Don't call someone a lover who feels happy when things go well and feels upset when they don't. That person only trades for themselves."

Implicit in Guru Angad's statement is a point on which we can all agree: True love is not conditional, nor can it be quantified or measured.

His message is larger than that, too. Guru Angad conveys that true love is not transactional. Lovers don't keep tabs on giving and receiving. Anyone who does so is more invested in themselves than in those they claim to love.

Saint Paul says the same when he announces that love is not self-seeking (1 Corinthians 13). Love is not about personal gratification or even about receiving some type of reward. There is no desired outcome of love because love is itself the desired state. As we have learned from Guru Arjan, love is the end and the means together, the goal and the process in one.

We don't always recognize what love is when we see it, but we certainly notice the force of its beauty when we witness it. Let me explain what I mean by being a bit provocative.

I think many of us today pay lip service to solidarity. We say we will have one another's backs when push comes to shove—but when the difficult moments come, we're nowhere to be found. We calculate our risk and our reward, and then we show up when it's safe and comfortable—and usually when the cameras are rolling.

Our solidarity is not authentic. Our solidarity is performed for show. Our solidarity is not selfless. Our solidarity is self-seeking.

So what would going beyond ourselves look like? What would it mean to truly love our neighbors?

One powerful example of authentic solidarity comes from my friend Dr. Larycia Hawkins. Larycia was the first Black female professor to receive tenure at Wheaton College, a private evangelical liberal arts school in the western suburbs of Chicago. In December 2015, Larycia began wearing a headscarf as a demonstration of embodied solidarity with Muslims in the wake of rising Islamophobia. She announced her decision on Facebook: "I don't love my Muslim neighbor because s/he is American. I love my Muslim neighbor because s/he deserves love by virtue of her/his human dignity. I stand in religious solidarity with my Muslim neighbor because we are formed of the same primordial clay."

Wheaton College placed Dr. Hawkins on administrative leave, a decision that ignited a national and international conversation on multifaith solidarity. Larycia was in the national spotlight for several months, during which she received multiple threats of violence, including death threats. People protested for her and against her, and she had little certainty about whether she would be fired or if she would have to leave the profession entirely. Yet through it all, Dr. Hawkins remained steadfast—she was not backing down from her commitment. Ultimately, her embodied solidarity cost Larycia her dream and her job. On February 8, 2016, Dr. Hawkins and Wheaton College issued a joint statement announcing they had "reached a confidential agreement under which they will part ways."

When I spoke to Larycia about her decision, she stood by it as unequivocally as she had then. And she had no regrets about standing her ground unflinchingly. She told me she felt proud to have opened up conversations about Islamophobia and anti-Muslim hate, and that she would always be willing to bear the costs of standing up, no matter what they may be. She admitted that it was scary, and that she took solace in knowing that she was doing the right thing for the right reasons.

This is authentic solidarity. It is selfless love. And it's a goal that we all—including me—must begin to strive for. It's not enough for us to pay lip service to showing up for one another. That's not getting it done. It's time for us to ask ourselves a fresh question, one that will make us uncomfortable but also will help us grow:

What are you willing to give up today to help produce loving justice in your own community?

Thirty-two

LOVE ERASES
SELF-CENTEREDNESS

I n addition to affirming that love is not self-seeking, Sikh wisdom also reveals that love is self-effacing. Love is the only force in the world capable of erasing our egos. In deepening our love, we transcend our own self-centeredness.

This is a critical point because, if you accept the teachings of our world's greatest spiritual leaders and philosophers, human ego is the root cause of our unhappiness. Guru Ramdas describes ego as a thorn in our foot. If we walk without removing it, it becomes more deeply embedded and causes us more pain over time. The pain only subsides once we remove the thorn.

Our inflated sense of self keeps us from feeling connected with the world around us. Love helps us feel more connected because love deflates our egos.

Anyone who has experienced love before can understand how this works. When we love someone dearly, we put their needs and desires before our own. The more we're immersed in love, the more we give of ourselves; and the more we give of ourselves, the more selfless we become.

Guru Angad defines love along these lines: "What sort of lover is attached to something else? O Nanak, the true lover is forever immersed." He is describing the ultimate state of love, where the lover and beloved entrench themselves in each other to the point that it's unclear where one begins and the other ends.

This is how love effaces our egos. Love erases the boundaries of our individual identities and opens us up to a new way of being—interconnected and fully immersed. Being immersed renders us incapable of distinguishing our sense of self from everything and everyone around us.

All is one. And one is all.

Ik oankar.

The idea of love as a merging together is embedded in the word "union," which comes from the Latin for oneness or coming together. It's what we mean by the phrase "two become one." Love is a complete integration. Guru Amardas says as much when he states that true life partners are not those who merely sit together physically; true life partners are those who become one light within two bodies.

I never experienced this depth of love through soccer because I was not in a reciprocal relationship; ultimately, I was only serving myself. But I did experience this through fatherhood. Becoming a parent opened up a new depth of love, and I find myself giving more of myself to my girls: time, resources, wisdom, guidance, love. It all comes naturally. I love my girls and feel motivated to do what's right for them without seeking anything in return or even wondering if they will do the same for me one day.

This is because my love for my girls is really not about me. I don't take it personally when they don't reciprocate my love or when they don't accept what I offer them. I'm moved to do what's best for my girls because my love for them is not self-seeking. It's that simple.

We all know deep down that selflessness marks a deeper kind of love. We have cherished and passed down stories of selfless human love for centuries, championing and admiring Romeo and Juliet, Heer and Ranjha, Cleopatra and Marc Antony. Communities have placed loving sacrifices at the centers of their collective memory, from the crucifixion of Jesus to the assassinations of Malcolm X and Dr. King. The principle of doing good for the sake of others runs so deep that it's even a thread that reaches through classic children's stories of heroism that my daughters and I love, such as *The Lion King*, *Charlotte's Web*, and *Toy Story*. In the words of Elsa from *Frozen* (which I know *way* too well), in order to open up love, we must all learn to "let it go."

The longevity of these stories in our cultural memories calls our attention to a simple fact. The greatest love stories we tell, and those of us who recall and share these stories, all share a common trait: We celebrate love as sacrifice.

The highest form of love entails complete selflessness. Reaching such a state of generosity requires one to prioritize their beloved over themselves. Guru Nanak acknowledges this truth when he declares: "If you want to play the game of love, come to me with your head on your palm."

Put simply, love is without ego.

We know this through our relationships. The closer we are to someone, the better it feels to give than receive. This is because when we truly care about someone, we want nothing more than for them to be happy.

Think about how hard it is to focus when someone you love is upset with you and how hard it is to be happy when someone you care about is in pain. Now think about how happy you feel when someone you love is excited about a promotion at work or about passing an exam for which they studied hard.

Love decenters our self-centeredness.

This was the spirit that moved Guru Tegh Bahadur to give his life for the Kashmiri Hindus who sought his help. He did not belong to their community, nor did he agree with how they saw the world. He didn't even know them. And yet he saw them as an inextricable part of himself.

This is what absolute selflessness looks like when it is rooted in the ground of ik oankar.

I love you because we are each other.

What we learn from Guru Tegh Bahadur's example is that selflessness is not just the hallmark of love; selflessness is also a quality we cultivate through enacting love. Once again, the process is the same as the endpoint. Our journey leads to our destination. All paths lead back to practicing love.

How have you experienced selfless love in your own life? What does it feel like inside you? How has it changed you? And what can you do to expand it to other relationships within your life?

Thirty-three

PRACTICING HUMILITY
AND SELFLESSNESS

I t seems obvious that we erase our selfishness by practicing humility, but what that means has not always been clear to me. For years I had conflated being proud of who I am with being prideful. I wasn't sure how to distinguish between modesty and lacking confidence, and I conflated humility with humiliation. My attempts at humility typically presented as self-deprecation—but this never felt quite right either. If I believed we all carry the same light, then how could I see myself as being less than others? And if I didn't respect myself, how could I expect others to respect me?

I was a senior at Trinity when I came across a helpful quotation from Christian luminary and writer C. S. Lewis: "Humility is not thinking less of yourself. Humility is thinking about yourself less."

These words felt right to me and helped me understand that we can quell our egos while also honoring our inherent self-worth. The two are not mutually exclusive. In the words of Guru Nanak, we're no better than anyone, nor are we any worse.

Lao-tzu pointed out that all streams flow into the ocean because it is lower than them: *Its strength comes from its humility.*

I realized that there's nothing wrong with feeling confident or being proud of who we are. The problem comes when we think of ourselves as superior. Such thinking is the parent of self-centeredness and ego-driven supremacies, like racism or misogyny. Honoring the idea of ik oankar is not just about seeing everyone around us as equal—we must also be kinder to ourselves and recognize that we are equally deserving. Humility is not about disparaging ourselves. Humility is about decentering ourselves. The difference between the two is critical.

I have been working on cultivating humility in the years since encountering Lewis's wisdom and have found that it comes most powerfully through generosity. The beauty of practicing generosity is that we can all incorporate and grow this practice in our lives.

Here is how I began. For the first month of my practice, I promised to take out either one hour or $15 each week (the cost of a movie ticket in Manhattan) to do something for someone else. The only rule was that I could not benefit directly from my own giving—my motivation had to be selfless.

My wife and I were both in graduate school when I started this practice; money was tight, but time was plentiful. I frequently opted to give my time to others. I reviewed papers for my classmates and helped them study. I sat with my friends from college and listened to their difficulties in relationships and frustrations with work. Once a month, I would collect leftover food from our neighbors and deliver it to our neighborhood shelter.

My daily practices of generosity were neither demanding nor earth-shattering. I didn't change the world, nor was I trying to. I was trying to change myself—and I could feel it working.

Giving to others helped accomplish precisely what I had hoped. I felt myself becoming less selfish. I was no longer the center of my own universe. And while that might sound scary and destabilizing, believe me when I say that it provided the most relief and freedom I had ever felt. No longer was I a prisoner to my own wants and desires. I could find happiness outside of myself.

By decentering myself, I felt more centered and grounded than ever before.

Perhaps you have felt something similar when you have given to others from the goodness of your heart, and perhaps you've also felt how even doing the smallest favor can draw you in. That's certainly true for me. My experience only made me want to be more generous with my own resources—a healthy addiction, like stretching or exercise or smoothies that are inexplicably neon green. Rather than asking *if* I was willing to sacrifice for the happiness of others, I was now wondering *how much*.

The more I gave of myself, the happier I felt. And the happier I felt, the more I wanted to give. This is how a simple practice of generosity helped me to begin decentering my ego.

———

There's another practice we can incorporate to help reduce our ego: confronting fear. Here's how it can work.

Our fears are based on actions or beliefs that can harm us. We do what we can to avoid physical pain. We worry about embarrassing ourselves in public. We feel anxious about our job security. We fear being disappointed by people we love, just as we fear disappointing the people we love.

At the end of the day, fear is about self-preservation. When we are constantly giving in to our fears and guarding against our insecurities, we are fueling our own sense of self. If I regularly tend to the garden of ego, how could my ego not flourish?

Don't get me wrong. A degree of cautiousness is helpful. It can protect us from stepping into a lion's den or falling off a cliff. But that incessant, crippling, paralyzing fear that we all come to internalize? This comes from disconnection—from ourselves and from the world around us—and it's a symptom of a flourishing ego.

Guru Tegh Bahadur states that the truly wise person is one who neither feels fear nor inspires fear. This is because a wise person has come out of their self-centeredness enough to have perspective.

When we are truly connected, fear leaves our consciousness. John 4:18 bears witness to this: "There is no fear in love. But perfect love drives out fear." If fear leads us to tend our egocentric gardens, then confronting our egos can help us trim them down. Embracing vulnerability can help each of us minimize our desire for self-preservation and, as a result, reduce our self-centeredness.

While each of us experiences and deals with fear differently, let me share a personal reflection on practicing fearlessness to give an example of how it might work for you.

For as long as I could remember, I had been terrified of speaking in public. As a student in high school and college, I would never talk in class because I worried about what my peers would think. I would do whatever I could to avoid class presentations. I conveniently slipped to the restroom when it was my turn to give any sort of feedback or remarks. I was once interviewed during an antiwar protest while in college and my hands shook so much while holding the microphone that my former roommates make fun of me for it to this day.

I was living in Boston as a graduate student when I had a particularly rough experience with racial profiling at airport security. My college roommate Bill was getting married in Los Alamos, New Mexico, and a bunch of our college friends were going to meet up there. I arrived at Boston Logan Airport two hours early. I knew from past interactions with airport security that, for people who look like me, it's best to allot buffer time for additional security measures. I had become accustomed to that, but on this trip the TSA agent insisted that he needed me to un-wrap my turban to prove I wasn't hiding any explosives in there. I resisted the urge to shout out his racism at the top of my lungs. Instead, I politely explained to him that his request violated TSA policies and asked to speak to his supervisor. When his supervisor also insisted that I remove my turban, I was incredulous. I urged him to look up the official policies for religious headwear. I explained to him the personal and religious significance of my turban. I even pulled out one of my brother Darsh's old jokes—that if a turbaned Sikh goes to a nude beach, they'd still be wearing their turban.

None of this changed the manager's mind, and ultimately we agreed that we could go to the airport bathroom, where I would have relative privacy to untie and retie my turban. This was the best compromise we could find, but I was still upset and unhappy. They were still treating me like a threat, presumed guilty until proven innocent.

After the security agent confirmed that there was nothing under my turban but my long, uncut hair, TSA gave me permission to go catch my flight. I was fuming. Wanting to vent, I wrote a brief description of what had happened and did something I had never done before—I posted about the racist encounter on Facebook. Within minutes, I received a text message from Marshall, one of my best friends from high school.

"I can't believe that happened to you, man. I'm so sorry."

I felt shocked and hurt. Marshall had been there during the violent backlash following 9/11 and had supported me through it. How could he *not* know the racism I had dealt with my whole life?

I picked up the phone and called him. I asked him exactly that, and his response surprised me.

"I knew you dealt with a lot of hate then, and I assumed that you still did years later. But you never really talked about it. Even when I asked, you would dismiss it. I'm really sorry."

I realized that Marshall was right. I had never even given him the chance to know what I had experienced, nor had I let anyone else. I had felt uncomfortable drawing attention to racism that came my way because it seemed selfish to call attention to myself. When other people in communities I knew—including in my own—were dealing with more direct discrimination and severe persecution, it felt inappropriate to complain about my own experiences that paled in comparison.

I was unsure how to move forward. I sat down to read some of my favorite writers with the hope of finding clarity on what humility and selflessness might look like in a situation like this. I came across a gem while reading James Baldwin: "If I love you, I have to make you conscious of the things you don't see."

This insight transformed my own spiritual outlook and political philosophy. I resolved in that moment to never again shy away from speaking up. I would share my experiences with others so that they could see the truth they wouldn't ever see otherwise. Doing so would be an act of love and justice. Sharing about my life could do more than simply draw attention to myself. I could share with the intention of teaching and illuminating, but only if I could get over my fear of opening up. Education is service.

I began by telling my close friends about brushes with bigotry when they took place. Their supportive responses made me feel comfortable about sharing more publicly, on social media, niche blogs, and eventually popular media outlets. The flood of positive and supportive responses made me feel affirmed, especially when people responded and shared similar experiences. The compassionate outreach made me feel less alone and helped restore my faith in humanity.

In addition to building trust, this practice transformed me in a more profound way. It helped me overcome my fear of sharing with the people around me. It is only in retrospect that I can see what was probably apparent to the people who knew me well: My self-consciousness around speaking and sharing was rooted in my own self-centeredness. I was afraid of what people would think about *me*, so I tried to protect *myself* from their opinions.

My fear was rooted in self-interest. The more I tended to it, the stronger it grew. It was once I finally confronted that fear head-on that I was able to decenter my own selfishness. These experiences were no longer about me. They were now about sharing insights with people I loved, to help them see more and to help them grow.

My fear of speaking in public has by no means gone for good. Confronting it remains an ongoing process, requiring attention and practice.

But doing so has helped me overcome my sense of self and find more comfort in my own life.

My guess is that you might also benefit by making a commitment to practicing fearlessness. Why not begin now? What's a fear you're willing to confront? And what would it take to challenge it in a way that helps decenter your own self-centeredness?

Part IV

CULTIVATING
OUR VALUES

A good friend once told me that self-help books are for people in their thirties. "We spend our first few decades trying to figure out who and what we want to be when we grow up. And then we're grown and realize we're not that good at life and nowhere near where we wanted to be."

I found this insight hilarious because it speaks to my own experience. I can remember being a child and thinking that grown-ups had it all figured out. Now I realize we're just as confused as we were then, stumbling our way through the dark until we find some semblance of direction.

One challenge is that there is no single answer for any of us. We are all unique, and we each experience the world based on our own identities, upbringings, and social contexts. Another challenge, though, is a more difficult one for many of us: Following directions can be hard, and staying on course can be even harder, especially when the benefits of that path aren't easily measured or quantified.

Yet when we're stumbling through the darkness of life, trying to find ways to make ourselves feel whole, there is a clear and proven method to finding meaning and happiness. This is the path of values-based living. It's not an easy path to traverse because it requires active engagement.

Thinking and talking about our values can be deceptive. Both are important steps in the journey, but efforts limited to reflection and discussion are incomplete—they make us feel like we're transforming, but nothing ultimately changes. The path toward growth is not only an intellectual one, but one of practice, too. One gives us an idea of where we want to go. The other takes us there.

Living by our values is easier said than done. We all know that, because we've each struggled in our own way to do so. The reward, though—as with a marathon—is not just at the finish line, but in each step we take along the way. This is because our journey into our values is precisely what transforms our aspirations into core parts of our character. Values-based living is like the paaras of Indic lore—though rather than turning iron into gold, it offers something far more valuable: a way to bring our values to bear, and in doing so, make us feel like we have value, too.

Thirty-four

How We Prioritize

hen the COVID-19 pandemic first hit New York City in early 2020, I wanted to leave town quickly. We worried about being infected, about being quarantined in our small apartment in an overcrowded city, about food supplies being cut off if they shut down the bridges and tunnels to our island of Manhattan. My wife, Gunisha, worked as a physician and human rights researcher at one of the city's larger hospitals, so treating patients would mean increased exposure to the virus and likely infection, especially given that she would be on the frontlines.

As New York City became the global epicenter of the pandemic, we discussed our options every evening. We could leave town to find relative safety. We could stay home and maintain a semblance of normalcy. We could split up our family, with me taking the kids somewhere else while Gunisha stayed home to serve patients.

We ultimately decided to stay in New York City. As far as anyone knew at the time, the virus was not supposed to have serious health effects on younger children like ours, or even on people in their mid-thirties like Gunisha and me. We also agreed that if death did come knocking at our door, we would rather be together. What we didn't realize was that we would be infected as quickly as we were.

While my wife was at work, I spent my days with our young girls, who did what kids of that age do to pass time: play, read, cook, eat, and dance. More of my time went into cleaning than doing my own work. And since we were cleaning so much anyway, we decided to potty train the baby early. Which of course led to *a lot* more cleaning.

Schools were closed, as were all other forms of childcare. It wasn't easy, and it took some adjustment, but I was finding joy in it. Anytime I felt tired or frustrated, I would simply look over at my wife. Gunisha would come home each day emotionally and physically exhausted. We had been married for eleven years, yet it still amazed me to see her as a real-life superhero, so selfless and committed that she would risk her own health to serve others in need. My heart would fill with gratitude: for her service and for our own relative ease in the midst of this pandemic. A little perspective can go a long way.

About ten days into our physical distancing, Gunisha started to feel sick. She had a low-grade fever, runny nose, shortness of breath, and a dry cough. Testing wasn't yet available, so we did the best we could. The guidelines from the World Health Organization and the Centers for Disease Control directed us to presume she had been infected. She notified the hospital that she was symptomatic and placed herself on quarantine.

We had all been exposed at this point, so there was no point in any of us leaving. We were in it together, just as we had promised ourselves. There was no going back now.

Gunisha's symptoms, though serious, did not turn out to be completely debilitating. She felt miserable and low on energy for about ten days. She fought the sickness with the same resolve I've come to know and love. Fortunately for us, she was never miserable enough to need admission to the hospital.

I got sick, too, though I wasn't as badly affected. My symptoms were muted for the most part, which meant my task was to support Gunisha while managing our girls.

But when our kids got sick, the situation started to feel untenable. For three straight days, our two-year-old pushed a fever of 104 degrees. We stayed with her day and night, trying everything we could to break her fever. The pediatrician urged us to avoid going to the hospital unless the fever exceeded 106 degrees. We still couldn't confirm that we were infected, so to visit the hospital would be to risk a potentially deadly infection.

About forty-eight hours into the baby's illness, our four-year-old's body started burning up. The thermometer read 104 degrees. We looked at each other with panic. For the first time in our ten-plus years, I looked at Gunisha and said out loud: "I'm feeling really scared." She replied with a soft, "Me too."

The baby's fever broke the next day, but the toddler's fever kept climbing. We did everything we could to keep her from passing the 106-degree mark. We woke up every hour throughout the night to check her temperature, doing cold compresses when she woke up in discomfort and blowing cool air on her face and neck to keep her comfortable while she slept.

On the third morning of her illness, our toddler seemed lethargic and asked for a late-morning nap. Gunisha noticed her shivering and a blue tinge to her lips and fingernails. She stripped off our daughter's clothes and ran her to the shower. Gunisha later told me that we had been minutes away from a visit to the emergency room.

After five full days of intense caregiving, our bodies were starting to give out from exhaustion and worry. Our spirits were on the cusp of breaking.

Just as we felt we might break, our daughter's fever broke first. The fever left as quickly as it had come, dropping nearly 7 degrees in less than two hours. We collapsed onto our couch with relief, knowing that we weren't yet out of the woods but also that the risk was much lower now. We hadn't slept in five nights. We had both worried like never before. And yet we couldn't have felt more thankful. We had survived the deadliest virus in generations.

There was something about staring death in the face that reminded us how fragile and precious our lives truly are. Our experience was a sharp reminder of how suddenly catastrophe can strike in life, even with every advantage: no preexisting conditions, young patients, a comfortable home, *a physician on hand.* It's also a humbling reminder of how little we ultimately control. We spend so much of our lives trying to control and plan every detail that we sometimes forget how much we actually can control. That's a frightening idea to wrestle with, and another lesson I took away from the pandemic: There's something liberating about letting go and accepting what is. In Sikhi, we refer to this acceptance as "hukam."

Being reminded of our smallness also led us to care more for the well-being of our loved ones and our communities. My worry was most poignant while walking around our neighborhood during those months. I had never seen the streets so bare. My beloved city had been stripped naked, completely exposed. I had become used to people looking at me as a foreigner in my own neighborhood, but now it felt as if our roles had reversed. Now my neighborhood of over a decade felt foreign to me.

Physical distancing had already left me feeling disconnected and empty; walking through our neighborhood-turned-ghost town amplified that void. Here I was, pushing a stroller with my two most precious pieces of cargo in the place I called home and yet I felt as empty as the city around me. I was living in a metaphor of my own unfulfilled life.

Within a few weeks of the pandemic, we began to settle into our new routine. Nothing about our lives felt normal. Our daily schedules, social interactions, family schedules had been entirely disrupted. Yet we felt ourselves adapting. The fog of uncertainty still hung over us, but we no longer felt we were drowning in it. Perhaps this was because living in crisis mode is only sustainable in short bursts; operating in constant fear is mentally and emotionally draining. Or perhaps the difference now was that we felt as if we had some control over our lives. It's scary to be reminded of our own smallness. As Sikh wisdom posits, how can a drop of water hope to understand the ocean? At the same time, there's nothing more powerful and more humbling than being reminded how delicate our lives are.

In one of our nightly check-ins, I confessed to Gunisha how much I was enjoying quality time with the kids and how nice it was that life had slowed down enough to enjoy time together.

She said something to the effect of, "Of course you love it. It's what you care about most and it's something you always talked about doing."

She meant it kindly, as an affirmation that it was appropriate for me to find a silver lining in this difficult time. But something about what she said really bothered me, jabbing underneath my skin in the way that only truth can. *What does it say about me that I've always talked about living this way but never actually lived it?*

Sometimes, kindhearted words can flip you more rapidly than angry ones. When someone comes at us with anger, we put on our armor and pick up our shields, preparing to defend ourselves for attacks that might come our way. It's when our defenses are down and our hearts are open that we expose ourselves to deeper truths, some that we have buried and some that we have never before seen.

In this moment, it came to me unexpectedly. I could see clearly the disconnect between who I was and who I *thought* I was. I could also see how the dissonance between those two had caused me so much pain. No wonder there was a constant tension in my life.

This reflection revealed to me a danger in how we manipulate ourselves and cause ourselves pain. I had tricked my mind so effectively and buried the truth so deeply that it was easy to believe my own lies. The more I repeated the mantra *Family comes first*, the more it became a part of my own self-understanding. It was how I described myself and the goal I set for myself, but I didn't fully live by it. Believing my lie hurt because it left a gap between who I was and who I wanted to be. It hurt even more because I was unaware that this gap existed. I was regularly afflicted by this tension inside me, but until this moment I'd had no idea why it was hurting or how to fix it.

Addressing this issue was more acutely painful than I'd anticipated, but I was able to channel that painful revelation to create a positive change in my life. The first step was to revisit my list of priorities—family, physical health, emotional-spiritual wellness—and conduct a quick assessment. How was I doing on these priorities? Did I actually live by them, or were they priorities in name only? In what ways might I be lying to myself about how I'm doing?

These questions offered a helpful starting place, but I still found it hard to get specific. I could give myself a rating or could distinguish between satisfactory/unsatisfactory in each of these three areas. But I needed more granular feedback. In reflecting on the problem of our distorted self-perceptions, I recalled that sometimes we have to step outside of ourselves to get a different perspective; that sometimes seeing ourselves through the eyes of others is our only way of sidestepping our self-delusions and truly seeing who we are.

Cognizant of this paradox, I created a thought exercise to help simulate the perspective of an outside observer. I imagined that aliens were coming from outer space and selected me as a case study. They would observe my behavior and report back on what humans spend their time doing. Their thesis was that whatever one spends most of their time on is what they consider most precious.

These were the specific questions I asked myself through the exercise: What does your daily schedule look like? What do you do? What do you consume? What do you think about?

This exercise gave me a new vantage point. Now, instead of seeing myself from inside my thoughts and feelings, I could see myself from the outside through my actions and behaviors.

First of all, if aliens came from outer space and watched me for a day, they'd probably be bored as hell. They would say unequivocally that my main priority is work. They would notice that I spend the first few hours of the morning with my girls, getting them fed and ready for school. If they had access to my thoughts, they would also notice that I was only half present during our morning routines; part of me would be thinking about what was on my calendar for the day or what I was hoping to cross off my to-do list.

Then they would follow my commute to work, which is about a thirty-minute jog, subway trip, or bike ride away, depending on the weather and my workout schedule. They would watch me work on my computer and meet with colleagues, usually from about nine a.m. to five p.m. If the aliens hadn't died of boredom by then, they would watch me head home, have dinner with the family, get my girls to bed, tidy up the house, and then sneak in a workout before heading to bed for the night.

Any observer would see clearly that my day centered around work. I had never fully grasped that, and up until this exercise I would have argued with anyone who said work was one of my top three priorities. But even I can see that now. An outside observer would also conclude that family is a clear second priority, albeit a distant second, and that there are other priorities and activities scattered in there, like reading good books, hanging out with friends, and playing basketball.

Here is a startling takeaway from this exercise: There is such a big gap between who I am and who I think I am that, when I look at myself from the outside, I can't even recognize myself. This realization is as powerful as it is painful, especially when you realize that your entire self-understanding has been built on a faulty foundation. It makes you wonder how much longer until it all comes crumbling down.

The long and the short of it is that I was short on a lot of it. Even when I was engaging my top priority (family), I was thinking about a lesser priority (my work). When I blocked off time for family on the weekends, I would often add a few hours of work—not because I needed to, but because I wanted to. It's not that I was disengaged as a father or partner or son or friend. I'm self-aware enough to know that I care and that I show up for family regularly. The problem was that I wasn't fully engaged with any of them. I wasn't meeting my own potential and I wasn't showing up with my whole being. Seeing that discrepancy for the first time forced me to reflect on how I was spending my time and what my life was actually about.

One of the big lessons for me in surviving this pandemic—a lesson that hadn't hit me this same way before—is the deep and constant pain that comes when we misalign our priorities and our behaviors. Now that I have seen it, I can't unsee it.

I am not writing this to beat myself up over my shortcomings, and I wouldn't want you to either. We have to be gentle with ourselves. None of us is perfect and we all have room to grow. Extending ourselves compassion is an important part of spiritual growth and justice work. Self-compassion is healing because it prevents us from feeling guilty or shameful about our imperfections; mistakes and missteps are part of our human experience. Approaching our shortcomings with self-compassion is also hopeful because it enables us to transcend shame and embrace our shortcoming as opportunities for growth. We can all do a better job of closing that gap between what we prioritize and how we actually behave. Finding coherence in our lives and overcoming our internal dissonance is no easy feat, but at least the pathway there is clear: We have to align our thoughts, our speech, and our actions.

We can start our journey by asking ourselves these three questions: What would an outsider observe while watching your behavior? How might this differ from how you see yourself? And what could you change so that you might feel proud of how you live every single day?

Thirty-five

RESETTING AND REBALANCING

S ocial science research and spiritual wisdom tell us that we're un-happy when there is a gap between how we behave and how we claim to behave. But we don't need scientists and prophets to tell us that these misalignments cause us disappointment and dissatisfaction. Part of what makes us human is making commitments to ourselves and others and not being able to keep them. I'm as guilty of this as anyone. So many of us make resolutions every year to improve our lives, only to see our resolutions fade away just weeks or months into our efforts.

This is why the greatest spiritual teachers all announce that our internal disconnection is the greatest source of unhappiness in our lives. Having found peace and joy in their own lives, they have let us in on life's most open yet least tapped secret: True fulfillment comes with finding alignment and connection within ourselves. I accept this truth for four reasons:

1. This wisdom makes intuitive sense.

2. This teaching lines up with scientific research.

3. The beauty and grace of spiritually accomplished figures reflect the power of this wisdom.

4. This teaching matches my own lived experience.

It may not be radical or unique to say that true happiness comes from within—and yet the insight can be both profound and transformative. When we truly believe this and commit ourselves to honoring it, then our next question essentially asks itself: *What can we do to move beyond our internal anguish?*

The first step is to acknowledge this disconnect within our own being. As I realized through my own journey, we spend far too much of our lives covering up uncomfortable truths with comforting lies. And we keep burying these lies until we don't even believe that they exist anymore.

The less we listen to our conscience, the softer the voice sounds. It's not that we don't know what the right thing to do is—it's still very much inside us. It's just that we haven't trained ourselves to listen.

Listening is hard. Listening to ourselves is even harder. There's a reason Guru Nanak devotes four of the thirty-eight stanzas in his seminal composition *Japji Sahib* to the importance of listening (sunniai) as a spiritual practice. I had buried my own voice so far down that rescuing it has required an entire excavation, a deep digging that has uncovered quite a bit along the way. It's an arduous process and one that I'm still undergoing—and it's also one that has been personally rewarding.

I have learned along the way that one doesn't have to complete the excavation to begin reaping its benefits. The remarkable thing about personal development is that we can see tangible results every step of the way. Self-growth is a treasure hunt in which the very act of searching is like finding buried treasure.

Acknowledging my own disconnect has helped me accept that I haven't yet achieved my goal of finding happiness and that there is a better way than the ones I have tried so far. This has given me permission to be imperfect and to stop pretending to be perfect. It has opened me up to my own discontent and to accepting my feelings instead of constantly trying to mask them.

In this way, accepting my internal disconnection is a way to acknowledge my vulnerability and, at the same time, to take a first step toward progress and healing. I can see now that the coronavirus pandemic gave me a unique opportunity to reset. At the time, many spoke of resetting as a function of powering down and recharging. I appreciated slowing down as much as anyone. We all work hard. We could all use a break.

But there can also be more to it than that. For me, it meant undergoing a more meaningful kind of resetting, one that had a more transformative effect than powering off just to power back on. It was about restoring balance to a life that had fallen out of equilibrium. The more I invested in resetting myself, the fuller my heart felt. This led me to ask the question we all ask when we find something that brings us joy: Why don't I do this more often?

Rebalancing is a standard practice in so many other spheres of our lives. Our supervisors conduct performance reviews to tell us where we're succeeding and where we're falling short. We go to our doctors for annual checkups to see how we're doing physically. We review our bank accounts and credit cards to make sure we're in good financial health. We tune up our cars and bikes to make sure we're physically safe.

So why don't we take time to tune up ourselves internally?

The simple answer is that looking at ourselves honestly is hard and uncomfortable. It takes conscious, concerted effort. It requires us to set aside the distractions of our outside world and take time to go within ourselves. All of it feels like a big price to pay for a reward that we can't ever measure or hold in our hands.

But the input cost is nothing compared to what you get out of it. It's easy to see this when we break through our obsessions with materialism. We can remind ourselves that the greatest joys of life are all intangible.

If someone told me that there was a Fountain of Eternal Happiness and that the price of admission was regular time commitment, sustained effort, and a spoonful of initial discomfort, I'd say it was a no-brainer. I think most of us would.

It feels silly that so many of us are open to this idea in theory yet resist it when it's right under our noses. We keep telling ourselves that we will take our first step when we feel ready for a new challenge. We put off and postpone, giving excuses for why we need more time. I did the same thing. I changed when death came knocking on our door in the robes of COVID-19, reminding us that time is not guaranteed for any of us. If we want to experience joy, the time to act is now.

———

Embarking on a new journey can feel intimidating, especially when we expect it to be an onerous one. Yet the best trips are the ones we enjoy all along the way. When I spoke with people during the pandemic, friends and strangers alike, I kept hearing the same thing: "Physical distancing is hard because I just don't know what to do with myself when I'm alone."

Being physically isolated from our daily routines showed us just how disconnected we all are from ourselves. We don't know who we are. We don't know how to value ourselves. We don't even know what to do when we're on our own.

This is the paradox of our unhappiness. We have become so accustomed to seeking temporary happiness through external sources that we never think to seek long-term fulfillment within ourselves.

Now imagine a world in which we flipped that, a world in which we all lived knowing that true fulfillment comes from within ourselves. Imagine how much less painful our day-to-day existence would be, how joyful our lives would be.

This is what resetting can do for us. It can help us get closer to achieving oneness within our own lives. It can help us find a more fulfilling kind of happiness. And it can protect us from being sucked into the inevitable ups and downs of life, no matter what's going on in the world around us.

What are the central priorities of your life? Where do you spend your time? And how can you adjust your behaviors to better align with what matters most to you?

Thirty-six

WHY WHAT WE DO MATTERS

Money was tight when my brothers and I were younger. We rarely went to restaurants because, as my mom would say: "Why should we pay for someone to cook when I can make it at home better?" My father would follow that up by saying: "Your mother's cooking is so good that you can't even buy it at a restaurant." We would roll our eyes, knowing that they just didn't want to pay for a night out. Now that I'm older, I find myself in the opposite position: Whenever it's my night to cook, everyone in our household pleads for restaurant food instead.

My mom's cooking was what first made me love going to the grocery store. Every aisle was an adventure, every conversation a lesson. It was where my mom first started treating me like an equal, asking my opinions and requesting my help. She taught me how to look for bruises on tomatoes, just as her mother had taught her. She told me stories of acquiring food back in India, a place with no grocery stores or even centralized locations for food supplies. She would talk about her family's own food insecurity, how they skipped meals at times to ensure they wouldn't go hungry later, or how her parents quietly rationed their own food so their children would have enough to eat.

It was from her that I learned to think of an American grocery store as a refuge, with its wide aisles, high ceilings, and more food than she could have ever imagined growing up in India. Every time we entered through the automatic doors of H-E-B, the local Texas grocery chain, she looked around with amazement and gratitude. Seeing my mother like that is my favorite childhood memory of her.

I was twelve years old when our weekly ritual came to a sudden end. One afternoon we were at the store's checkout counter, and when she wasn't looking, I grabbed a Snickers bar and shoved it into my pocket. I glanced up and caught her eyes widen. I didn't have the courage to hold eye contact. I looked away quickly, pulled the bar out of my pocket, and handed it to her. She placed it on the counter and paid for it, along with the rest of the groceries. Neither of us spoke the whole way home.

I put away the groceries in silence and then went into her room to apologize. The words hardly squeezed past the lump of shame in my throat. I stood patiently, waiting for her to announce my punishment. Instead, she looked toward me and asked a question that felt unrelated.

"Do you know why you wear a turban?"

I didn't know what she wanted me to say. My mind raced through the different explanations I had heard throughout my life. Nothing seemed to connect with shoplifting, so I shook my head no.

She asked if I had heard the sakhi of Guru Tegh Bahadur's shaheedi (martyrdom), and I nodded yes, recalling the story that had already made such a huge impression on me: When a group of Kashmiri Brahmins were facing religious persecution by the Mughal emperor, Guru Tegh Bahadur stood up for them. He didn't believe the same things as them, yet he was willing to die for their right to live freely.

My mother smiled for the first time since the incident at the store. She then asked pointedly: "But do you know what happened after that?" She then shared a story that was new to me, a story that changed how I saw myself and how I wanted to live in this world.

Because Guru Tegh Bahadur was seen as a powerful leader with a sizable and growing community, the emperor decided to make an example out of him; publicly imprisoning, torturing, and executing such a figure would intimidate others from dissenting. After Guru Tegh Bahadur's public execution, none of his followers immediately stepped forward to claim their guru's body or decapitated head. Their inaction bothered Guru Tegh Bahadur's son and successor, Guru Gobind Singh, who felt that these Sikhs were blending into the crowd instead of stepping forward to do the right thing. The young guru also felt that truly devout people should live by their beliefs unconditionally and that they wouldn't have been able to hide in fear if they were more publicly visible. Many believe it was this feeling that prompted Guru Gobind Singh to bestow Sikhs with their unique appearance.

"There's nothing sacred about looking like a Sikh," I remember my mother saying. "Your turban is a public statement that you wear on your head. It's a crown that announces to the world that you will always do the right thing. If you're not willing to honor that, then maybe you should think about not wearing it."

Her concluding words caught me off guard. For years, my mother had encouraged me to resist anyone who told me to take off my turban. Now she was asking if I deserved to wear one in the first place?

The sting made me feel defensive. Instead of focusing on her point, I focused on trying to refute her. I wanted to explain that my decision to pocket the Snickers bar was an anomaly, a relatively minor mistake that didn't hurt anyone. That no one besides her even saw that I had stolen something. Each of those refutations dissolved before making it to my tongue, because I knew in my heart that my mother was talking about something different. She was talking about the importance of always doing the right thing, whether people are looking or not. Integrity.

My mother's guidance in that moment was calm yet firm, simple yet transformative. This was a lesson on living honestly, public accountability, and inner happiness.

The point about the grocery store incident is this: There was no question in my mind that I was doing wrong. I was old enough to know better, which was why I tried to make sure no one could see what I was doing. I realize now that I wasn't just ashamed of being caught. There was a deeper shame that came in knowingly doing the wrong thing. I *knew* I was betraying my values, even prior to reaching for the candy bar. Yet I chose to do it anyway.

Being caught meant that I had to deal with the discomfort of being reprimanded. It also meant that I had to deal with my internal disconnection. Why did I choose to do something I knew was wrong? What did it mean that a momentary desire for something so trivial as a Snickers bar had overpowered my inner voice? Could I really trust myself to do the right thing when the stakes were higher?

The grocery store incident may seem like a random moment, but for me it was an inflection point. I share it because we all have moments like these; my account reflects the decisions that we all make each and every day. We are all making choices constantly, and it can be easy for us to dismiss or minimize the impact of each. It can also be easy for us to justify or cover for poor decisions by making excuses to ourselves and the people around us.

"It's okay to eat this because I had a hard day at work."

"I couldn't call you because I ran out of time."

"My shouting was merited because they messed up."

We may be fooling the people around us, but we know deep down that we are being dishonest, with ourselves and with the people we love. We can't fool our own hearts, and the cost of such self-deception is too high. It breeds negative feelings that we come to internalize and embody.

When we act in ways that don't match up with our ideals, we feel more disconnection, disappointment, and guilt. We feel ashamed of our behavior, and over time we come to feel ashamed of ourselves. Those were the feelings afflicting me in that moment after shoplifting, and although they have waxed and waned over the years since, those feelings are still very much familiar to me. I think they're familiar to all of us.

When we betray our values, we also weaken the trust we have in ourselves. Doubt creeps into our hearts and minds, corroding our self-confidence. How can we love ourselves if we don't respect ourselves?

On the other hand, the opposite is also true. Aligning our ideals and our behaviors can instill self-confidence. Each decision can be empowering and trust-building because it can show us that we have the capacity to do what's right.

Think about the last time you successfully resisted something tempting: an extravagant purchase, that last slice of cake, skipping your weekly fitness class. Now think about how you felt the moment you resisted. Didn't you feel proud? Weren't you energized by knowing you could do it?

We each have these struggles, and we each have our victories. After all, we're only human. The problem is that we don't realize our daily decisions can make the difference between a life of joy and a life of shame. Every decision matters because every decision shapes who we are and who we become.

As Guru Angad asks so eloquently, what sense does it make for us to plant poison and expect nectar?

Our daily actions are seeds that grow into our habits and, ultimately, our character.

We tend to focus on the decisions that have tangible results: Will executing this project help me secure a promotion? Will I get caught if I cheat on this homework? Yet, as with so much in life, the real treasure is not something we can see with our eyes or feel with our hands. The real power of what we do is that our behavior will either take us toward happiness or away from it. This is why we must stop measuring *what we do* exclusively on the basis of tangible outcomes; *what we do* matters first and foremost because our actions and behaviors shape *who we become*.

Our actions matter not because they are inherently sinful or pure, or because there is some formula that determines what happens to us based on what we do. Our actions matter because of how they form us internally. This is why integrity is not about the outcomes of our actions or about what other people see us doing. Integrity is being integrated on the inside. Integrity is about oneness—or in the words of Guru Nanak, ik oankar.

To be clear, this is not a point about morality. I am not here to proclaim what is right or wrong or even what values you should ascribe to yourself. Our ideals are personal and context-specific, so only you can determine what is right or wrong for yourself. My point here is about unlocking something powerful that is already available to us: If we can see our everyday choices as opportunities to practice our values, we can strengthen our own feelings of self-connection and self-worth.

When we are unaware of how our choices affect us, we tend to choose without intention. Our decisions become a randomized series—some may make us feel proud, others may make us feel regret. But they don't really take us anywhere. We get little out of them aside from the momentary pleasure or pain of each decision. Without intention, it becomes hard to see our actions—positive or negative—as anything more than random. At best, that makes it hard for us to replicate what makes us joyful. At worst, it leaves us dazed from the constant twists and turns of our lives. Without purpose behind our actions, we are stuck on our emotional roller-coasters, going through the same ups and downs, wanting nothing more than to get off the ride but not sure how to do so.

There is a way out of this constant cycle, a simple exit strategy rooted in Sikh wisdom that we can all internalize and engage. If we can learn to see our daily decisions as devices to help us produce patterned behavior and build our personal character, then we can become more mindful about our actions.

The religion scholar in me wants to point out that, although this concept feels intuitive and sensible, it's also at odds with how so many of us have been taught to view the world. Many of our belief systems posit that what we do matters because it determines our place in the afterlife. This may or may not be true. I won't pretend to know what happens once we breathe our last. Having read countless philosophers and theologians and scholars, I think it's safe to say they all agree on one point: No one truly knows what happens after we die.

What I do know, though, is that we don't need the prospect of an afterlife to compel us into rightful action in the here and now. If that were the case, how would we explain all the kind and generous people in this world who don't consider themselves religious?

Sikh spiritual teachings illuminate a different way of understanding why *what we do* matters. Our daily decisions are not a portal to a heavenly world but to our own self-fulfillment. If we can learn to cultivate integrity within ourselves, we can achieve a different kind of liberation within our own lifetimes. This is what Guru Arjan meant when he said that he was not concerned with power or salvation—because the only skill that guarantees us happiness in the here and now is learning to live with oneness and love.

Thirty-seven

IDENTIFYING OUR VALUES

J agmeet Singh is a prominent Sikh in Canadian politics, currently a member of the Parliament of Canada and leader of the New Democratic Party. At a 2017 campaign event in Brampton, Ontario, a white woman began yelling racist hate speech at him. Jagmeet and his supporters responded by chanting, "Love and courage," a campaign slogan derived from his own core values. Jagmeet patiently responded to his attacker by leaning into those values, explaining that, despite her anger and hate, he loved her, respected her, and would protect her rights—echoing a sentiment that many in the Sikh community endorse and live by.

"Once allowed to grow, hate doesn't pick and choose. It spreads like fire," Jagmeet said after the incident. "Once we say it's okay to hate someone based on their religion, we're also opening the door to hate based on race, gender, sexuality, and more. It's important that we stand united against all forms of hate. It takes love to understand that we are all in this together. It takes courage to come together, demand better, and dream bigger, so that we can build a world where no one is left behind."

Jagmeet Singh won his election that year and went on to become the first person of color to lead a major political party in Canadian history—and he also won more than that. His ability to maintain his poise and values in the face of a racist tirade in public showed that anyone can respond to hate with love, even in extremely upsetting situations. Jagmeet's example also shows how helpful it can be to have clearly identified values to lean on in times of difficulty; it was clear through his words and actions that these two values—love and courage—guided his response to this woman. Moreover, his response shows how powerful and beautiful it can be when we can adhere to our values with integrity and authenticity.

Where does this type of real and unflinching commitment to love and courage come from? And how could we get some of that for ourselves?

This form of ethical living entails two key components:

1. Clearly identifying, articulating, and understanding our values.

2. Putting our values into practice.

It is only when we know our values and practice them daily—so that they are ingrained in our hearts and minds—that we will be prepared to respond with them even in the toughest of situations.

———

My personal introduction to values-based living came far before I was ready for it, and only because my parents were intent on instilling values in my brothers and me at a young age. When we were in elementary school, we had to complete two rituals before our family dinner every evening. First, we had to offer a prayer of thanks for all our blessings, including the food sitting on the table. Then my father would ask, "What makes the world go around?" My brothers and I would all groan and roll our eyes. We would sit there giving smart-ass answers like, "Evil scientists!" or "The secret leprechaun within all of us!" We'd all laugh, including our parents. But that didn't mean they gave in. We'd sit there until finally one of us would run out of patience and blurt out the answer: "Love makes the world go around." We would then shovel food into our mouths as our parents facilitated a dinner conversation on the power of love.

When we were in middle school, my parents brought home *The Book of Virtues*, a large anthology of poems, parables, and stories from Western traditions. The book, thematically organized by individual virtue, became like a second scripture in our home. It sat on top of the living room mantel, and every day, after reciting the Sikh evening prayer, Rahiras, we would take turns reading a selection from the book. Whatever we read would then become fodder for our dinner conversation.

When we got to high school, my parents began organizing quarterly family meetings. To our chagrin and in spite of our protests, we were expected to block off an entire Saturday once every three months just for these meetings. My parents would arrive at them with a glimmer in their eyes, excited to share their latest wisdom from leadership trainings they had undergone themselves. My three brothers and I would complain through it all, even when we were secretly appreciating what we learned.

The most memorable family meeting was also the one we protested the most—a two-day session in the middle of our spring break with a leadership executive my parents had recently befriended. For weeks my brothers and I refused to set up a time to meet with him. Finally, our parents mentioned that he led leadership training for our beloved San Antonio Spurs and that he might share some details about Tim Duncan, Tony Parker, and Manu Ginóbili. Twenty minutes later, we had a date on the calendar.

Larry Mills was a stranger to the four of us, and yet he had no problem commanding our attention. He talked insider basketball with us for the first half hour before shifting to business. He announced that our plan for the weekend was to develop a document that articulated our family's mission statement, vision statement, and a set of shared values.

Our excitement evaporated as we looked at one another with incredulity. What we thought would be a basketball-filled weekend turned out to be real work during our precious spring break. We agreed to sit there respectfully, though, engaging with Mr. Mills and one another through the painstaking process.

I was surprised to find that it actually did take us two full days of conversation to achieve our goals. It was less that our views were at odds with one another and more that we were getting into the process. We started by listing everything that felt important to us and then spent the next two days organizing, narrowing down, and refining what we meant. I wouldn't have mentioned it to our parents then, but even as a sixteen-year-old, I found it instructive to spend so much time thinking and talking about what mattered most. It helped me to better understand myself and my family.

At the end of the two-day session, we had a mission and values statement that reflected our family's priorities: "We are the Kaur/Singh family, committed to developing and supporting ourselves and each other in all aspects. We do this to achieve continuity, harmony, and stability, strengthen individual and collective well-being, maximize our potential, and develop strong future generations. We accomplish this by implementing and living our core family values: faith, integrity, love, service, and excellence."

My brothers and I participated in this process that weekend out of respect for our parents and Mr. Mills. I had no idea then that this single exercise would serve me for years to come. Two decades later, I still consult it almost daily as I work through decisions. It hangs in a frame over my office desk, and I keep a digital version on my phone so I can review it on the fly. I even facilitate different groups, from large corporations to family units, seeking to develop mission and values statements like ours.

I think our family values document resonates with me for the same reason that Sikhi resonates: a values-based approach is not a set of rules that dictate our lives for us. Rather, it offers us a framework that we can interpret and apply to our own life situations. I appreciate that this approach accounts for the particularities of our lived realities. Detailed instructions and rigid rules have always been hard for me; life is too

dynamic and complex for formulas. Anytime people give definitive di-
rectives, I find myself rebelling and wanting to do the exact opposite.
How could one specific prescription apply to all of humanity when no
single one of us is the same? There is no predetermined recipe that can
tell you how to live your best life. Each of us needs to figure this out for
ourselves.

That's why I believe our family values document has worked so well
for me. Undergoing this exercise is useful because the values are specific
and tailored enough to offer us real guidance based on what we feel matters most and who we aspire to become. At the same time, it's nimble
enough to be broadly applicable in a variety of life situations—personal,
professional, social, and so on.

The framework's openness also allows for the reality that we all
change over time and that we don't always see situations from the same
perspective. It took me some time to understand that honoring the diversity of our experiences also means honoring that diversity within ourselves. Reflecting on my values in one scenario doesn't mean that I now
have a one-size-fits-all solution for all the potential scenarios in my life.
Instead, each decision gives us a chance to revisit our values—and every
recalibration further reinforces these values within our character.

What is your personal mission statement? What are your core values?
When push comes to shove and there's no easy answer for how to respond, what would you use as a guide so that you feel proud of your actions rather than ashamed?

Thirty-eight

HOW OUR VALUES
CAN SAVE US

I first joined Twitter in 2010. Being the nerd that I am, I saw it as a great platform for education and activism. I loved sharing views on justice and introducing people to fresh perspectives. I didn't mind differing viewpoints, though I would get fired up when people sent me bigoted tweets. I would want to answer with something equally angry or hurtful. I knew it wouldn't be constructive, but I wasn't sure what else to do. On the one hand, I felt like it would be best to turn the other cheek and not give racists a platform. On the other hand, I felt a duty to respond, inform, and educate.

Sometimes I would respond positively with the hope that I might create a moment of humanizing connection. Sometimes I would respond angrily, hoping to put open racists in their place. Sometimes I would use humor, trying to show them the absurdity of their thinking and trying to win over people who might see me as unrelatable. The results varied, but one outcome remained the same for those first several months. Each interaction would set off a long internal dialogue, mixing anger, outrage, hope, and confusion. I felt exhausted from putting all this energy into dealing with strangers online and frustrated that my effort seemed to be making little difference.

In the midst of this emotional confusion, I received my first credible death threat since those first few weeks after 9/11. It came via mail, an envelope addressed to me at home with no return address. I opened it up and saw something I thought only happened in movies: To prevent their handwriting from being traced, the sender had cut letters out of a magazine and glued them to the paper.

It was frightening enough to know someone would take the effort to create that letter. It was even more frightening to realize that whoever had sent this knew where we lived. I went to bed that evening feeling even more angry, frustrated, and powerless than I usually did in situations like these. I remembered what my friend Carina once told me: "If you think American hate is ugly, imagine what activists go through."

I was too bothered to sleep that night, so to distract myself I flipped through photos on my phone. I scrolled right past our family values document, and something told me to go back and read through it for the millionth time. Reading it, I could start feeling my power return.

I may not have been able to change how this person viewed me, but I could control how I chose to deal with the situation. Instead of being trapped in fear and rage, I made the conscious decision to respond based on the five values we had articulated all those years before.

To live with **faith** meant that I would not compromise those aspects of my religious appearance that bothered racists.

To live with **integrity** meant that I would continue to do what I thought was right in terms of racial justice and social justice activism.

To live with **love** meant that I would continue on the path that James Baldwin quote had put me on: that loving people means showing them what they cannot see on their own.

To live with **service** meant that I would continue engaging and educating, not for my own benefit but for the enrichment of those around me.

To live with **excellence** would mean to continue doing all of the above to the best of my abilities, fearlessly and unapologetically, and without compromising our family's physical security.

Articulating each of these points helped me then and in the years since as threats of violence have increased. I share this approach with you because knowing my values turned out to be my saving grace at a time in the midst of confusion. Getting this clarity didn't happen immediately and it didn't happen on its own. It took intention and sustained effort—and that worked.

I no longer find myself infuriated and outraged by attacks online, despite how toxic they might be. My entire online persona is now oriented around those five personal values: faith, integrity, love, service, and excellence. Maintaining authenticity between the virtual world and real world has made it much easier to navigate the two.

This is not just because adopting a values-based approach has made me feel more at ease with my responses or even that engaging authentically comes more intuitively—it's also that I now spend far less time and emotional energy on things that upset me. I am still cautious about risking our family's safety and still mindful when I receive credible death threats; this comes with the territory of being visibly different in today's America. The difference now, though, is that I no longer carry the psychological weight of these toxic and life-sucking emotions.

Values-based living is life-giving because it releases us from the bondage of other people's hate. Where my focus was once on responding to what happened to me, this document has given me a way to act with clarity and purpose. The circumstances may be the same, but how we experience them can be radically different.

I was fortunate that my parents had the wisdom and wherewithal to instill these concepts in us from a young age and to build them into our family structure. When we first articulated these values together, we believed they would serve as guideposts for better decision-making. I didn't realize then that this values-based approach could help protect the things we held most dear.

Another example that comes to mind most immediately has to do with the time I almost lost my dream job within a month of getting it.

Since day one of my ten-year (!) journey in graduate school, I set a goal of returning to teach at my alma mater, Trinity University. Just before completing my PhD, I was hired to teach there. Although I would have preferred to teach Sikh studies, there were only a handful of jobs in all of North America in that field—and all of them were filled. I knew this going into my training, and my advisers had insightfully suggested that I become proficient in teaching multiple traditions—including Islam, Hinduism, and Buddhism—in order to be more flexible in my teaching abilities. This advice proved to be wise. I couldn't have been more thrilled to receive an offer from my alma mater to return home and teach in their religion department about the Islamic tradition, including its history, the Qur'an, and global Muslim communities.

Before joining Trinity's faculty, my new department colleagues and I agreed that I would not slow down my social justice activism. I would continue working on civil rights with the Sikh Coalition, participating in racial justice campaigns at the national level, and speaking against hate openly and unapologetically.

Here I was, a turbaned Sikh guy teaching about Islam and talking openly about racism in the middle of Texas. I knew my activism would rub some people the wrong way, but I didn't realize how many within the local community would be upset and how quickly they would organize against me. Within a month of my arrival (and before I even made it onto the Professor Watchlist), there was a campaign to have me fired. I know this because I received a call from our university president's office one morning informing me that their phones had been ringing off the hook with people demanding that I be removed from the job. The day before, school authorities and police officers in Irving, Texas, had detained and arrested a young Muslim boy, Ahmed Mohamed, because they wrongly presumed the clock he had brought to school was a homemade bomb. I had a sense of how humiliated the boy must have been and I felt moved to post a note of solidarity. I tweeted a photo of myself holding a clock with the caption: "Brought my clock to work today in solidarity." Unbeknownst to me, that tweet went viral, making it on national morning and evening news shows. Because of this tweet, people were calling on the university to fire me.

When asked why they were upset, the complainants claimed that I had a track record of making hateful statements online—a charge I knew was untrue. I hid the concern in my voice and asked what I could do to address the accusation. The representative with whom I was speaking, an assistant vice president at Trinity, told me to hang tight and that she would reach out again after their team reviewed the facts.

The next two hours felt like two weeks. I sat in my office staring at my phone, willing it to ring. When it finally did, I was relieved to learn that the university would be putting out a statement on my behalf. I breathed a second sigh of relief when the vice president assured me that my job was safe. When I thanked her and asked why, she explained that university administrators had gone through all my social media history and couldn't find a single post or comment to suggest the kind of hate or anger people were accusing me of. Scrolling through my posts had showed her that, if anything, I was consistently posting about two topics: love and justice.

I had never planned to create an online persona that would help protect me. The idea had never crossed my mind. Yet one month into my professional career, the reward couldn't have been more evident. Having a clear sense of my values had rescued me from emotional tumult years earlier. Now it had just saved my dream job.

A values-based approach to life is like a compass, both clarifying and instructive. It's so easy for us to get caught up in the ups and downs of our busy lives, losing sight of what we're doing and why. This is normal. It's part of being human.

We fall into problems when we're not purposeful about our decisions. So where do we turn in times when we realize that we have lost our way? How do we deal with these moments of crisis so that we come out stronger and not weaker? And what are we actually doing proactively to save ourselves from the pain and difficulty of personal crisis?

If you feel like you could be doing more to find coherence and direction within yourself, try this simple exercise. Create a list of twenty or so qualities you wish to embody. From that list, identify five that feel central to who you are and who you aspire to be. For instance, your list might include honesty, generosity, courage, service, and humility. Once you have identified your top five values, try to come up with one action you will take each day to practice each of them. For example, if you chose generosity, you might commit to giving three compliments a day to people in your life. Now ask yourself: What will you do to hold yourself accountable to each commitment? Will you record it in a daily journal? Will you have an accountability buddy you check in with at the end of each week?

This exercise may feel anodyne, but it has real import. It can help you develop more clarity around what values matter most to you; more intention and power behind your actions; and more self-love and self-confidence as you begin taking steps toward becoming who you truly aspire to be.

⌐━━━━━━━━⌐

Thirty-nine

EMBODYING OUR VALUES

W hen we were kids, it wasn't uncommon for my poor mom to show up with all four boys in tow: on errands, to birthday parties, even to doctor's appointments. Where else could she deposit so many kids?

Once when we were young, years before 9/11, the five of us arrived at the skating rink, excited for my older brother's fifth-grade class party. But as soon as we walked through the doors, a large man rushed at us from across the room, pointing at our turbans and wagging his finger. "Y'all can't skate here with those rags on your head," he announced in his Texas drawl, loud enough for everyone to hear. "Take off them damn rags or leave right now."

We hoped to ignore him, but the large print on his shirt announced that he was the rink manager. There was no sidestepping this one.

We were young, but we had encountered racism enough to know the routine. We slid to the side and left our mother to handle it.

Typically, it only took a minute or two to resolve, so when there was no resolution in sight after two minutes, my brothers and I walked over to the arcade. After a few minutes of pretending to play games and look-ing for coins in change return slots, we were both bored and eager to skate with our friends. I ran to the counter to ask my mom for an update. I tugged the back of her kameez, and when she turned around, I saw tears streaming down her face. I had never seen her cry before, and I must have assumed the worst because I burst into tears, too. "It's not fair. Why are they picking on us? They should just let us skate!"

My mom came over to me quickly, gently grabbed my shoulder, and explained in her subtle Punjabi accent, "I'm not crying because it's unfair. I'm crying because we're so lucky. All the parents and teachers have agreed to protest the skating rink. We're all going for ice cream instead. Aren't we blessed to have such amazing friends?"

I was dumbstruck. Her tears actually came from the show of solidarity that touched her deeply.

Thirty years later, I am still moved by my mother's strength and her unwavering commitment to doing what is right. It must have taken enormous courage and self-control for her to try to convince a racist manager to let her sons skate, and then explain to the other adults why we had to leave. As a parent now, I can empathize with how hurt and helpless she must have felt, watching someone discriminate against her children and not having the power to stop him. I am inspired even more to see how, in spite of the tough situation, she still managed to maintain her values.

It would surely have been easier for her to let us take off our turbans and enjoy the party. And yet she chose the harder path because she was unwilling to betray her principles.

Carefully honed fortitude is the backbone of resilience. It's not something we encounter often in our lives, but we know it when we see it. And when we see it, we know that it's special. We also know in our hearts that capturing this fortitude and bringing it into our own lives could change us for the better.

I am equally struck by my mother's optimism in that moment. In a situation where most would have felt powerless—and understandably so—my mother found grace and gratitude. She could have easily dwelled on the injustice of the situation, how her children were being hurt by exclusionary rules and their heartless enforcement. But instead of being swallowed up by her pain, she immediately found the silver lining. Her chardi kala, gratitude, and strength in the face of injustice have remained with me to this day.

My mother's decision to lead and mobilize our community provides a powerful insight into how much stronger we are in solidarity. If my mother had walked out with just the four of us in tow, my brothers and I likely would have internalized the feeling that we didn't belong. What's more, no one else would have gained anything from the incident. By sharing the situation with our teachers and classmates, she gave them the chance to care and stand up; by bringing everyone together for a collective action, she showed her own kids that their friends cared for them. Whether or not this had any effect on the roller-skating rink or its manager isn't the point. What's most important is that my mother, in that moment, showed all of us—parents and teachers and students alike—how one fights for justice with grace and love.

When I look back on why my mother made such an impression on me that day, I realize that this was the first moment in which I saw idealized values come to life. We had talked about these ideas over dinner and had shared stories about how people embodied them, but I had never truly witnessed them firsthand. Now, through my mother's example, I could see the transformative power of this wisdom. And more than that, I could see how they transformed me.

Sikh wisdom teaches that, while it may be priceless to *know* how we want to live, knowledge is worthless when it just stays locked in our brain. Knowledge without action is hypocrisy. Not that this would ever happen, but when I know in my heart and mind that I should help my partner empty the dishwasher yet instead just sit on the couch and watch the game, I'm being a hypocrite. The same is true when we go through the motions without putting our heart into it. Action without heart is disingenuous, and living life this way prevents us from ever living in the present.

Authenticity, on the other hand, is when we bring together our thoughts, words, and actions. When we align what we say, think, and do, we can unleash the true power of any ideal into our being and into the world.

This is a lot easier said than done, and it certainly does not happen by accident. At the same time, seeing integrity in the people around us suggests that it is not as unattainable as we may presume. I saw this internal clarity in my mother at the roller-skating rink that day. And since realizing that, I have felt one question recurring with urgency: *How do we nurture authenticity within ourselves?*

The answer, it turns out, is simple. We nurture authenticity the same way we cultivate anything else we want within. In the famous words of Allen Iverson: "I'm talkin' 'bout practice."

The practical wisdom here is both obvious and profound. The more we practice our values, the more we internalize them. The more we internalize them, the deeper we forge them into our being. The deeper they are forged, the more intrinsic they become to us. And the more intrinsic they become to us, the more we become them.

You'll see by now that practice is a common theme that emerges. That's because practice is the alchemy of values-based living. We begin with the basic ideals of how we want to live and who we want to become. Through sustained and intentional practice, our idealized values transform into embodied qualities.

We can summarize the difference between them like this: Values can be learned. Qualities have to be earned.

This is why so many spiritual thinkers place emphasis on embodied practice. It's not because there's something magical or supernatural about these practices that help us skip over the process of self-development. Rather, embodied practice is powerful because it *is* the process of self-development. Creating routines and rituals to cultivate our ideals is how we optimize incremental, transformative change.

It can feel easy to dismiss this point because it feels so intuitive. But the truth is that, despite how obvious it seems, we consistently overlook the direct relationship between practice and outcome. How did my mother have the capacity to meet a tough situation with grace and resolve? She had spent her entire life cultivating these qualities. So of course she was ready when she was put to the test.

This is the underlying and untapped promise of living our values. Practicing these ideals can change each of us from within, transforming us from everyday people who have aspirations and values into superhuman beings who derive power from their embodied qualities.

We don't just *value* love. We *are* love.

We don't just *value* integrity. We *are* integrity.

We don't just *value* service. We *are* service.

I wonder sometimes what our world would look like if we started defining success based on who we become rather than what we have. Perhaps we would stop pursuing fame and material wealth, and perhaps we would begin collecting the treasures already within us.

When we embody our values, we no longer feel insecure about ourselves and how people perceive us. It rids us of our self-doubts and transforms our feelings of guilt and disappointment into lasting happiness. This is why authenticity is the ultimate form of self-love.

I wish I had stayed in touch with all the soccer coaches, music teachers, and swim instructors who told me that "we practice because practice makes perfect." I want to go back to them and share what I've learned. If practice truly made us perfect, how could we explain that after a lifetime of practicing baseball, hitting the ball just four out of ten times (.400) is seen as a phenomenal accomplishment that hasn't been done in sixty years; yet even this achievement means the batter didn't meet their goal in 60 percent of their attempts. Similarly, the best shooter in basketball history—Steph Curry—still misses 5 percent of his free throws, the easiest shot in the sport. He's historically great, but he's not perfect.

Perfection is unrealistic, and if we make it our goal, we will spend our entire lives chasing the unattainable with perpetual disappointment. On the other hand, if we practice to make ourselves better and stronger and closer to meeting our full potential, then we can find joy all through the process.

Embodying a values-based framework can change our lives. It can help us navigate situations, mold us into the people we hope to become, and bring us a new level of happiness, ease, and solace. I want to share a few examples of how this has worked for me.

Forty

THE VALUE OF CREATIVITY (KARTA PURAKH)

As turbaned teenagers in Texas, my brothers and I were constantly aware that we had a different heritage than the people around us. We had accepted our unsolicited role as community ambassadors and had become comfortable answering basic questions about our traditions. It may seem burdensome, but I thought it was an easy way to make a positive difference. It felt especially easy because, even when they thought they were being creative, most people asked the same questions:

"Do you shower with your turban on?"

Only if I'm having a really good turban day and don't want to mess it up.

"Were you born with a turban on?"

Yes, Sikh mothers have magical wombs that make turbans and tie them in utero.

"Is your car shaped like a turban?"

Of course it is. We call it the Turban-Suburban.

Even conversations with my friends hardly went beneath the surface. It may have been because they were afraid to ask, but my bet is that none of us were all that interested in talking about life. We'd rather be enjoying it in our kayaks on the lake or playing pickup basketball at the park.

So it came as a surprise when Lisa, a close friend from my high school cross-country team, once asked earnestly what Sikhs believe. Lisa's family is Catholic, and she was studying her own faith as she prepared for the sacrament of confirmation. She told me that she had stayed up late the night before talking to her father, trying to understand how someone she loved could be a good person but not be allowed into heaven because he didn't accept Jesus as his savior. She said that, during the entire conversation, she kept thinking about me.

I answered Lisa's initial question by sharing some of the basic Sikh teachings. She asked if we believed in God and if it was the same God as Christians. I told her about a teaching from Guru Nanak that came to mind—that there is only one God, no matter how many names we might use. As I said that, I remembered visiting a famous megachurch in San Antonio and hearing its pastor, John Hagee, preaching about God's anger, wrath, and vengeance. (He also preached that day about how children's books with magic and sorcery are evil, but that's another story.) What I had heard sounded so different from what my tradition taught about God being love. Observing the difference between the two made me wonder: We may ultimately worship the same God, but do we really have the same idea of who God actually is?

Lisa's question prompted me to investigate my own tradition further. I began at the same place many Sikhs begin their spiritual journeys— with a composition called the "mul mantr," the first verse in the Sikh scripture that we all learned as young children.

Ik oankar

Satnam

Karta purakh

Nirbhau

Nirvair

Akal murat

Ajuni

Saibhang

Gur prasad

I had recited these words and their translations so many times as a child that their meanings felt self-evident:

> One Divine Force.
> Identity of Truth.
> Creative Being.
> Fearless.
> Without Enemies.
> An Eternal Form.
> Never Born.
> Self-Created.
> Through the Guru's Grace.

I had memorized these terms as a child, and as I grew older, I began to understand that the mul mantr was seen to outline some of the foundational qualities of divinity. Now that I was revisiting these terms, I noticed that they fit into a larger pattern. Throughout their writings, the Sikh gurus did not use just one word to refer to divinity. Instead, they used hundreds of descriptors, each of which reflected a particular quality: compassionate (miharvan), enduring (akal), creator (kartar), fearless (nirbhau), giver (devanhar).

Why would they have placed so much importance on these specific qualities? Perhaps we can best answer this question by construing it more broadly: Why does it matter what we believe?

I felt stumped until I remembered my own experience with this question. The time we'd spent with Larry Mills to identify our family values and mission statement helped me live into them more intentionally. And therein lay the answer: Our beliefs are more than hypothesis and more than even theory. Our beliefs can shape how we act and behave. The gurus were not just describing the nature of divinity; they were also outlining ideals to which we can all aspire. This made perfect sense based on how I saw the world already. If we all share the same divine light and potential, then doesn't it follow that we have the opportunity to realize these divine qualities?

We could describe this in secular terms as cultivating our best selves. In spiritual terms, we might say that we are tapping into the divine potential inherent within us. In any language, the fruits of virtuous living are clear: Cultivating these qualities would put us in harmony with the world around us and in harmony with ourselves, too.

All this made sense in my head, but I wanted to test it out. I decided to start with the third term of the mul mantr—karta purakh—which literally translates to "creative being." I began by asking myself a simple question: *What is the value of creativity?*

My first reflection took me to the idea of contribution. Creativity is powerful because you are giving something to this world rather than taking something away. There's something generous and generative about creativity. Creativity is also selfless and life-giving because it brings people together. In a world marred by destruction and division, we all know how easy it can be to break things apart and cause chaos. Building and growing requires much more investment—love, concern, attention, care, patience. These ingredients bring us together and strengthen our cohesion.

In studying the teachings of Guru Nanak, I have also come to see creativity as a key element of justice. When we are dissatisfied and outraged with the injustices happening all around us, there is a more constructive way to deal with our frustrations. Doing so takes innovation and ingenuity. Guru Nanak's life offers a fresh model for activism. While many biographers have softened his image to present him as a typical spiritual figure, anyone who reads Guru Nanak's writings knows that he pulls no punches. Yes, he was a spiritual mystic who sang of divine love and beauty. But he was also a political activist who called out injustice unapologetically. To be spiritually connected is to care about the people around you, and to care about the people around you is to pursue justice. The two, Guru Nanak taught, are not mutually exclusive but mutually reinforcing.

Guru Nanak was open with his social and political criticism. He rejected the social hierarchies that he saw in his communities, whether on the basis of caste, gender, religion, language, etc. His conviction of ik oankar would not allow him to discriminate, because in his eyes all were equally divine. Guru Nanak did not just announce his frustrations and disagreements, and he didn't just reject what he didn't like as wrong or evil. He always offered a solution, an alternative vision that resolved his core disagreements.

One of the more common accounts that Sikhs share is that of a young Nanak, who upon reaching a suitable age was brought to the local pandit (Hindu priest) for a rite of passage: the sacred thread ceremony. The sacred thread is a thin cotton cord that higher-caste Hindu boys and young men typically wear over the left shoulder and across the body. Traditionally, and even today, low-caste Hindus and women are denied the sacred thread. Nanak's parents were practicing Hindus who belonged to a higher caste, which meant that the thread placed on his body would bestow Nanak with social and religious privilege.

Nanak refused to put on the thread and expressed his disagreement with two core ideas undergirding the ceremony and central to the logic of the caste system: the claim that some people are better than others; and that everyone in society could be organized according to how pure or impure they were perceived to be. In a pointed criticism of the sacred thread practice, Nanak declares: "When this thread is worn out, it's replaced by another one. If it truly had enduring strength, it would have never broken in the first place." Guru Nanak also criticizes the religious elite for manipulating the masses by falsely presenting this twisted yarn as an article of purity.

Guru Nanak did not hide his views against caste; his criticisms are preserved in Sikh scripture. He clearly had no problem sharing how he felt about the sacred thread and what it represented.

Guru Nanak could have stopped here, and yet he wouldn't. Even rhetorically, his way of engaging was inspired by creating. So instead of just disavowing and rejecting, Guru Nanak offered another way of thinking about the sacred thread: "Make compassion the cotton, contentment the thread, modesty the knot, and truth the twist. This is the sacred thread of the soul. If you have it, then go ahead and put it on me. It won't break, and can't be soiled, burnt, or lost. O Nanak: the people who wear this thread are truly blessed."

As Guru Nanak formed his own community, he ended the practice of wearing a sacred thread among his followers. He also challenged the caste hierarchies embedded within the ritual. For instance, Guru Nanak established a free communal meal (langar) at each community center (dharamsala) established for his budding followership. The meal incorporated a radical rejection of caste norms: Whether you were a high-caste king or an untouchable pauper, everyone broke bread together and sat on the floor together as a sign of collective equality. Guru Nanak created a way to simultaneously lift everyone up into shared dignity while also confronting and dismantling the social inequities that frustrated him.

That the practice of sitting together at langar continues more than five hundred years later is a testament to the power of creative activism. Guru Nanak's way was not to simply call out those with whom he disagreed. Guru Nanak sought to meet them where they were and offer alternative perspectives and opportunities. He then baked his solutions—rooted within his own values of oneness and love and creativity—into the institutions he was building.

Guru Nanak's approach to engaging with the world constructively requires a lot more commitment than our current approaches of virtue-signaling, performance outrage, and call-out culture. Guru Nanak's way calls on us to invest more of our time and effort and emotions into the injustices of our world. It also asks us to let go of the short-lived gratification that comes with things like social media attention. Anyone can post an opinion online. The difference is that the guru followed through with action, taking the initiative and ownership to make the change he wanted to see in the world.

Guru Nanak's model gets us away from constantly complaining and bickering and moves us into positive action. It illuminates our way out of our personal malaise and collective polarization. No longer do we have to feign our outrage or tear one another down in order to lift ourselves up. Bringing the ideal of karta purakh into our lives offers us all a way out of the toxic negativity and into the more life-giving and heart-filling approach of creativity.

Forty-one

THE VALUE OF
FEARLESSNESS (NIRBHAU)

As someone who came of age during the "war on terror," and as someone whose very presence often makes people feel afraid, I have thought a lot about fear: as a human emotion tied to our safety and security, as a tool for political manipulation, as an evolutionary instinct critical for our survival, as a hurdle that keeps us from reaching for our goals and finding true happiness. That we keep fear at the forefront of our minds speaks to how deeply it has been ingrained in our psychologies.

As part of my desire to experience a more immersive and fulfilling type of love, I have committed to digging deeper into my own fears. Until we confront the fears buried within, they will continue to haunt us.

In my own process, I have learned that one of my deeper fears is that people may not like me. This is not an entirely new revelation. My childhood friend Kiran first made me aware of this while we were sophomores in college. I remember shrugging it off with a laugh, saying that being called a people-pleaser paled in comparison to the other, racist names I'd been called. My reaction was defensive and dismissive because I saw my people-pleasing as a strength. I felt that it made me sensitive and empathetic and confident among peers. I didn't realize then that she was trying to help me see something I couldn't see on my own—that this strength could also be a liability if I only relied on the opinions of others to validate my self-worth.

As I began digging into my fears, I was able to identify some of the origins for these feelings: internalizing some of the negative assumptions people have about me; living with parents who took the little they had (minus the $3 spent on that omelet) to create a beautiful life for my brothers and me; belonging to a community enduring genocidal violence back in the homeland. Each of these raised questions about security and safety and stability. Being liked was a way for me to feel I belonged. How people saw me wasn't the only source of my self-confidence, but it was an important one.

Through exploring my memories, I realized that my deep concern with perception related back to that conversation with my mother after the shoplifting incident years ago, when she said that my unique appearance as a Sikh meant I had a responsibility to represent the community at all times. That put a lot of weight on my shoulders. And it didn't just come from her. We heard often from our parents and elders that we would probably be the only Sikhs other people met anywhere we went— especially in South Texas—and that whatever impression we made on them would last forever.

Many people who come from the margins of society can relate to this. We feel pressure to behave well in public because we care about our communities and want to put our people in a positive light. Every interaction feels like a meaningful opportunity to erase someone's negative assumptions and paint a fresh picture in their minds. Making a good impression can feel like the critical difference between your loved ones being accepted or rejected, being embraced or murdered. The stakes feel incredibly high. That's why it feels as rewarding as it is exhausting.

Growing up in Texas long before we learned about systemic and institutionalized racism, my brothers and I clung to the naive belief that if people knew who we were, then their fear and animus would evaporate. We believed that racism was purely a result of ignorance. The solution to our problems, then, was education. My personal experience and world-view propelled me into a lifelong journey in education. This is also why I believe that, for people on the margins, cultural and religious literacy is about social justice.

Over time, my views on the nature of racism have changed substantially. I now see that it is about more than ignorance—that it is also about racist ideologies embedded in our government and social policies, institutions and systems, all of which produce negative biases in our minds and deep inequities in our societies. A complex problem requires a complex solution, and resolving a social disease as pervasive as racism will take all of us working together.

And yet, while my understanding of racism has broadened and deepened, the specificity of my own experience still rings true. The belief that our family was mistreated in Texas because "people don't know who we are" speaks to the formation of my own psychology and the critical importance I have always placed on education and representation. Anytime I felt discouraged by a setback, I would remind myself: *If people just knew who we are and saw our humanity, life could be so much better for so many people I care about.* Education and self-representation aren't our golden tickets out of racism, but they're the vehicles to which I feel most drawn and to which I have devoted my life.

My desire to be liked was never so extreme that I was pretending to be someone I wasn't or changing my personality to fit into different social groups. I was fortunate enough to have good friends wherever I went and enough self-confidence to feel worthy in new settings. My real challenge came in moments when I felt people were uncomfortable around me. I would try to compensate for their discomfort, bending over backward to appease them or avoid upsetting them. I would take on their discomfort as if it was my problem, and then I would take on the burden of finding a solution.

Without fail, I would walk away feeling upset and dissatisfied. Upset because it felt like I was being forced to justify my right to exist and share space on this planet. Dissatisfied because, despite having done these contortions my entire life, I still didn't have a satisfying way to deal with these situations.

This brings me back to one of my favorite topics and least favorite activities: air travel.

Imagine entering the airport knowing that people have already been conditioned to fear people who look like you. You check in to your flight and approach the security checkpoint, knowing that racial profiling is official policy: Anyone with a turban and beard will be automatically set aside for secondary screening.

Imagine knowing your own government is sending the message to everyone around you that it's not just okay to *feel* scared of you, but that it's also prudent to *act* on those fears, no matter how humiliating or dehumanizing it might be.

Imagine knowing you have the right to moral outrage and protest, but also knowing that those rights are equal in name only; knowing that if your brown-skinned body misbehaves at airport security, you won't get the benefit of the doubt—and there's no telling what the outcome might be.

Imagine being already hypersensitive to what people think about you, but also knowing that those misperceptions could be the difference between someone seeing you as their enemy or their neighbor.

How would you proceed? It might feel natural to lower your head and avert eye contact, hoping that no one will see you as you wish for it all to be over. It might feel natural to raise your voice, or speak rudely, or even glare at the officers as they aggressively pat down your body.

But for people like me, who know the stakes, what choice do I have? We stand there with a soft smile on our faces, desperately hoping that people in line will see that smile as genuine, not devious. We stand with our heads held high, but not too high, because we don't want people to think we don't know our place. We know that how people perceive us really matters for our own safety and security.

Passing through airport security is only the first back-bending exercise in our journeys. Imagine what it feels like to board an airplane with some of my physical features: brown skin, facial hair, and a turban. Do you think people *don't* notice me as I walk down the aisle to my seat? Do you think people are clamoring for a chance to sit next to me?

Let me assure you that they're not. I can affirm this by the countless open-seating flights in which I get a whole row to myself. People often choose to sit in far less comfortable middle seats than have a window or aisle seat in the same row as me. I'm not complaining about that—I'm happy to claim the extra legroom and stretch myself out for a cozy nap. I don't feel bad about that either. I'll take whatever few advantages racism has to offer.

What I'm saying is that it's as stressful for me to board an airplane as it is to pass through airport security. My mind flashes through the numerous instances of people being removed from airplanes for nothing more than flying while brown: the young man removed for speaking Arabic on the phone to his mother; the Sikh religious leaders removed because of their "threatening appearance"; the elderly woman removed for reading the Qur'an; the MIT professor removed for writing math equations that a fellow passenger thought looked suspiciously like Arabic.

As absurd as these stories sound, they are all real cases from the past few years. And in each case, the "suspects" were barred from flying because other passengers felt uncomfortable. This is part of why it can be hard not to fall into the trap of trying to appease those around us. Repeated life experiences have taught us that it is our responsibility to justify our existence, and that when we fail to do so, we are the ones who suffer the consequences.

So what do we do?

When talking to my wife or parents on the phone, I would let them know I was getting on the plane and then switch from speaking in Punjabi to English. If I'm being honest, a small part of me wants people on the plane to hear my American accent and perhaps feel like I am one of their tribe. My wife and I have even made an agreement that, once we got onto an airplane, she would take the luggage and I would carry the kids. One thing I have learned about racism is that nothing softens people's hearts like carrying cute babies. It's sad that we even had to think of this, but truly, these are real questions for people in my skin.

In the years that I taught Islamic studies in Texas, I would commute from my home in New York City. Each week, I would struggle with the question of preparing for class while on the airplane. I wondered if it might scare people to see a turbaned man reading books about Islam on the plane. Each week I seemed to have a different answer. Sometimes I wouldn't want to carry the burden, so I would stay up late the night before to complete my reading. Sometimes I didn't want to appease people's Islamophobic discomforts, so I just read my books openly. I remember one week, when we read Ayesha Jalal's book on jihad, *Partisans of Allah*, I used another book jacket to disguise what I was actually reading. Another week, a white passenger sitting across the aisle saw me reading Omid Safi's *Memories of Muhammad* and spent the rest of the flight asking me about every anti-Muslim talking point he had ever encountered.

All this performance was in the service of other people's perceptions. And it was exhausting.

The breakthrough for me came when I realized that I was operating out of fear. All of my actions were actually reactions. I wasn't living for myself, nor was I truly serving others. I had fallen into an ocean of victimization. And I was drowning.

Just realizing this was a saving grace. Sikh wisdom warns against the victim mindset; there's not even an equivalent word for "victim" in Punjabi. Instead, Sikhi teaches about survival and resilience, that life may not be fair for everyone but we take on our challenges with grace and fortitude and dignity. This is what chardi kala is all about.

While I knew all this intellectually, I needed practical wisdom to help me deal with my fear. I thought back to Guru Tegh Bahadur's teaching that had helped me so many times in my life already: "The truly wise person is one who fears none and frightens none." Sikh traditions maintain that the ninth guru uttered these words while sitting in a Delhi prison, awaiting his execution mandated by Aurangzeb, the most notorious of Mughal emperors. If Guru Tegh Bahadur could be fearless in the face of his own impending death, then surely I could find a way to embody fearlessness while boarding an airplane.

The takeaway is that, while perceptions matter, our own internal workings matter more. It may be important that we try to appease the people around us—but only to an extent, and certainly not at the cost of our own dignity. Guru Tegh Bahadur is trying to tell us that true fearlessness comes from within us, and that we must also be sensitive to other people's fears. Both are important. One without the other tips us out of balance.

This is what my friend Kiran had been saying years ago when she pointed out my fear of not being liked. If we don't like ourselves in the first place, how happy can people's perceptions make us?

I have been implementing this wisdom as I have faced my own fears the past few years, and it has completely transformed my experience of air travel—although perhaps not in the way you might think. I am still subjected to racial profiling every time I pass through airport security. I still loathe that our government reinforces dangerous stereotypes that have violent consequences. I hate that my daughters have to watch me get patted down and that I have to explain to them why we are treated differently. And I withstand it all, with my head held high and a smile on my face.

The difference is what's on the inside. No longer am I putting on a show for people to affect how they see me. That feeling of anxiety and desperation is now gone. I want people to see me for who I am, but not at the cost of my own happiness. Removing fear from the equation has liberated me from that burden.

The same is true when I board an airplane. I remain sensitive to the fact that people might be scared when they see me, but I no longer feel the need to justify my existence to them. I know now that we all have equal claim to this world and that while we all have a responsibility to one another, we also have a responsibility to ourselves. And I have learned that I don't have to compromise my own being in order to help others.

When we resist confronting and overcoming our fears, we are constrained by the same pathologies that leave us feeling the way I used to during air travel: upset, dissatisfied, undignified, and victimized. While there may be comfort in accommodating what others need and ignoring our own, there is no joy it. It will not give us liberation. True joy comes when we can free ourselves from the fears that keep us from realizing our potential. And then we can walk around with our hearts feeling full and with our heads held high.

This is the gift that practicing fearlessness has given me. I can walk down the airplane aisle with the dignity we all deserve. I can speak in Punjabi to my family *and* exude kindness to the people around me. I can read books on different topics and in different languages *and* engage in conversation with fellow passengers. And who knows? One day, I may even do a math problem or two.

Forty-two

THE POWER OF DISCIPLINE

I didn't always enjoy running. In fact, I pretty much hated it until my twenties. It was while living in Boston that I began to change course (pun intended). My friends and I were watching football one evening when a new commercial came on that caught my attention. It was part of a new Adidas "Impossible Is Nothing" campaign, featuring two of my all-time favorite athletes—Muhammad Ali and David Beckham—as well as an elderly Sikh man in a tracksuit and bright yellow turban. I was stunned. It was the first time I'd ever seen someone who looked like me depicted positively on TV. And standing with two sports legends?! I had to know more about this man.

I learned quickly that he was ninety-seven years old, his name was Fauja Singh, and that after shattering a number of running records, he had set a goal to become the first hundred-year-old to ever run a marathon. I began following his training and career, and three years later I watched with the world as Fauja Singh crossed the finish line of the Toronto Waterfront Marathon. It took him more than eight hours, but he had done the impossible: Fauja Singh completed 26.2 miles after being on this earth for an entire century.

I felt inspired by his feat (and his feet). I also felt a little embarrassed. If Fauja Singh could run a marathon at one hundred, what excuse did I have? The day he set the record, I signed up for my first marathon. That was when I decided my goal would be to run the world's largest marathon, which takes place every year in New York City. Fauja Singh had run it a few years earlier, so it would be a way to follow in his footsteps. I thought it would be a fun experience, a nice task to cross off my bucket list, and a good way to stay in shape. I didn't anticipate the impact it would have on other aspects of my life.

Training for the marathon in 2011 started as a drag. I especially dreaded pulling myself out of bed early on Saturday mornings for my long runs. But after a few months of consistent practicing, it became easier—not the running itself, but the act of getting myself out to run. I also found myself eating healthier, talking more to my loved ones, being more efficient in my teaching and research, and feeling an all-around sense of happiness and positivity.

I still disliked the physical act of running. But I loved how it was making me feel. My wife must have noticed, too, because she commented positively on the person I was becoming. I had been making resolutions to do better for years. Why was I able to finally achieve some of those results? Did marathon training have anything to do with it?

By this point, I had come to anticipate the same answer for any self-improvement question. *How does one become more grateful?* Practice. *How does one become a better listener?* Practice. *How does one become more compassionate?* Practice. Practice. Practice.

When it came to self-growth, practice seemed like an important, well . . . practice. But in this case, it could only really explain so much. By running every morning, I became a stronger runner. But what about the rest of it?

According to Foucault (here he is again), running had everything to do with my transformation. In his words, I had accessed a "technology of the self," a regular discipline that helped me cultivate internal fortitude. By committing myself to the training schedule wholeheartedly, I was practicing one of the most basic Sikh teachings, kirat karni, which calls on us to harness and use our skills and abilities to the utmost for improving the self, our communities, and the world around us.

What we're talking about here is a different kind of practice. Discipline strengthens our inner character and fortitude. Through running, I was building power internally, which was making it easier to do the right thing in other aspects of my life. There was something liberating about this inner strength, because I felt more comfortable following my own internal compass and less beholden to what society expected of me.

Practicing discipline is not just about honing a particular value so that it becomes a quality; it's also about training ourselves to make the right choices. The more we train, the easier it becomes to align our thoughts and actions. As with any sort of practice, repeating something over and over helps make it second nature. This is why training for a marathon helped me improve in so many other aspects of my life.

Developing inner strength was the key to unlocking my agency because that strength helped me develop the behaviors I had long aspired to adopt: eating better, sleeping better, and managing my time better, to name a few. As I improved in these areas, I felt more like the person I wanted to be. God knows that practice hasn't made me perfect (and a lot of other people know this too), but practicing discipline has definitely made me better and happier.

We live in an age when people are moving further away from disciplinary practice and closer to an à la carte sort of self-care that calls for immediate self-gratification. And while that may have its place, we lose something important when we only embrace the things that feel good and let go of practices that feel challenging.

Living without discipline comes with a cost. By ignoring our conscience rather than engaging it, we quash the voice inside us that encourages us to do the right thing. This is what I was missing that day I took the candy bar from the grocery store. It's what we're all missing when we think of our daily choices as random acts rather than what they really are: a constant set of opportunities that, when embraced and engaged, can help us achieve our goals and become the people we want to be.

———

I'll never forget where I was when I first encountered Foucault's idea of technologies of the self. It was one of those *aha!* moments when I felt something click. The kind when, if I was a cartoon character, a lightbulb would have popped up above the turban on my head. The idea was illuminating, shining a light inside me and helping me understand something about myself that I had not been able to uncover on my own.

I was assigned Saba Mahmood's *Politics of Piety* in my graduate theory course at Columbia, a book in which the author speaks with Muslim women about their experiences with veiling practices. Mahmood explains that her book was born from the realization that we hear so many people explain what covering means for Muslim women (usually oppression and misogyny), yet somehow we never ask Muslim women who cover what it means to them.

Reading Dr. Mahmood's interviews with these women felt like an out-of-body experience. So much of my self-identity was wrapped up in my Sikh appearance: the turban wrapped on my head; the hair wrapped in a neat knot beneath my turban; my beard wrapped up in a smaller knot and held by tiny bobby pins underneath my chin. I always had this nagging feeling that, because there was something important I didn't quite understand about the Sikh identity, there was something important I didn't quite understand about myself.

Let me explain. Aside from the turban, there are five Sikh articles of faith. Each begins with the letter *k* in Punjabi, so we often refer to them in English as the Five Ks:

○ **Kanga**—a small wooden comb typically worn in one's hair

○ **Kara**—an iron or steel bracelet worn on one's wrist

- **Kirpan**—a dagger or small sword typically worn in a sash (gatra) on one's body

- **Kesh**—long, uncut hair

- **Kachera**—long soldier shorts worn beneath one's clothes

Sikhs are expected to maintain these five articles of faith after undergoing initiation (amrit), so this appearance figures into their disciplinary practice. This identity was formalized at the turn of the eighteenth century by Guru Gobind Singh, the tenth and final guru-prophet. While all Sikhs are expected to aspire toward initiation, only a small percentage are ever initiated. The most common article of faith maintained by Sikhs is the kara; when someone greets me in Punjabi, I often look at their wrists to see if they identify as Sikh. The next most common of the Ks is the kesh—long, uncut hair. These were the two articles I maintained as a boy growing up in San Antonio. I began to wear the other three Ks in my teens when I began planning to become initiated. The way I experienced it matched up with the way the Sikh identity was explained to me: the external discipline is interlinked with inner practice; as one grows in their commitment to the faith, one also embraces additional commitments to the Sikh identity.

Guru Gobind Singh never gave a reason for these five articles or explained what they mean. In the centuries since, Sikhs have often explained the Five Ks through their perceived functions. For instance, some say that the kirpan is a reminder for us to defend everyone's right to justice, or that the kachera is a reminder for us to practice sexual restraint.

These explanations make sense to me, especially when they match up with core teachings within the tradition, but they have never felt fully satisfactory on their own. If, for example, the only reason to wear a kara on my wrist is to remind myself to always do good deeds, then couldn't replacing the kara with a simple string serve the same function?

Of course, anything *could* function similarly. And yet, anytime I have asked a fellow Sikh this question, they have responded by saying the meaning goes deeper than its ascribed function. I agree with this sentiment, and it's why the functionalist explanation feels insufficient on its own. It's also why Sikhs tend to avoid describing their articles of faith as symbols.

Another common explanation lines up with what my mother told me all those years ago. The Sikh identity is like a uniform so people can identify us in public. It holds us accountable to the ideals we proclaim, and it creates cohesion among a pan-global community 27 million strong. It's why, as kids, we were able to easily identify Sikhs when we visited New York City, and why, despite having never met them, we felt comfortable greeting them.

There's a lot of truth to the uniform metaphor, especially in how it helps me feel connected with Sikhs across the world, past and present. Yet it doesn't fully capture my own relationship with my Sikh identity either. It also comes with a set of unintended consequences. For instance, by equating our identity with our physical appearance, it becomes tempting for Sikh men to justify trimming their beards short and saying they are still just as identifiable in public. This explanation of our identity as uniform also has the impact of erasing the experiences and existence of Sikh women, most of whom are not as easily identifiable by appearance as Sikh men. This is a sore spot for many in the Sikh community today, and rightfully so; the representation and discussion of Sikh experiences is overwhelmingly from the perspective of men. What does it mean for Sikh women—whose community is already overlooked and underrepresented—to be rendered doubly invisible?

The most compelling explanation I have found for the Sikh identity is through the analogy of a wedding ring. We don't try to reduce the significance of a wedding ring to its function, because its value is so much deeper than that. We cherish our wedding rings not because of what they do but because of what they mean to us: A wedding ring is a gift of love from one's partner, and its value is deeply personal. Similarly, Sikhs cherish their five articles of faith primarily because they see them as a gift from their beloved Guru. Trying to understand these articles solely on the basis of their function misses the point.

This analogy spoke to *why* I valued my Sikh identity so much, but there was still something missing in my understanding: I still couldn't quite articulate how my external Sikh appearance shaped me as a person.

This was the gift of Saba Mahmood's work. Through her, and through Foucault's notion of technologies of the self, I finally had language to express what the Sikh identity did for me. It was not just that it reminded me of my core values, or just that it made me feel spiritually and emotionally connected to those I admired most in this world. It was also that the public accountability that comes with this unique appearance compelled me to consciously live my values.

Ever since the day I snuck that Snickers bar at the grocery store, I have been highly conscious of my behavior in public. My mother had told me that we all carried the responsibility of representing our entire community and that whatever people saw of us would be the impression they carried forever. At first, I experienced that as a weight on my shoulders, an unfair burden placed on minority groups the world over.

As time went on, I came to see it as an opportunity. To be able to change hearts and minds in a single interaction? To create a positive impression of a community that might otherwise be demonized? What an incredible gift. My unique identity was not a cumbersome weight to carry from one interaction to the next. It was an energizing force that carried me through the world. I didn't just feel a release from the pressure; I felt empowered, as if that same pressure was now propelling me through the very spaces I had once dreaded.

Here's another change that came with this outlook. I sincerely believed that I had to act in accordance with my values in order to portray our community in the best light. What this meant practically is that I worked hard every day to show these values. And however empty these behaviors may have been when I started, they begin to take full form only by repetition. The more I practiced them, the more they became a part of who I was.

Some may say that this is faking it until you make it, but the truth is that there's nothing fake when your practice is sincere. If you really believe in what you're doing, then it's just practice. Growing internal strength was not my intention, and I didn't even know it was happening until very recently. But I see the wisdom in it now. Feeling accountability for our actions and ideals is an instrument for creating our best selves. I have learned this through two entirely different experiences with disciplinary practice: training for a marathon and maintaining my Sikh identity. In both cases, I have seen my internal fortitude strengthen and have experienced more calm and joy. Both have also given me an appreciation for the irreplaceable power of discipline.

When we come to see all the challenges before us as opportunities to strengthen ourselves internally, then we will have embraced a mindset that helps us build character and resilience—and that helps us access an ever resounding joy that's no longer subject to the ups and downs of our lives. In that way, every moment becomes a chance to cultivate, every breath an opportunity to take another step toward liberation.

Part V

SEVA AS A SPIRITUAL PRACTICE

There's one aspect of childhood that I didn't like: We didn't get to keep the birthday presents that people gave us. We'd unwrap all the gifts, note who gave us what, and stack them up in our closets. We could select two gifts to keep. The rest were for giving away, donations to children in need through San Antonio's Elf Louise program. My parents probably thought it was a brilliant way to instill a spirit of generosity. To my ten-year-old self, it instilled resentment. I wanted four different Nerf guns, damn it!

Now that I'm a parent, I find myself trying similar methods with our own daughters. Not because I want them to feel resentful, but because I want them to learn, as I learned, what it means to give before we take. Not give *as* we take. And not give *after* we take. The Sikh ethos is vand chakna, which literally means share *first*, and then partake. We practice this every time we visit the gurdwara, following the tradition of distributing langar before sitting down to eat. It comes through in our hospitality, serving others before we serve ourselves.

Seva, as we call it, is a natural expression of love. It's worshiping with our hands—or, as Rabbi Heschel famously said after marching with Dr. Martin Luther King Jr. in Selma, it's praying with our feet. Love-inspired service has produced some of the most beautiful expressions of love the world has ever seen, from the tens of thousands of people fed for free at

Darbar Sahib of Amritsar daily to the single mother working three jobs to support her babies.

The spirit of giving lives in all of us. It can come in the form of charity, volunteering, philanthropy, and more. And while all of these are valuable and beautiful, our current models of generosity fall a step short. Seva offers us a fresh approach to service and justice, one rooted in love and oneness. When implemented wholeheartedly, practicing seva can help us reduce suffering in those we serve and also in ourselves.

Forty-three

SERVING OTHERS, SERVING OURSELVES

The COVID-19 pandemic affected more than our physical and emotional health. It affected our spirits, too. We grieved our loved ones who died and worried for our loved ones who lived. For the first time in our lives, we felt the overwhelming pain of collective loss and suffering.

For many people, this feeling of connection was both new and unfamiliar. We no longer had time to focus on the differences that set us apart. Our survival depended on the more basic elements that bind us all together: health, food, water, shelter. We also realized how interlinked our well-being is and how our own decisions may affect others—even making the difference between life and death. Through it all, I heard echoes of what Guru Nanak had been trying to tell us all along: *Our lives are inextricably interconnected.*

We appreciated the feel-good stories that came out of the pandemic and took heart in moments people stepped forward to serve their communities: health-care workers who risked their own lives to save the lives of strangers; restaurant workers who made sure their communities were fed; delivery persons who transported supplies to people in need. When news outlets first started sharing stories of everyday heroes, we saw them as exceptional and applauded their superhuman efforts. But the more we heard these stories, the more we began to connect the dots and see the big picture. These were not just random acts of kindness and these heroes were not superhumans. This was humanity at its finest. People all over the world were making sacrifices to serve their communities. Our governments may have been failing us, but we were not going to fail one another.

At a time when it felt easy to give in to hopelessness, witnessing this selfless generosity gave me real confidence that we could get through the pandemic if we continued to take care of one another. At the same time, I felt uncomfortable with my own contributions. We were living in New York City, the global epicenter of the pandemic early on, and we saw firsthand the devastation wrought by the coronavirus. My wife was doing her part to serve those in need. Why wasn't I doing more?

Much of my discomfort came from my inactivity. I was used to being on the frontlines of activism and addressing urgent needs, whether guiding responses to hate crimes or advocating for better policies. Now I was trapped at home with little to contribute. I had no doubt that the best thing to do was care for our young kids while my wife served COVID patients at the hospital. But this didn't feel significant or even adequate, given the stakes; it didn't feel right to use her service as a proxy for my own.

Our lives were so different during this period that it was almost as if Gunisha and I—while living in the same small apartment—were living in two separate worlds. She was doing everything in her power to keep sick people from dying, while I spent my days constructing unicorn-princess castles and riding scooters with our babies. I was loving my time with them, but I also felt ashamed.

My guilt felt slightly sharper each day until one afternoon, while cleaning our apartment, I came across a folder from a racial justice and activism training I had led for high school students. A note scrawled in the margins reminded me of a lesson I always emphasized when speaking to young adults on social justice: *Don't confuse activity for activism.* I had shared this pearl hundreds of times with people all over the country over the years, yet somehow I had lost sight of it in my own life. Seeing this note was helpful because it reminded me that my guilt had less to do with what I was *doing* than how I was *thinking*.

We value our physical contributions because they are tangible. We can feel them with our hands and see them with our eyes. We can measure and quantify them and—perhaps just as noteworthy—others can, too. Their observations can make us so accustomed to receiving recognition for the work we do that going unnoticed can become painful.

Seeing the note and reflecting on its message helped me see how my own specific experiences of activism had colored my views. My bias was that being an activist meant being on the ground and in the middle of everything. I had become so wrapped up in my way of doing things that I had overlooked and forgotten all the people around me who played critical roles in our justice efforts. My outlook had become self-centered and self-serving.

To be clear, this bias is not part of my worldview or even my theory of change. I share it to show how easy it can be for dissonant perspectives to enter our mind and disrupt our internal wholeness. Being vigilantly mindful is our best bet in protecting against that.

In this moment, I had to reckon with how this newly discovered bias was distorting my view of what social justice looks like. Whereas I had come to view it as direct, hands-on, and on-the-ground, I knew in my heart that there's no single pathway to progress and that justice work is as diverse as the people who carry it out. I also knew intellectually that social movements are most successful when we make space for multiple approaches to work together.

What do we lose by insisting that our way of doing things is the only way, or even the best way? And who gets hurt in the process?

In my self-reflection, two touchpoints emerged that felt especially clarifying.

First, I had to grapple with the idea of serving directly versus serving indirectly. I knew that caring for our kids and household meant that my wife could spend more time with patients who needed her—and that felt good. Yet when she came home each evening and debriefed about her day, a small part of me felt diminished. That my contributions were less meaningful made me feel like my existence was less valuable. My identity had become so wrapped up in being an activist that not being fully active in this moment made me feel useless. When the people around us are described as essential, what does that make the rest of us?

The question hovered over me like a dark cloud, and I wanted to get out of its shadow. I resisted the urge to simply make myself feel more useful by busying myself with more activity. Instead, I decided to take a step back to get a clearer view. For the zillionth time in my life, I reminded myself: *Our worth is not determined by what we do. Our worth is inherent and priceless and cannot be diminished.*

The problem comes when we try to quantify and compare our value, because in doing so we devalue ourselves and others in the process.

Similarly, our seva is not more or less valuable. Some of us may have a chance to make more direct interventions than others, and some may have more resources to give than others, but none of this is a measure of who we are as people and how we give of ourselves. What truly matters is that we do our best with the capacity and skills we have. As Toni Morrison wisely advises, the question we should ask ourselves is: "What can I do from where I am?"

This is why the sakhi recounts that, during his travels, Guru Nanak chose to stay at the home of the humble, sincere carpenter Bhai Lalo and rejected an invitation from the wealthy but dishonest merchant Malik Bhago. The merchant could offer more material comforts, but the lowly carpenter was elevated by the sincerity in his heart. The truest measure of our humanity is the sincerity in our hearts.

The other touchpoint from my reflection related to the knowledge that staying home and keeping physical distance was the best action I could take for other people, including my own family. This felt counterintuitive because I was so used to thinking of activism as activity. Being an activist meant *doing* something, and suddenly so many of us were sitting at home and doing very little.

Seeing activism as activity works for us in most situations because it keeps us busy. But it falls apart in moments like this one where we realize that the most compassionate way to engage is to do nothing. Sometimes the best we can do is to sit with openness and silence. Sometimes activism is nothing more than listening.

Digging into the tension I felt during the pandemic revealed to me the problem of my perception. When we see activism as activity, we center ourselves instead of those we are hoping to serve. In this moment, I let my own desire to feel useful supersede what others actually needed. This was the source of my internal conflict.

We need to expand the way we think about activism. Because our current model spurs us to see activism as action, we measure our outcomes to determine if our activism is successful: Did we achieve the policy change we sought? How many people did we register to vote? How many reporters responded to our press release? These metrics are important to effecting change, and we should continue putting energy into them—but we can also demand more.

While our current model of activism measures results and outcomes, it neglects to account for our intentions and our processes. Without rightful intention, our efforts can make us more self-centered rather than less. Without valuing the ends and means equally, we set ourselves up to cut corners and compromise our ethics along the way. These two shortcomings can be devastating to our pursuit of achieving wholeness and justice.

On the other hand, a model of engagement that accounts for what we accomplish *and* what's on the inside can take us toward wholeness and justice rather than away from it; such a paradigm would enable us to transform the world around us while also transforming us from the inside. According to Guru Amardas, sincerity—not outcomes—is the ultimate gauge of our efforts: *Seva, consciousness, and devotion are true when we eliminate selfishness within.* This is the vision of seva, the Sikh version of activism that accounts not just for what you do but also how and why you do it.

Forty-four

SEVA AS AN
EMPATHY PRACTICE

I also have to admit that, like many people during the COVID-19 pandemic, I was quickly absorbed by my own immediate world. The uncertainty made me feel uncomfortable, and watching the news sent our worry into overdrive. It felt less like a snowball effect and more like an avalanche; destruction was inevitable and escape was impossible. I knew the death toll was rising quickly, but I had a hard time caring for others when my own safety felt threatened. My concerns were limited to the four walls of our apartment as we prepared to bunker down.

I did not anticipate how this approach would transform my own psychology. Rather than feeling more safe and secure, I felt more stressed and anxious. I realize now that I was cycling through a victim mentality: the more I focused on my own situation, the more wrapped up I became in my own world. The universe of my self-centeredness was expanding rapidly.

To get out of this, I began to change how I consumed the news. Instead of focusing on the stories that exacerbated fear, I sought out positive news stories of people serving those in need: nurses and physicians coming out of retirement to serve understaffed and overwhelmed hospitals; community groups leading fundraisers to purchase protective equipment for essential workers; kids donating the contents of their piggy banks to people who'd lost their jobs; religious groups delivering free meals to those going hungry. These stories helped balance all the negativity—especially appealing to me in a moment of self-absorption. I admired what these volunteers were doing, even if I could not fully wrap my own mind around their selflessness.

I was so moved that I began reaching out to volunteers. I wanted to write about their stories and share them with the world. I also wanted to learn for myself what motivated their selflessness.

I learned that each person had different reasons for stepping up in this time of need. I also noticed that there were a few threads that tied their stories together.

Some shared how they felt compelled to serve because it felt like the right thing to do. Others mentioned that they felt the responsibility of their privilege. Others still explained that they saw it as part of their religious training. Each of the volunteers talked in some way about how serving others helped engender positivity within them. Serving those who need it helped the volunteers notice their own blessings and feel sincere gratitude for them. It made them feel good to show up for others in a time of need. And most unexpected to me, it helped them feel connected with people they didn't even know.

This point about connection hit home for me. I had long thought about seva as a way to help minimize one's ego. I had never thought about its corollary: seva is also a way to cultivate empathy.

Connecting these dots encouraged me to begin serving others during the pandemic in whatever way I was able. I asked myself a simple question each morning when I woke up: *What is one thing I will do today to extend beyond myself and truly love my neighbors?* It did not have to be a grand gesture or something that changed the world's trajectory. What I really wanted to do was reconnect with the people around me, to the point where I cared about others at least as much as I cared about myself.

Adopting seva as a practice in this moment helped relieve the pressure that was building inside me. At a time when I had retreated into myself, sincerely caring about others helped draw me out of my self-centeredness. It provided perspective and positivity at a time when I needed it most. Perhaps more than anything else, it has become a daily practice that has helped me nurture empathy for people across the board, whether I know them personally or not.

Forty-five

SEVA AS A PRACTICE OF LOVE

I first learned the golden rule in third grade: "Do unto others as you would have done unto you." Mrs. Pendergraff explained it then as a way to think about fair treatment and equality. I loved the idea from the first time I heard it (and not just because I used it that afternoon to convince Shannon to share her brownie with me). I also loved it for the vision it offered: Wouldn't life be so much better if we all lived this way?

I came across the golden rule often in the years that followed, most often in interfaith settings. Religious leaders loved to invoke it as a fundamental precept shared across faith traditions. I accepted that as a beautiful connection, too, and I dreamed of a world where people of all backgrounds shared this value.

I first began to question the wisdom of the golden rule in graduate school. We were studying European imperialism, and something about the rhetoric justifying colonial intervention sounded familiar: *We are more advanced than others, so we know what's best for them better than they do. If we really care about them, we must conquer and civilize them, even if they resist.* It bothered me to see how misguided their logic was and that, however noble their intentions may have been, they operated from an assumption of cultural superiority.

We can now look back and see the problem with such paternalistic thinking. It is egocentric, both in its stance of supremacy and in its approach to solutions. Rather than learning what others might want and trusting their judgment, the colonialists presumed to know better and imposed their views on those they colonized.

It struck me that a similar impulse underlies the golden rule: Whatever I want for myself is what others want, too. This assumption may be well intentioned, but it's also problematic. It's self-centered to think that everyone wants the same things we do, and to boot, it could result in a savior mentality in which we presume to know what's best for others. Misguided outlooks like these give us the sense of being generous while also masking the harm we might cause others.

Has anyone asked the colonized if they would rather stay free?

On May 4, 1493, just a year after Christopher Columbus arrived in the New World, Pope Alexander VI issued the papal bull *Inter Caetera*, which announced that any land not inhabited by Christians was open to be "discovered by Christian rulers" and that the "Catholic faith and Christian religion be exalted and be everywhere increased and spread, that the health of souls be cared for, and that the barbarous nations be overthrown and brought to faith itself." This document, which enacted what would come to be known as the Doctrine of Discovery, was foundational to European colonization of the Americas, to its presumptive claims of Western expansion (later known as Manifest Destiny), and to the genocidal killing of Indigenous people.

One of the most celebrated writers in English, Rudyard Kipling, propagated the same mindset. Here's a short excerpt from his 1899 poem "The White Man's Burden," which speaks to the duty superior people have to reform those who are uncivilized:

> Take up the White Man's burden—
>
> The savage wars of peace—
>
> Fill full the mouth of Famine
>
> And bid the sickness cease;

And when your goal is nearest

The end for others sought,

Watch sloth and heathen Folly

Bring all your hopes to nought.

Kipling saw imperialism as a generous gift that European colonialists brought to the rest of the world. He did not see it as an unwanted imposition because he told himself that the heathens did not know any better. His holier-than-thou attitude prevented him from seeing the humanity in whomever he considered inferior. Thinking we're better than others can cause real damage to those we deem inferior, and it also harms those of us who come to believe in our own supremacy.

The problem with this mindset is not one of sincerity but one of perceived supremacy. The colonizers' measure for intrinsic human value relied on their own self-perception. Seeing themselves as ambassadors of advanced civilization, they would appraise those they encountered according to how closely they mirrored themselves. When "savages" and "heathens" inevitably failed to live up to this measure, imperialists felt justified and duty bound to intervene. Had they truly approached people different from them with humility and compassion, they would not have perceived or treated them as inferior.

Studying colonialism was fascinating because this new information challenged so much of what I had learned in my history classes growing up—a stark reminder that history is the story told by the winners. And it became personally challenging when I realized the supremacist mindset that propelled this outlook was not exclusive to colonialism, nor was it a remnant of the past; it lives on in every one of us. Our minds are adept at keeping distance from the injustices we seek to address. We tell ourselves that we are not susceptible to misogyny because it's outdated. We perceive racism as a thing of the past. Yet we know that both are so entrenched in our current world that they continue to affect and shape our everyday lives. Employing this defense mechanism protects us from having to grapple with the truth: We all carry these biases, whether we are aware of them or not.

Like colonialism, the golden rule may be noble in its intentions, but it leaves no space for empathy or humility. Without compassion, our activism can become dehumanizing and violent rather than enriching and equalizing.

I remember how torn I'd felt upon first realizing this: dejected for not having been as open and inclusive as I had considered myself to be; grateful to have learned this so I could grow from it going forward; horrified to think about all the people I may have harmed in trying to place my own feelings and wants onto them.

I was clear in my heart that none of this was malicious. My intentions had been purehearted. At the same time, I remembered the lesson I learned in the racial justice world: *Intention is not the same as impact.* We can mean well, but in acting without open ears and open hearts, we may very well cause harm.

By this point in my life, I had learned to accept my imperfections and to not feel ashamed of them. I understood that revelations like these only merit shame if we fail to act once we become conscious of them.

I had unconsciously been living by a Western concept that I had internalized, whereas the truth had been with me all along—the Sikh concept of seva. I just hadn't connected the dots. Seva offers a more sensitive approach that brings in listening and authentic connection with those we seek to serve. Seva calls on us to remove ourselves from the equation and seek instead to treat others how they want to be treated. When met with seva, the golden rule is reborn in a more evolved form: *Do unto others as they would want.*

The difference between these two approaches may seem marginal, especially in cases where the needs seem more obvious: food for the hungry, water for the thirsty. What happens, though, when what we want for someone and what they want for themselves is at odds? Without ever asking and without ever listening, how could we know what they want in the first place?

Here is where the two approaches diverge: While the traditional golden rule centers ourselves while extending compassion to others, seva calls on us to decenter ourselves and to center those we aim to serve. This is because seva has its roots in oneness and love.

Each of these three—oneness, love, and seva—share the element of selflessness. Through connection, we open up the boundaries that separate us. Through love, we enter into a state of union. Through service, we go beyond our sense of self.

Seva is not done to feed our egos or to make ourselves feel good. Seva, like love, is not self-serving. Seva is animated by concern and compassion. We serve because we love.

Seva is a natural expression of our love. Think about someone you love and how much pain you feel when they are upset or hurt. Your natural response is to help minimize their pain. You don't act because you expect something in return. You're moved into action because you love them.

We all feel this kind of compassionate pain for the people we love because they are a part of us. Despite the universality of this experience, there is no good English word to capture it. Perhaps the closest we come is when we say something like "I know what you mean" or "I feel your pain." But even these phrases place ourselves at the center and therefore fail to capture the selflessness of love.

Not having appropriate vocabulary is significant because we rely on language to help make meaning. Being unable to articulate this feeling makes it exceedingly difficult to act on it intentionally. Bringing selflessness into our language can help us bring it into our lives.

The Persian word for such aching compassion is "hamdard," a term so useful that it has been adopted in many South Asian languages, including Punjabi, Hindi, and Urdu. The celebrated thirteenth-century Persian poet Sa'adi has a timeless poem that speaks to this idea of shared pain through human connection. He shares that if we recognize all of humanity as extensions of our own being, we will experience their suffering as our own and their joy as our own—just as the branches of a tree are all affected when a single branch is afflicted. Sa'adi's point here is that deep connection means experiencing our pain and our liberation as being bound up with one another's. This is what it means to love and serve our neighbors.

Understanding the unique logic of seva helped me through the personal dissonance I felt during the COVID pandemic. It reminded me that while activism is about what we *do*, seva is about our motivations as well. When we are coming from a place of selfishness, our actions will never feel as satisfying, no matter how much impact they might have. On the other hand, when our engagement is selfless, we will be perfectly content doing whatever is best for other people. We leave behind the feelings of guilt and shame and the need for external recognition, because our seva is not about us.

The most empowering aspect of the seva paradigm is that there is no prescription for what we should or must do for our efforts to count. According to this mode, anything and everything we do can be seva, if our heart means it to be: parenting or protesting, teaching a class or serving sick patients. These may not fall within our rubric of activism—but each of them can be a form of seva. All we need is the right mindset.

Cornel West's pronouncement that "justice is what love looks like in public" resonates with the core of seva. And yet seva offers us even more. Seva is a spiritual practice that transforms the world around us while also transforming us within. Seva is justice work that feeds our souls and nourishes our hearts, a way to bring more happiness to others while also firmly planting the seeds for our own long-term happiness.

Forty-six

CHALLENGING THE DARKNESS

A silver lining of our current political climate is that we are more socially and politically engaged than ever. We are in the midst of a cultural shift that prioritizes civic engagement and social activism—from record voter turnout in 2020 to massive transnational movements like Black Lives Matter, the Women's March, and March for Our Lives. In 2020, Americans gave a record $471 billion to charity. Sports icons like Colin Kaepernick, Megan Rapinoe, LeBron James, and Simone Biles have inspired people all around the world with their public commitments to activism and justice.

The passion is exciting, hopeful, and inspiring.

Yet what we are seeing is also problematic. So much of our activism is rooted in anger, a reactive emotion that can itself be harmful, to ourselves and to others. When we limit ourselves to viewing anger as a foundation for our activism, or vengeance as the only fuel for our passion, we may find ourselves more interested in destroying the people who hurt us than in creating a new environment that would engender more justice.

Don't get me wrong—I'm not saying that there's no place for rage in activism, or even that those who have been wronged by injustice aren't justified to be angry. Of course there is, and of course we're justified. But there's a difference between our raw human emotions and how we choose to channel them. When we fail to process them through our values—like love, service, and creativity—won't we end up reproducing the very inequitable structures we seek to abolish?

Another problem with activism anchored in rage and negativity is that our conversations about injustice remain at the surface. In 2017, the world watched in shock as white supremacists gathered in Charlottesville, Virginia, for a rally called "Unite the Right." That shock turned to outrage after learning that a white supremacist murdered Heather Heyer, a thirty-two-year-old Charlottesville native who had gone to protest racist hate.

When asked to comment on the rally, President Donald Trump infamously stated that there were "some very fine people on both sides." People across the globe channeled their outrage into social media posts, tweeting their disgust and anger.

The revulsion inspired by Trump's response was wholly justifiable. And yet, to me, the outrage felt rooted in a different sort of fear—as if it had unintentionally exposed something about all of us. How many of us cared enough about real justice for the victims of white supremacy? How many of us worked to hold the perpetrators accountable? How many of us changed our behaviors to align with the outrage that we felt and displayed? And did any of it create meaningful change, either within our hearts or within our communities?

We have entered peak outrage culture. Far too often we announce on Facebook: "I changed my profile picture in solidarity with refugees," without donating financially, opening up our homes, or calling our elected officials. Or we tweet, "I absolutely reject this new policy because it's racist," without actually having read the legislation, examined its significance, or even learned what consequences it might have. What are we actually accomplishing when we make pronouncements without taking actions to follow through? And what does this approach say about how much we really care?

I call this "performance outrage" because it is registered primarily for its social value. It carries so much cultural currency today that even marketing agencies now advise their clients to display social concern as a way to attract consumers. We gain social standing by publicly announcing our position on a particular issue. The more outraged we seem, the more points we score.

Social media has become a forum for us to gain social points by performing outrage. We can't possibly care about every single issue, and yet we worry about being judged for not doing so. The charade is unsustainable, which is why so many of us burn out online. Pretending to be someone we're not is soul-crushing.

It doesn't take much to announce to the world that we care. This is part of its appeal. Performing concern requires little investment—little time, treasure, or talent. All it takes is the literal click of a button.

Social media culture capitalizes on and encourages these sorts of behaviors. The more polarizing our behavior, the more likely we are to get likes and retweets. The more outrageous we are, the more followers we score. It doesn't matter so much that our information is accurate or constructive or even meaningful. What really counts is that we have a hot take or, better still, that we call someone out and drag them.

Social media can be a tool for doing good, but too many of us have become tools, letting social media use us and abuse us. We've lost control of our own lives, and we have to ask ourselves who we're serving by participating in such discourse. Audre Lorde warned us: "The master's tools will never dismantle the master's house."

We have become so used to this form of empty engagement that anything more meaningful captivates our imaginations and energizes us. This is one reason the grassroots activism around gun violence has been so refreshing to witness. Groups such as Everytown, Moms Demand Action, and the Parkland high school students have risked their own lives to demand positive change. It's why the Black Lives Matter protests have inspired people all across the country and all over the world. It's also why the Indian farmers' protests of 2020 and 2021 speak to our souls. People engaged in all these movements have shown consistently—despite insults, death threats, and violent attacks—that they genuinely believe in what they're doing. We admire their sincerity and seek to emulate it in our own lives.

True engagement is not just about giving our wealth to worthy causes or publicly announcing our concern for others. To be truly engaged with the world requires human connection, selflessness, and, ultimately, love.

Sincere caring also goes beyond finger-pointing. Anyone can do that. And frankly, it seems like that's what most of us do. We can blame ourselves for this. We train our students to problematize; the students who can poke holes and find the problems are the ones who receive our highest honors. But what if we were to add a step to our process, one that brings in the value of creativity? What if, in addition to rewarding those who can identify problems, we also began to train and incentivize our children to develop constructive and compassionate solutions? What could our world look like then?

Here's what I know: When our activism is without creativity, and when our outrage is not grounded in true love and connection with those in need, our actions will inevitably be short-lived. It either becomes toxic and vengeful, destroying everything in its path, or it simply burns itself out until the next incident of injustice manages to gain public attention. Most of us announce our discontent on social media, follow the story for a day, and then move on within twenty-four to forty-eight hours.

Lather. Rinse. Repeat.

Performance outrage is ineffective, delusional, and maddening. Ineffective, because it does not inspire meaningful action or change; delusional, because we trick ourselves into thinking we are caring and compassionate even though it's superficial; and maddening, because it offers no real nutrition for our souls.

The payout of embracing love, sincere caring, and seva as a way of life is immense. This approach is not just an effective social or political strategy, though this approach has been proven incredibly effective by visionary leaders such as Harriet Tubman and Nelson Mandela. Seva isn't about branding or marketing, though it can have incredible impact there, especially among people who appreciate the values you espouse and admire how you embody them. The primary outcome of seva as a way of life is perhaps the most valuable one for the modern age: the ability to stay engaged with the world—even when confronted with injustice—without self-defeating rage and without sacrificing one's inner peace and happiness.

A way of life that prioritizes love, sincere caring, and seva—as a *practice*—gives us agency. Freeing ourselves from the chains of empty performance makes it harder to point to the systems and people around us and shrug our shoulders; harder, too, to seethe with rage while we blame others for the injustice or suffering around us. Like Jaswant Singh Khalra's parable of the lantern, seva sets us free to call on ourselves to do the right thing based on what is actually within our control, to accept what we cannot change with fortitude, and to keep our lights burning as we challenge the darkness.

Forty-seven

SEVA AS MINDFULNESS

T he logic of seva resonates because we are so used to words without actions, or actions without heart. I remember how dishonest it felt in high school to spend time volunteering just so I could mention it on my college applications. Decades later, it still irks me whenever I think about it. We know insincerity because we all say things out loud without any intention of following through, whether at home, at work, or with friends. It's also why we feel outraged when our politicians offer thoughts and prayers after a school shooting but fail to follow up with meaningful action. It's why my kids roll their eyes when, anytime they ask me for something, I say, "We'll see."

Claiming to love our neighbor is different from actually loving our neighbors. Whereas sincere caring builds relationships and cultivates connection, our empty claims damage us in ways we don't realize.

We convince ourselves of our own lies. When we claim to care sincerely but don't feel it in our hearts, we create dissonance within our own being. Our internal discord may not be noticeable on a day-to-day basis, but when it does show itself, it can cause extreme confusion and strife. We then have to grapple with our own hypocrisy and figure out the disconnect between our beliefs and our actions.

We damage relationships. When we announce to people that we care about them but do not show up in their time of need, we breach their trust. When I have been on the hurting side of this kind of betrayal, it frankly would have been less painful if people had never claimed to have my back in the first place. Actions speak louder than words.

We place an arbitrary limit on ourselves. When we come to believe that empty words and actions are the limits of sincere caring, it becomes difficult to push beyond these boundaries. We reduce our capacity to experience a more expansive kind of love, a love that is fulfilling and enriching rather than desolate and transactional.

Seva is an antidote for our malaise, because when we ground our lives in love and selflessness, we will be moved away from empty speech and actions and toward authenticity.

While seva feels right intuitively, it also runs counter to so much of what we learn from childhood: that the ends justify the means, that some lives matter more than others, that we will find happiness if we just care for ourselves. We have been hardwired to live with pretense and dissonance; our socialization makes it difficult to live with authenticity.

The good news is that our incongruous ways of thinking are taught, not inherited. If we have learned to live this way, we can also unlearn it and learn something new. Recognizing this reality presents an opportunity as much as a challenge: What can we do to ensure we are not tripped up by ideas we have learned from childhood?

Embracing seva is an intervention and a tool at the same time. When we can accept its wisdom for improving our lives, we can use it as a daily mindfulness practice to help us live with more authenticity. Returning to the seva principle in moments of confusion can help us push past older ways of thinking when they come back to tempt us.

There have been moments when approaching seva as a mindfulness practice has helped me cut through the fog to find clarity.

=====

As a student, and now as an educator myself, I've had the fortune of learning from and working with incredible teachers in my life. But I've also seen the deep deficits that can occur when teachers are disinterested, unprepared, or disconnected from their students.

The best teachers are those who approach their work as service. Good teachers don't make teaching about themselves; they make it about meeting the needs of those in the room. It takes incredible humility and an ability to decenter oneself to meet people where they are and to prioritize what's most important to them. I'm reminded of our many coaches over the years—Coach Dan, Coach Leo, Coach Dave, Coach McKenna, Coach Stone—who were ready to boycott games when referees said we couldn't play with our turbans.

Often, leadership and service are taken separately, as two discrete ways of engaging with the world around us. We typically think of leadership as how someone with power influences those who follow them, and service as a way of supporting those without power.

What Sikhi has taught me, though, is that power and service go hand in hand: We each have our own forms of power, and we can each deploy that power for the betterment of our world. This is servant-leadership.

Leadership is at its best when rooted in compassion and humility. The worst leaders are those who work for their own gain and seek to serve themselves. The greatest leaders are those who are connected to their people and work for the benefit of those they serve. One approach is self-centered and leads to disconnection, while the other is inspired by love and produces justice. We have seen with our own eyes the difference between the two.

Seva is both the natural expression of love and the way to cultivate it. It's the goal and the practice, the destination and the way to it. More directly, seva *is* love.

One of the most commonly sung praises of Guru Gobind Singh, the tenth Sikh guru (d. 1708 CE), announces: "*Vaho gobind singh aapay gurchela.* Amazing, amazing is Gobind Singh, who is both the guru and the servant."

For Sikhs, this is not just empty praise. We aspire to be like Guru Gobind Singh and embody his qualities, including his unique approach to leadership—to lead and to serve in the same breath. We can all learn from his approach to leadership as a form of service. As we move toward building a more just and loving world, we would all do well to follow in his footsteps.

The words of Guru Angad ring true: *Those who focus on the Truest of Truths in their service—they find true satisfaction.*

What I take from this wisdom is this: For our seva to give us the peace we desire, what truly matters is what is in our hearts. What are we focused on? What do we dwell on? If the underlying motivation is to serve one's self, then this is a lower form of service—not seva. Being pure of heart is the true measure of seva. Buddhist teachings refer to this in the Eightfold Path as rightful intention.

Understanding this gave me clarity on how to approach teaching: with humility, empathy, and love. Without employing seva as a mindfulness practice, this could very well have been a path not taken.

Seeing the value of seva as a mindset has encouraged me to return to it frequently over the years. Life is so complex and full of entanglements. It is not easy to continue down a narrow path with purpose and vigor. It can be easy to get lost.

For instance, it has been tricky to maintain a balance between maintaining a sincere, selfless humility on the one hand and, on the other, bringing attention to the justice issues about which I am passionate. Marketing and promotion are important components of activism and movement building, and it can be easy for us to build these efforts around personalities. There have been moments when the praise I received for this work went to my head and made me more interested in promoting myself than serving the cause.

You don't notice at first when this is happening because you tell yourself what you want to hear: "Enhancing my own brand will enhance the work; building my platform will create more opportunities for justice." The problem is not that these are untrue. The problem is that we delude ourselves into thinking that our intentions are still selfless.

When I eventually realized that I had fallen off the path of seva, I returned to the practice of seva as mindfulness. What are my intentions? Am I serving myself or others? How do I create alignment across my thoughts, speech, and actions? Asking myself these simple questions helped return me to solid ground.

By leaning into seva as a mindfulness practice, I remind myself that I can do my best to be transparent and share myself with people, but I cannot always control how people perceive or receive me. All we can truly control is that we try to do the right things with our hands, say the right things with our tongues, and carry the right things in our hearts.

Viewing my life through the lens of seva has been a compass and a refuge. It has given me direction in moments of confusion, and it has given me comfort at times of self-doubt. While applying it sincerely has required more courage and commitment than I'd ever anticipated, it has also helped me to live with more authenticity and joy than I ever imagined possible.

Forty-eight

PUTTING SEVA INTO PRACTICE

O ne of the first sakhis that Sikhs learn recounts that when Nanak is a boy, his father gives him some money to invest. While walking from their village to another town, Nanak comes across a group of penniless spiritual people. He gives this group all his money with the understanding that they need it more than he does. He returns home full-hearted but empty-handed, and his father becomes furious upon learning that his son has wasted all his money. Young Nanak simply replies by asking: *What could be a better investment than giving to those who need more than us? This is the true investment (sacha sauda).* The term Guru Nanak used—sacha sauda—remains a common term in Sikh vocabulary for a form of generosity tied to connectedness and love.

In a later account, Guru Nanak meets with some spiritually accomplished ascetics (siddhas) living in the mountains. He acknowledges their spiritual prowess, then asks pointedly: "What good are your accomplishments if you don't use them to serve society?"

These memories of Guru Nanak resonate with Sikhs today, who invoke these accounts to share the importance of charitable giving and social responsibility. This is how the Sikh idea of seva bridges the realms of spirituality and justice.

Through these sakhis we also see a basic precept of Guru Nanak's worldview: Our desire to divide our world into the spiritual and the political is a false dichotomy. Truly enlightened people know that these divisions are figments of our imaginations, human machinations that take us away from the oneness of reality rather than toward it.

We buy into this division because it fits with how we want to see the world. We are jaded after seeing people of all stripes use religion to justify all sorts of heinous behaviors, and we prefer softer approaches of spirituality, where people keep their beliefs and practices to themselves. We feel a tension between spirituality and politics, assuming that no one could genuinely straddle both worlds. In our jadedness, though, we forget that some of the greatest spiritual leaders—including Jesus, Mohammad, the Buddha, and Guru Nanak—were also some of the greatest social activists and political revolutionaries.

In Guru Nanak's view, to live a fully integrated life means that we see the world as integrated, too. There is no heavenly realm set apart from the physical realm. There is no sacred space set apart from polluted space. There are no chosen people set apart from the rest of us. Everything is one, ik oankar—and our lives must be also.

Sikhi coined its own terms to articulate this worldview, which brings cohesion through seemingly disparate notions. The tradition calls on every Sikh to live as a saint-soldier (sant-sipahi) and to practice service and spiritual cultivation (seva-simran). Guru Hargobind, the sixth Sikh guru, famously pronounced allegiance to the political-spiritual (miri-piri). What we see here, and what we see all throughout their teachings, is a consistent attempt to destroy our senses of duality. By bringing together these worlds that seem at odds with each other, the Sikh tradition is reminding us of our inextricable oneness. Spiritual cultivation and social contribution are not mutually exclusive or even practically separable; they go hand in hand.

This idea can help us understand the simultaneous importance that Sikhi places on nurturing us through internal reflection and external disciplines: What is on the inside informs what we do on the outside—and what we do externally informs who we are within. The challenge before us is learning to live with this paradox.

How are you using your gifts—time, talent, and treasure—to help serve those around you? To put it more bluntly: What might you do to become less of a burden on this earth and help bring more light into the world?

Forty-nine

SEVA AS AN
AUTHENTICITY PRACTICE

I 'll never forget the first class I walked into as a PhD student at Columbia University. I arrived twenty minutes early, nervous about going to the wrong place. About a dozen of us sat around the conference table. Everyone seemed to know one another already, speaking excitedly in different languages about their summers and their research progress. Then the door swung open and in walked a world-renowned scholar of Hinduism I'd long admired and who had drawn me to this school. I recognized him from the jacket photos of books I'd read—Dr. John Stratton Hawley, known universally as Jack. My heart fluttered and then began to sprint. My palms started sweating. Who knew intellectual crushes could have the same effects on us as romantic ones?

Jack welcomed us and invited us to introduce ourselves. I sat at the far end of the conference table (the best place to hide), and my turn came after listening to four others announce who they were and their impressive experience in the field. I was mortified and couldn't string a sentence together about who I was or what I was doing there. I asked them to come back to me and wondered if the whole thing was a mistake, that someone would find out I didn't belong. While everyone else sounded intelligent, I just wanted to sound intelligible.

Eventually I was able to stammer out an introduction, but the feeling of not belonging stuck with me. Since that moment in 2008, and for years before that, I have been haunted by the fear that someone might find out who I really am and that I don't truly belong. I never shared this with anyone all those years ago. For one, I didn't yet have a handle on this new feeling. Second, to confess this would be to risk being exposed. I kept the feeling to myself and worked hard to live up to expectations.

I remember exactly where I was upon first learning that I was not as alone as I felt: the Hungarian Pastry Shop near campus with my Persian study group. Emily first confessed the feeling of not truly belonging, and everyone in the booth affirmed her before admitting the same. I was surprised and relieved. I had no idea other people felt the same way. I learned a term for what we all felt: *imposter syndrome.*

I now felt doubly relieved. I had been unable to pin down that feeling before, but now I had conceptual language that would help me better understand myself. Knowing a term existed for my feeling made me feel less alone, too; if there was language for it, that meant more people must have experienced this feeling, too.

One of my most unexpected insights from meeting and interviewing an array of different leaders from various fields—politicians, athletes, comedians, actors—has been learning that imposter syndrome is deeply embedded in so many of us, even the people we admire most and even those we put on a pedestal. I find myself asking about this frequently, perhaps because I find it heartening to know we're not on our own. The most touching response came from Cecilia Muñoz, then President Obama's chief domestic policy adviser, when I interviewed her for my podcast. When I asked if she had ever felt imposter syndrome, she laughed and shared openly that she felt it every single day. She explained that she was often the only woman and the only person of color in a room with powerful world leaders, and that she often would have to remind herself that she belonged.

Ms. Muñoz's response struck a chord with me because it brought home the psychology that animates this feeling. When a society consistently sends messages that certain people do not belong, those messages get embedded in the minds of those who receive them. Without being fully conscious of this, I had responded by creating a false narrative in my own head—that if I could somehow reach a certain level of perfection, then I would start feeling like I belonged. My approach led me to work harder and reach higher, and I am grateful for that. But it also led to frustration and disappointment. I had neither achieved the unfeasible goal of perfection, nor did I feel any more like I belonged. That feeling of being an imposter stayed with me.

The answer to my discontent was more intuitive than I'd anticipated. Belonging does not require perfection. Belonging comes with connection and sincere caring.

This realization can answer a variety of questions that arise as we journey through life. When I speak about the power of merging our justice work with our spiritual practice, someone inevitably asks: "How will we know when we are ready to start serving? Shouldn't we perfect ourselves before we start helping others?" I want to talk through this question because it has tripped me up in the past.

If we embrace our imperfections as part of our collective humanity and can learn to see humility as an asset rather than a liability, then we will no longer be confined by the illusion of perfection. This is how we can move from feeling like imposters to feeling truly connected. It is also how we can embark on a journey that is as enjoyable as the destination itself.

The Sikh gurus, who lived less than five hundred years ago, modeled this form of activism throughout their lives. They lived in a context of immense inequity and injustice, and they actively confronted discrimination in its various forms. They did everything from explaining why gender discrimination was wrong to confronting emperors who persecuted innocent citizens. They called out injustice unapologetically, modeling what it looks like to align our values with our actions.

When we understand seva as a spiritual practice that can serve us as much as it serves others, then we realize that we don't need to separate the two; to engage in seva is to refine our inner being *and* to help others. Speaking practically, this integrated approach enables us to get in the game immediately. If we wait to achieve perfection to contribute, we will sit around working on ourselves forever, no more relevant than those ascetics (siddhas) in the mountains who Guru Nanak called out.

Asking ourselves to refrain from service until we're spiritually enlightened places artificial limits on our own happiness. It's like telling a parent they shouldn't take care of their newborn baby until they know everything there is to know about parenting. Even seasoned parents (like my own beleaguered mother) would admit that there's no such thing as perfect knowledge. To sit around and wait for perfection is to deny ourselves the gift of living in the present. To delay our generosity is to decline giving to others whatever we have *right now*. If we truly believe that wisdom comes with experience, and that our lived experiences make us who we are, then what sense does it make to live in the hypothetical? In other words, why not start giving now while also working on yourself? You might find, as I did, that these practices buttress one another.

Fifty

SEVA AS A
HUMILITY PRACTICE

In 1991, after a lifetime of service, eighty-seven-year-old Bhagat Puran Singh was nominated for the Nobel Peace Prize, a distinction usually reserved for the greatest humanitarians among us. His contributions are hard to capture in words.

Bhagat Puran Singh grew up in India in poverty. His father died soon after Bhagat Puran Singh was born, and his mother served as a domestic worker. He volunteered in refugee camps after the violent partitioning of India and Pakistan in 1947, an experience that led him to establish Pingalwara, a home that cares for those rejected by society: the sick, the disabled, the orphaned, the destitute. He worked tirelessly as an environmental justice advocate during India's Green Revolution, and he famously returned the prestigious Padma Shri Award to the Indian government after its attack on the Golden Temple in 1984. For Bhagat Puran Singh, justice was intersectional and every moment of life was an opportunity to serve.

Every morning, people would see him walking through the streets of Amritsar, bending over to pick up the trash he found along the way. He continued this practice through his advanced age, at which point people started asking him questions.

"You have been doing this for years, babaji, and yet our city is still polluted. Don't you realize yet that it makes no difference?"

Bhagat Puran Singh's wisdom would shine through his smile as he explained: "It may not make a difference to you, but it makes a difference to me. My aim is to leave this world better than how I found it."

This simple insight encapsulates Bhagat Puran Singh's superhuman contributions. Even in the most mundane of actions, like picking up trash on the street, we can see something unique about how he approached it. Seva is about the *ethic*, *attitudes*, and *intentions* that inspire service as much as the actions themselves. True seva is selfless love.

Serving with love is a powerful practice because it can help us eradicate a key source of our suffering—our egos.

Our egos cause us pain because they create a mental wall between us and the world. Our self-absorption causes us to view our perceived disconnections rather than our intrinsic connections, and these perceptions lead us to feel disconnected and isolated. This is why performing service out of self-centeredness is ultimately unfulfilling. We may be helping others, but we are hurting ourselves. Misguided intentions enlarge our egos and produce more suffering. In the words of the Guru Angad: *Lasting satisfaction comes when we engage in loving service (seva) while erasing selfishness.*

If we can buy into the idea of realizing divine oneness by effacing human ego, then to live with love is to see *no* distinction between the self and the other. When we truly begin to believe that our well-being is interconnected—that my liberation is tied to your liberation, and that your suffering is tied to my suffering—then we can see that the only way forward is through loving, selfless service: seva. When we serve with this motivation, we also eliminate the *fear* of being vulnerable, or of losing out in some way ourselves.

I heard these ideas about seva in theory long before I saw them in practice, and I remember questioning their efficacy: Can we truly claim that something is selfless if we expect a reward at the end? Isn't there some self-interest built into the pursuit of selflessness?

My best answer to this question is one that affirms and negates. Yes, there is a degree of what we might call self-interest here. But no, the term "self-interest" falls short because it is not fundamentally about the self. The gurus talk constantly about conquering our egos so that we may live truly and freely. The intention and goal of Sikh wisdom is to annihilate the ego, not expand it. While both approaches share in common that they carry a sense of urgency and a particular agenda for a perceived benefit, the substance underneath each is entirely different. Whereas our natural inclination is to focus on our own wants and needs, Sikh wisdom calls on us to actively engage in a process of decentering. Seva helps us do this work.

Fifty-one

PRACTICING SEVA

erhaps it is in our nature to take. Guru Nanak points this out in *Japji Sahib*: "We constantly plead, 'Give! Give!' And the Giver keeps on giving to us."

Who could we be if we were more like the Giver?

We know in our inner hearts that it is better to give than to receive. Taking gives us momentary happiness; generosity brings us lasting joy. As Kahlil Gibran wrote: "There are those who give with joy, and that joy is their reward." This is the promise of adopting seva as a mindset and practice for everyday living. And another luminary tells us that this approach is not for the elite or for a select few; seva is for all of us. Dr. Martin Luther King, Jr., told us this when he said: "Everyone can be great because everyone can serve. You don't have to have a college education to serve. You don't have to make your subjects and verbs agree to serve. You only need a full heart of grace."

Any of us can adopt a seva mindset, and all of us can benefit from it. Love-inspired service can help us challenge the darkness around us without internalizing its causes: fear, anger, hatred, and more. Here are some simple reflection questions you can incorporate for your own seva practice:

1. What will I do today to help someone I do not know?

2. What is one act of kindness I can do anonymously this week?

3. Who is suffering most in my community this month, and
    what can I do to help them?

4. Who has been most neglected in the past year, and how
    might I serve them?

You may find, as I did, that the more you practice seva, the happier life feels. Here's the secret that the gurus identified: with seva, the giver and the receiver are mutual beneficiaries. When you see others as part of yourself and serve them out of love, bring them joy, or relieve their pain, without hidden agenda or selfish motives; when you reach out to a stranger in need or a coworker to whom you owe no obligation; when you stand in solidarity with those whose rights are being violated even if they don't look like you—they are not the only ones who are benefiting. You are, too. True seva is transformative to the giver. Humility grows, the ego diminishes, gratitude blossoms, and joy springs forth. This is what true living feels like, how we transform from dry, barren branches to lush, enlivened greenery.

So how do we shift our mindsets so that our actions produce more love and wholeness, both within ourselves and within the communities we serve?

When we identify our core values and commitments, and when we begin to put these into practice consistently, then we have set ourselves up to engage with the world around us in a way that is rooted not in our emotions and attachments, but in our principles and convictions. Our actions, words, and thoughts are all aligned. This is what it means to live with wholeness and integrity.

This is also how we know that love, sincere caring, and seva are all interrelated. Practicing all three together enables us to deal with injustice, hatred, and even annoyances with equanimity, grace, and rightful action. This is the payoff of making seva a spiritual practice. When asked what we want more of in this world—in our lives, in our families, and in our communities—it strikes me that this is the answer we're all looking for.

EPILOGUE

The other night, as I tucked my daughters into bed, one of them asked: "Dada, do you ever get tired of taking care of us?"

I was weary from our day together and felt tempted to say yes, but my heart was full, and kids in polka-dot pajamas are *so* cute. I responded the way most parents would: "Of course not."

"Why not?" she asked, pointing out that my entire day had consisted of cooking, cleaning, and playing with them. I gave her the truth in its barest form: "Because I love you."

This is the hardest thing about parenting. I wanted to share more, but realized she wasn't ready for it: that although everything in life looks like a give-and-take, there's a better way to interact with the world; that we expect receiving to bring us happiness, but our hearts don't work this way; that life is abundance and true fulfillment comes in caring for those we love.

Instead, I offered her a pearl from Guru Nanak that she had heard before: "The Giver keeps on giving, while the takers get tired of taking."

Reflecting on our lives together, I knew this to be true. I might be weary at the end of each day, but I will never tire of caring for them. Giving out of love is a bottomless well that can never be exhausted.

I shared this insight with my girls not because I expected them to understand it, but because I wanted to plant a seed in their hearts. My hope for them is that, one day, they will experience an expansive love that nourishes them, sustains them, and brings joy to their daily lives. This is my hope for you and your loved ones, too.

Acknowledgments

Guru Ramdas writes that we do not find our people (sangat) without great fortune. I feel fortunate and grateful to have so many incredible people in my life, all of whom have contributed to my formation and the formation of this book. To everyone in my sangat who has helped shape the person I am today, words can't convey my gratitude for you.

Many of you also had a direct hand in writing this book, and I want to thank you personally.

To my wonderful agent, Tanusri Prasanna, for being the first to see the potential in this dream and for working tirelessly—from start to finish—to help bring it to reality.

To my brilliant editor, Jake Morrissey, for encouraging me to share myself openly and for helping me write the book I've always dreamed of.

To Jackie Shost, Ashley Sutton, Shailyn Tavella, and the entire team at Riverhead for all your support in creating this book and for helping us share it with the world.

To my editors and writing partners, past and present, official and unofficial, including Kiran Kaur Bains, Megan Goodwin, Kali Handelman, Dave Levy, Ilyse Morgenstein-Fuerst, Paul O'Donnell, Paul Raushenbush, Deepjyot Sidhu, Prabhjot Singh, and Bob Smietana.

To my teachers, professors, coaches, and mentors who have invested countless hours in preparing me for the world, teaching me life's lessons.

To my colleagues at the Sikh Coalition who do so much, who care so much, and who have taught me so much about humility and seva over the years.

To my colleagues at the Aspen Institute for believing in me and in this book.

To the organizations and institutions that supported my time in writing this book, including the American Council of Learned Societies, the Open Society Foundations, NYU's Center for Religion and Media, and YSC.

And of course, infinite thanks to my family, without whom I would be lost. To my partner, Gunisha, who is effortlessly smarter than me and spent countless hours reading drafts and giving feedback. To our two daughters, both of whom give me light and inspiration daily. To my brothers, their partners, and their kids—Amandeep, Gurbans, Harpreet, Lakhpreet, Darsh, Raj, and Harmann—all of whom make life fun and meaningful.

To our grandparents and our parents, in San Antonio and Buffalo, who have sacrificed so much to give us the opportunities we have today. To Pritam Uncle and Harminder Aunty, and their kids, Gurpaul Virji and Seema Didi, who helped raise us, too. To my extended family, in the U.S., in Punjab, and elsewhere, who have showered us with unconditional love.

To Guru and Vahiguru. Thank you for all our gifts. May I always live with remembrance, gratitude, and love.

Glossary

Chardi kala

Chardi kala loosely translates to "everlasting optimism" or "rising spirits." Sikhs repeat this term daily in their regular collective prayer known as "Ardas."

Guru

Guru literally means "enlightener." While the term in English has come to refer to an expert in any domain (e.g., basketball guru, real estate guru), it carries a particular institutional meaning within the Sikh tradition. In Sikhi, "guru" refers to the line of religious authority beginning with the ten prophets who established and led the Sikh community. The first of these, Guru Nanak, was born in 1469 CE; the tenth in his line, Guru Gobind Singh, breathed his last in 1708 CE.

Before he passed, Guru Gobind Singh passed the leadership to joint entities: the Guru Granth Sahib (the scriptural canon) and the Guru Khalsa Panth (the community of initiated Sikhs). Sikhs revere these two as occupying the throne of the guru for eternity.

Guru Granth Sahib

The authority accorded to the Guru Granth Sahib, as well as its unique compilation, sets it apart from other scriptural texts of the major world religions. The Sikh gurus personally compiled the Guru Granth Sahib. The collection is primarily composed of devotional writings by the gurus;

it also includes writings by other religious figures, including Muslim Sufis and Hindu Bhaktas.

Unlike the prose narratives that characterize most Western scriptures, the Guru Granth Sahib is made up entirely of devotional poetry, most of which is set to music. These writings—primarily expressions of divine experiences and wisdom on spiritual growth—have played a central role in Sikh practice since the time of Guru Nanak. Sikh worship consists of singing these compositions in both private and congregational settings.

Guru Nanak (1469–1539 CE)

The founder and first teacher of Sikhi. Guru Nanak was born in 1469 to a humble family in western Punjab, which is now part of Pakistan. He observed the suffering and inequities around him and brought forward a new worldview premised on interconnectedness and a shared experience of the world. Guru Nanak spent much of his life sharing this new vision as he traveled across South and Central Asia. As he did so, he established a new religious tradition, Sikhi, rooted in the principles of love, oneness, service, and justice.

Ik oankar

The first term to appear in the Guru Granth Sahib and often the first idea that Sikh children learn, ik oankar refers to the oneness of reality, the one divine force that connects us all. This concept is the basis of core Sikh values, including love, equality, service, and justice.

Oneness and love serve as the foundations of Sikh theology—these are both the objective and the process. Sikhs aim to recognize the divinity within everyone and everything they encounter, and this daily practice helps people cultivate and embody their values.

Sikhs believe that the Creator permeates all of Creation and that every individual is filled with the same divine potential. The Sikh tradition emphasizes the collective familyhood of all humanity and challenges all social inequalities, including those on the basis of class, caste, gender, and profession.

SEVA

Realizing oneness and love within one's life compels individuals to seek unity with the world around them. Sikhi urges every follower to live as a sant-sipahi (saint-soldier), one who strikes a balance of cultivating spirituality while also contributing to community service and social justice. Sikhs call this tradition of love-inspired, selfless service "seva." In a global context, their service to humanity has become a hallmark of the Sikh community.

SIKHI

Some people mistakenly presume Sikhi to be an offshoot of Hinduism or Islam, or a blend of the two religions. Scholars and practitioners alike classify Sikhism as an independent religion.

The Sikh tradition carries the basic markers of organized religion, including its own founder-prophet (Guru Nanak), scripture (Guru Granth Sahib), discipline and ceremonies (rahit), and community centers (gurdwara). There are more than 27 million Sikhs worldwide, making it the world's fifth largest religion.

VAHIGURU

The Sikh gurus used various names from different traditions to refer to divinity—allah, ram, khuda, hari—as well as many adjectives to articulate divine qualities—akal (timeless), beant (limitless), miharvan (compassionate). The gurus openly shared their belief that people may use different names, all while referring to a single divine force.

The most prominently used term among Sikhs today is Vahiguru, which translates as "wonderful enlightener." Vahiguru is not the only term Sikhs use for the divine, but it is the most common.